The Arts in Nazi Germany

Previously published in this series:

Medicine and Medical Ethics in Nazi Germany: Origins, Practices, Legacies
Edited by Francis R. Nicosia and Jonathan Huener

Business and Industry in Nazi Germany
Edited by Francis R. Nicosia and Jonathan Huener

THE ARTS IN NAZI GERMANY

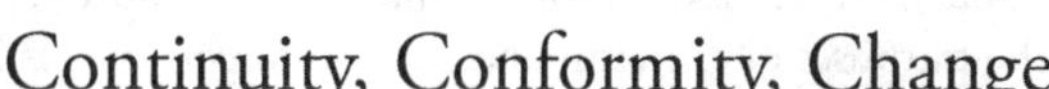

Continuity, Conformity, Change

Edited by

Jonathan Huener

and

Francis R. Nicosia

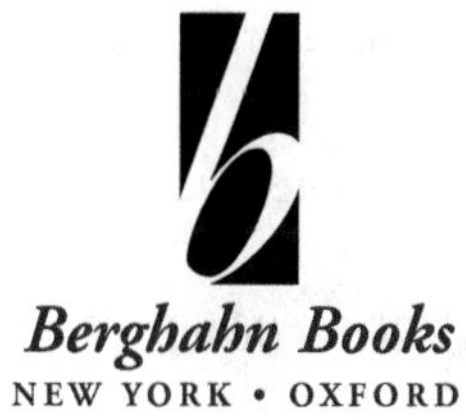

Berghahn Books

NEW YORK • OXFORD

Published in 2006 by
Berghahn Books
www.berghahnbooks.com

Library of Congress Cataloging-in-Publication Data
The Arts in Nazi Germany: continuity, conformity, change / edited by
Jonathan Huener and Francis R. Nicosia.
   p. cm.
Includes bibliographical references and index.
ISBN 1-84545-209-7 (hardback: alk. paper)
1. Arts, German—20th century—Congresses. 2. National social-
ism and art—Germany—Congresses. I. Huener, Jonathan
   II. Nicosia, Francis R.

NX550.A1A85 2006
700.943'09043—dc22

                                            2006042834

British Library Cataloguing in Publication Data
A catalogue record for this book is available from
the British Library.

Printed in the United States on acid-free paper.

ISBN 978-1-84545-209-4 (hbk.) 978-1-84545-359-6 (pbk.)

CONTENTS

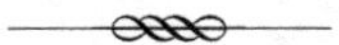

Contents

PREFACE

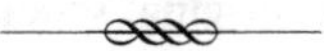

THE SIX ESSAYS IN THIS BOOK ARE BASED ON LECTURES delivered at the Miller Symposium on "The Arts in Nazi Germany," held at the University of Vermont in April 2004. Organized by the Center for Holocaust Studies at the University of Vermont, this was the third symposium bearing the name of Leonard and Carolyn Miller, generous supporters of the center's work and great friends of the university.

Established to honor the work of Professor Raul Hilberg, who served on the faculty of the University of Vermont for more than three decades, the Center for Holocaust Studies is committed to furthering the cause of Holocaust education and to serving as a forum for the presentation and discussion of new perspectives on the history of Nazi Germany and its crimes. Professor Hilberg's pioneering and ongoing research is a model and a standard for scholars, and it is his work in the field that remains an inspiration for the center's programming and for publications such as this. The Miller Symposia have contributed significantly to the center's efforts to explore insufficiently charted areas in the history of the Third Reich. Our goal in organizing them has been to address a topical, or even controversial, theme in the history of Nazi Germany and the Holocaust, relying on the expertise of some of the most accomplished authorities in the field.

The first Miller Symposium, held in April 2000, brought together some of the world's leading scholars in the history of eugenics and the German medical establishment during the Third Reich. It resulted in the anthology *Medicine and Medical Ethics in Nazi Germany: Origins, Practices, Legacies,* published by Berghahn Books in 2002. The second Miller Symposium, with its focus on German business and industry under National Socialism, took place in April 2002. It brought together scholars who are among the most respected and innovative analysts of business, industry, and finance in the years of the Third Reich. The resulting volume, *Business and Industry in Nazi Germany*, was published by Berghahn Books in 2004. The third Miller Symposium featured some of the most important scholars in the history of the arts in Nazi Germany. Their contributions to this volume address the roles of artists, writers, musicians, filmmakers, Jewish cultural institutions, American cultural influence, and German youth in the life of the Nazi state. Based on the authors' original scholarship, the essays assembled here serve as an introduction to some of the most current research and controversies in the history of the arts in the Third Reich.

These essays will be of interest to students and scholars of twentieth-century German history and the Nazi era, as well as those interested in the history of music, art, literature, and the cinema in Germany under National Socialism, and to general readers in the history of German culture, the Third Reich, and the Holocaust.

Both the Miller Symposium and this volume owe a tremendous debt to Leonard and Carolyn Miller, whose continuing support for the Center for Holocaust Studies has helped to sustain and expand its programming over the years. The editors also recognize and thank Wolfgang Mieder and the symposium's organizing committee, which included Kathy Johnson, David Scrase, and the editors of this volume. David Scrase deserves special thanks for his translations of some of the documents in the appendixes, as does Kathy Johnson for her tireless efforts, both in organizing the symposium itself and assembling materials for this publication. We are grateful as well to Kelly McDonald of Saint Michael's College for her help in the editing process. A final word of thanks is due to Michael Kater of York University for his contribution to the symposium and to this anthology. A contributor to the first Miller Symposium and to the volume on German medicine and medical ethics, and recognized around the world as a leading authority on the history of music in Nazi Germany, Professor Kater has played crucial roles in two of the three Miller Symposia and in the books that have resulted from them.

INTRODUCTION

The Arts in Nazi Germany:
Continuity, Conformity, Change

Jonathan Huener and Francis R. Nicosia

ON THE EVENING OF 25 JANUARY 1942, during one of his typically endless conversations at the Wolfsschanze that lasted long into the night, Adolf Hitler suggested to those in his company that the cultural life of the Reich, not politics, was his true passion and concern. He made the following confession to his guests:

> I became a politician against my will. Politics for me is merely the means to an end …. It will be the happiest day of my life when I can retire from political life …. I want to do that when I have completed my political tasks at the end of the war …. Wars come and go. All that remains is the value of culture.[1]

In different ways, Hitler always nurtured a sense of self-importance in the cultural life of Germany. In his 19 July 1937 speech opening the Haus der deutschen Kunst (House of German Art) in Munich, he stressed his central role and that of the National Socialist revolution in creating the necessary conditions under which German art could flourish: "[I]f now I venture to speak of art I can claim a title to do so from the contribution which I myself have made to the restoration of German art."[2] Moreover, his incessant observations about German culture and the role of the arts in its preservation and promotion after 1933 reflected what had remained a personal priority since his youthful obsessions with art, architecture, and Wagnerian music in Linz and Vienna before the First World War.[3] As a consequence, it helps to explain the central role of culture and the arts in the ideology and propaganda of National Socialism from the early years of the movement until the last months of the Third Reich in 1945.

Hitler and his followers came to understand German culture and the role of the arts primarily in political terms. Specifically, they believed that it was the responsibility of the party and the state to rescue German culture, through political means, from allegedly degenerate, largely foreign influences that threatened to destroy it. They believed that art and culture were expressions of race, and that "Aryans" alone were capable of creating true art and preserving true German culture. This was certainly a recurring theme in Hitler's early speeches and writings, and remained so after the National Socialist *Machtergreifung* in 1933. An observation in *Mein Kampf,* for example, certainly pointed in this direction for the future:

> As soon, however, as from this point of view one lets pass before one's eyes the development of our cultural life in the past twenty-five years, one will be shocked at seeing how far we already are on the way to this backward development. Everywhere we meet germs that represent the beginning of excrescences by which our culture is bound to perish sooner or later. Also, we are able to recognize in them the symptoms of decay of a slowly rotting world. Woe to the nations which are no longer able to master this disease![4]

The notion of a national mission to defend German culture from invasive, allegedly degenerate, largely alien music, art, cinema, and literature, as well as the practical need to use the arts to further the regime's propaganda, would seem to have placed the artistic professions in a critical position as instruments of Nazi domestic policy after 1933. But how did the arts really fit into the pattern of culture in the Nazi state? What kind of culture was it? Who were the people who generated it? And how did it coexist within a political culture of fascist totalitarianism and, ultimately, genocide? These are some of the questions that the essays in this volume seek to address.

Some historians and other scholars present a picture of a German artistic and cultural establishment coerced into conforming to a totalitarian regime determined to mobilize the arts in the pursuit of its ideological ends.[5] They have thus situated artistic and other endeavors within the confines of totalitarian political culture such as that defined by Antonio Gramsci: "A totalitarian policy is aimed precisely: 1. at ensuring that the members of a particular party find in that party all the satisfactions that they formerly found in a multiplicity of organizations, i.e., at breaking all the threads that bind these members to extraneous cultural organisms; 2. at destroying all other organizations or at incorporating them into a system of which the party is the sole regulator."[6] Gramsci further argued that this inevitably occurs when, among other things, "the given party wishes to prevent another force, bearer of a new culture, from becoming itself 'totalitarian'—then one has an objectively reactionary phase … and [the reaction] seeks itself to appear as the bearer of a new culture."[7] The Nazi regime, as both protector of traditional "German" culture and as cultural innovator for a future "new Germany," is often understood to have coerced German artists into producing art that was compatible with its ideology and policies. It did so by bestowing on artists honors and money or, if necessary, fines, bans, exile, and threats of incarceration in concentration camps, as incentives to cooperate. But does this approach alone accurately reflect the reality of the arts during the Third Reich?

On the initiative of Reich Minister for Public Enlightenment and Propaganda (Reichsminister für Volksaufklärung und Propaganda) Joseph Goebbels, the establishment of a Reich Chamber of Culture (Reichskulturkammer) in September 1933 prescribed the *Gleichschaltung* (coordination) of the arts and the media under the ideology and policies of National Socialism. The Chamber of Culture established under its auspices separate chambers for writers, journalists, radio professionals, musicians, visual artists, and those in the theater. Two months earlier, a Chamber of Film (Filmkammer) had been established for the film industry, and it was later incorporated into the Reich Chamber of Culture.[8] According to the Reich Chamber of Culture Law (Reichskulturkammergesetz) of 22 September 1933, the Reich Minister for Public Enlightenment and Propaganda was empowered to "enact legal decrees and general administrative guidelines" to govern the arts.[9] The law applied to several hundred thousand professionals and influenced the work of untold millions of amateur artists, musicians, and others. While the Chamber of Culture regulated the affairs and, in theory, the work of those in all the professions related to culture, it also contributed to the significant improvement of the economic conditions of many professionals working in the arts.[10] It allowed the Nazis to reward loyalty to the state with opportunities for economic gain and with some degree of professional autonomy.

But the realities under which those in the arts pursued their work in Hitler's Germany were complex, and not easily characterized by notions of a totalitarian state dictating artistic norms and directions to a regimented, docile, coerced world of professional artists. It is certainly true that the Nazi state used the arts for specific propaganda purposes, particularly during wartime. Hitler's fantasies and the dictates that they generated guided policy from time to time, and Goebbels certainly gave direction to the arts through the Reich Chamber of Culture, as did Hermann Göring as head of the Prussian State Opera, Alfred Rosenberg as head of the League for German Culture (Kampfbund für deutsche Kultur), and even Robery Ley as head of the Strength Through Joy (Kraft durch Freude) program.

Yet, substantial artistic creativity and cultural production did, in fact, take place during the Third Reich, in spite of Nazi values and tastes, and in spite of the dictates of Nazi leaders and state regulations. Moreover, too strong an emphasis on the regime's coercive nature tends to overlook many artists' "passive compliance and active collaboration" with the regime's cultural policies.[11] Finally, particularly in the early years of the Nazi regime, we can also identify artistic and cultural developments in the Third Reich that we would not expect to find in the context of the Nazi state. These include the persistence of creative expression in such musical genres as swing and jazz, in modernist art, and even in a flourishing and expanding Jewish culture.[12]

All of this points to the conclusion drawn by some scholars that there was considerable overlap in artistic and cultural developments between the Weimar and Nazi years. Of course, this must be considered within a larger debate over continuity vs. discontinuity in modern German history, or specifically, the efforts of historians and others to understand National Socialism and the twelve-year horror that was the Third Reich within the larger context of modern German history since 1871. This process, generating as it has some revision of our understanding of the relationship between the Nazi state and the German artistic and cultural establishment, is part of a larger tendency that has come to characterize other aspects of the history of National Socialism in Germany, in particular the histories of nationalism, racism, and anti-Semitism, as well as the geopolitical aims of German foreign policy.

In this instance, the perspectives of a political divide that separated a culturally open, progressive, and democratic environment during the Weimar Republic from a culturally reactionary and repressive one during the Nazi years have been complemented by arguments that suggest considerable confluence and parallels between the cultural politics of both periods.[13] In music, for instance, some scholars have identified many of the conservative and repressive elements in the cultural life of the Weimar Republic that one normally attributes to Hitler's Germany.[14] In pursuing the theme of cultural continuity after the Weimar years, Michael Kater has characterized the cultural environment in the Third Reich as follows: "In the end there was a mixture of aesthetic styles and forms, some mere copies of the tried and true, some syncretic and more interesting, and others bold new moves in the world of art and culture."[15]

Finally, scholars have also identified areas of continuity in terms of post–World War II cultural developments in occupied Germany. Indeed, the Allies encouraged the resurrection of a vibrant German cultural life as a political instrument in their occupation policies and goals,[16] a process that would necessarily rely on some of the initiatives and organizational foundations established under Nazi rule and even earlier. This was particularly so in music, as leaders of postwar musicology had little choice but to resurrect some Nazi-sponsored enterprises and established practices and, as in other areas of the arts, to permit the reemergence of prominent musicologists and musicians from the Nazi era.[17]

In the end, artists in Nazi Germany were essentially no different from other educated and professional elites. Although they represented a wide spectrum of political convictions, they were largely motivated by the same career considerations and political opportunism that prevailed in professions such as medicine, law, business, academia, and others. These factors almost always trumped moral considerations, as most possessed no more civil courage than the vast majority of ordinary German citizens. For the most part, artists, too, opted for compliance with the overall policies of the regime, adapting to circumstances in order to preserve their own interests. Primo Levi's observation about the catastrophic results of this compliance, by those in the arts or any of the other professions, is certainly instructive here:

> Whatever the case, since one cannot suppose that the majority of Germans lightheartedly accepted the slaughter, it is certain that the failure to divulge the truth about the Lagers represents one of the major collective crimes of the German people and the most obvious demonstration of the cowardice to which Hitlerian terror had reduced them …. Without this cowardice the greatest excesses would not have been carried out, and Europe and the world would be different today.[18]

Catastrophic compliance characterized much of the art world in Nazi Germany, but the essays in this volume, authored by some of the leading scholars in the field, demonstrate that the political and cultural environment of the Third Reich was complex on a variety of levels. Not only did artistic production in the years from 1933 to 1945 show continuities with the Weimar and postwar years; it also revealed creative developments that are both surprising and disturbing, especially when considered in the context of state intervention in music, film, literature, and the visual arts. State intervention, whether political, bureaucratic, or economic, took many forms, and all of the essays to follow contribute to the trend in scholarship that challenges the notion of the state as totalitarian monolith in its direction of cultural affairs.

Diverse and inconsistent as the Nazi state's role may have been, it was the conviction that the arts were to function in the service of the nation, race, and *Volksgemeinschaft* that guided the regime's *Kulturpolitik*. As Alan Steinweis's leading essay illustrates, an "ethnic cleansing of German art and culture," fueled by Nazi anti-Semitism, was a guiding principle from the earliest days of the movement until its collapse in 1945. Indeed, it was this racist view of culture, combined with the principle of state agency and intervention, that had such disastrous consequences for Jews in the art world and for artistic creativity in general. Art, like so much else in Nazi society, was a tool functioning in the interests of the *Volksgemeinschaft*, and as such it could not tolerate the contaminating influence of Jews. And as Steinweis's analysis reveals, there were striking parallels between Nazi racial ideology as it was applied to the arts and Nazi racial ideology as it was applied to people. Pronatalist policies and public health initiatives sought to increase the health stock of the *Volk*, while the eugenics program sought to "streamline" society by purging the *corpus Germania* of the genetically unhealthy and inferior. In similar fashion, a two-track cultural policy worked to weed out corrupting and parasitic influences while offering the regime's support and patronage to artists whose work was considered "authentically Germanic." This is not to suggest, however, that the application of anti-Semitism to cultural policy took the form of a coherent state program initiated in 1933. Like the regime's anti-Jewish policies as a whole, the discrimination against and purging of Jews from the arts evolved over time. From the Reichstag Fire Decree, the Civil Service Law, and the formation of the Reich Chamber of Culture in 1933 to the expulsion of Jews from that body beginning in 1935 and the subsequent organization and staging of "Degenerate Art" and "Degenerate Music" exhibitions, the regime effectively, if rather haphazardly, signaled and enforced the purge of Jews and their artistic production from German culture. No less disturbing is Steinweis's concluding observation that these measures appear to have met with widespread approval in the art world and German society as a whole.

The German public was reluctant to oppose Nazi measures against Jews in the arts, but at the same time it was also reluctant to conform to the anti-American aspects of the regime's *Kulturpolitik*–an anti-Americanism that was based, to some extent, in racial ideology. As Michael Kater's contribution makes clear, American popular culture in its various forms had a strong influence on Germany in the Weimar years, and this influence carried over well into the 1930s and 1940s. Kater grounds his analysis in the important historiographical transition from an early post-war emphasis on the Nazi state as a totalitarian monolith enforcing cultural homogeneity to a later tendency, beginning in the 1960s, to view the regime in terms of its diverse social transformations and structural incoherence. For Kater, the presence and influence of American popular culture is best understood within the latter framework, for that culture's modernism, embodied in technology, consumerism, film, fashion, and music, emerged in Germany in the years of the Weimar Republic and continued to manifest itself throughout the Nazi era.

Not surprisingly, elements on the political right condemned American popular culture, which they associated with heightened sexuality, women's emancipation, and faddish and decadent music and dance. The Nazis, too, vilified these aspects of American culture, which they also identified with the allegedly corrosive and socially subversive influence of blacks and Jews. On the other hand, Hitler's personal attitudes toward the United States were rather ambivalent, and for a time the regime seemed willing to tolerate a degree of openness toward American films, popular music, and German-American personal and cultural exchanges. Jazz and swing were immensely popular among young Germans, while the influence of Hollywood resulted in nothing short of an "American film craze" in Germany prior to 1941.

The relative tolerance of things American came to an abrupt end with the outbreak of war between Germany and the United States, as the Nazi regime launched an unrestrained propaganda war as well. Racist attacks on American Jews and African-Americans intensified, and American culture was increasingly characterized as the product of moral and social decay. The corollary to this ideological shift was the persecution of young Germans who were devoted to American popular culture. As Kater explains, this was nothing short of a "witch hunt" undertaken against American popular culture and its adherents. By the war's end, prohibitions against swing dancing, arrests of jazz fans, incarceration of young men and women in the Ueckermark and Moringen concentration camps, and other such measures taken against those engaging in activities defined as "offensive to the state" had "all but snuffed out in a brutal campaign" those young Germans devoted to swing, jazz, and American film. Thus, whereas the Nazi state was willing to tolerate some American influences in the 1930s, the regime's coercive character came to the fore in its brutal wartime measures against young supporters and patrons of an allegedly modernist, consumerist, democratic, and racially corrupt culture.

In the end, Michael Kater's essay alerts us to the "negative" and potentially violent character of Nazi cultural policy; by contrast, Eric Rentschler's analysis illustrates the regime's attempts to cultivate a more "affirmative" and persuasive approach to the arts via film as a political tool. It may come as a surprise to some readers that the overwhelming majority (86 percent) of films made in Nazi Germany were not openly political, but were intended for popular entertainment. Yet, as Rentschler makes clear, film could be put to political use in both explicit and subtle ways. "What is essential about Nazi films," he writes, "is not so much their explicit propaganda, but the way in which they gave shape to reality and promulgated a worldview through the means of audio-visual fantasy ware."

Focusing first on Leni Riefenstahl's well-known *Triumph of the Will* (*Triumph des Willens*), Rentschler reveals how this highly choreographed "self advertisement," in the guise of a documentary on the 1934 Nuremberg Party Rally, could express the Nazi fantasy of the *Volksgemeinschaft*. Many of the film's images are familiar, not least because they are early, vivid models for the sort of political aesthetics and "mass ornaments" that are deployed today in the service of social goals. As such, these images have made both Riefenstahl and her film enduring objects of public fascination and, no less, public controversy. Controversy and debate notwithstanding, the blending of mass culture and mass propaganda in *Triumph* is clear.

What, however, is the relationship between mass culture as expressed in film and the murderous racial agenda of the Nazis? Rentschler addresses this question through his analysis of Veit Harlan's *Jew Süss* (*Jud Süss*), the most popular and influential anti-Semitic film to emerge in Nazi Germany. The story of a Jewish confidence man who infiltrates the Württemberg court and endangers the citizenry, *Jew Süss* is a register of Nazi anti-Jewish prejudices and fears. Moreover, according to Rentschler, the film represents a call to action. Its violent conclusion served as an object lesson for the public at large, while its immense popularity at the box office suggested, as Rentschler argues, that the German population would be willing to tolerate the regime's intensified anti-Semitic measures in the future.

The legacy of these films is complex, and Rentschler invites the reader to consider what is really at stake "when audio-visual artifacts from Nazi culture continue to circulate in our own times." Should we forbid "the postmodern citation of the Nazi past" or, conversely, "free these signifiers from their historical calling and dispose over them playfully and irreverently?" Neither a rigidly proscriptive nor a wholly permissive approach is entirely responsible, for these films and, indeed, countless other cultural artifacts of the era are ultimately "testimonies in need of historical judgment."

While Michael Kater's and Eric Rentschler's analyses focus on state policy and artistic activity in what we might broadly call "mass culture," the final three essays in this volume turn our attention toward the traditionally "high culture" worlds of music, literature, and the visual arts. In her essay on music in the Third Reich, Pamela Potter challenges the conventional notion that the Nazis were rigorously "totalitarian" in their censorship of music and in the cultivation of a "Germanic" musical culture. In fact, as Potter illustrates, the "Germanization" of music personnel and the music itself were complex tasks that, contrary to popular belief, were undertaken in a haphazard and ideologically inconsistent manner. Contrary to popular myth, artistic license did not cease, Hitler and the Nazis did not strictly control (nor would they have been capable of controlling) the composition, performance, and consumption of music, and state intervention in music was limited. Nor, according to Potter, "is there any evidence that total control over musical production was ever a priority for Nazi cultural policy-makers in the twelve years of the Reich." Nazi ideologues may have decried "Bolshevism," "Judaism," or "Americanism" in music, but they were never successful in consistently transforming a vague ideology of music into concrete policy. Instead, jazz increased in popularity, allegedly "degenerate" music survived, and a coherent censorship policy failed to materialize.

Far more successful, however, was the regime's goal of "dejewification" (*Entjudung*). The purge of Jewish composers and performers was not entirely consistent, but nonetheless resulted in discrimination, mass emigration, and death. And it stands as a tragic irony that the purge of "degenerate" composers and performers proved far easier to organize and enforce than a purge of "degenerate" music itself. As Potter concludes, "[i]n the end, although no one could clearly distinguish between German music and Jewish music *per se,* the physical separation and ensuing eradication of Jewish musical personnel served to satisfy the requirements of Nazi ideologues and mitigate the insecurities among the German music professions and the German nation as a whole."

Like the other essays in this volume, Frank Trommler's analysis discourages any monolithic view of the arts under the Nazis, for state policy on and public consumption of literature were, as he demonstrates, marked by inconsistencies and variations over time. Some would suggest that literature during the Third Reich was characterized by poor quality and ideological conformity under an efficient apparatus of state control. Noting elements of continuity among the Weimar, Nazi, and postwar periods, Trommler accounts for the Nazi efforts to encourage, through literature, an allegiance to the national community. This was undertaken through an emphasis on *völkisch* writing and, at the same time, the cultivation of a reading experience and public consumption that emphasized collective nationalist goals.

Literature could serve the nationalist project in variety of ways, and the Nazis advanced this agenda through organizing annual "Book Weeks," financing the construction of libraries, supporting any number of book prizes, and enlisting radical student organizations as the vanguard of an "intellectual pogrom" against literary works that were believed to be symbolic of the hated Weimar Republic or representative of subversive elements in society. Thus, the regime was committed to supporting literature as a nationalist tool, but at a high price: according to Trommler, the Nazis settled upon a "retrograde aesthetic," purged Germany of some of its best literary talent, and allowed for (or arguably supervised) the consistent drop in book production from 1933 to1945. Thus, responsibility for advancing the regime's limiting literary agenda fell to authors such as Hans Friedrich Blunck, Hanns Johst, and Hans Grimm; or to the youthful, and at times poetic and theatrical, efforts of the members of the writers' group Junge Mannschaft; or perhaps to an earlier tradition of literature built upon the experiences of World War I. Even as the Nazis promoted those writers whose work was consonant with their nationalist goals, they also worked to direct the consumption of literature along nationalist lines. "Reading," as Trommler observes, "was not to remain a solitary activity, but to become the basis for a collective experience of a *lesende Volksgemeinschaft* [reading racial community]." As the Third Reich moved toward war, the regime increasingly emphasized reception over production, and even went so far as to condemn an excessively individualistic "reading rage" as antisocial.

Trommler makes clear that the Nazis never succeeded in transforming the act of reading from a private to a collective practice, and evidence of this is easily found in an analysis of German reading habits during the years of the regime. The results are perhaps surprising, for available data suggest that the reading public was considerably more likely to enjoy the work of foreign authors, humorists, and science-oriented writers than politicized Nazi novels. Research in this area is not yet conclusive, but it is a departure from other analyses of literature in the Third Reich that emphasize ideology, censorship, and coercion.

Trommler concludes that "there are many ways of participating in or digressing from" a "command performance" in a dictatorship; this invites the reader to consider how those in the world of the visual arts responded to Nazi ideology, aesthetics, and attempts at control. This is the subject of Jonathan Petropoulos's concluding essay on the art world. Petropoulos uses three personalities–sculptor Arno Breker, art dealer Karl Haberstock, and museum director Ernst Buchner–to analyze the ways in which these leaders in the art world made professional choices, how they rationalized those choices, and the extent to which they were brought to justice for their complicity in Nazi policy. Breker, the most prominent among artists sanctioned by the Nazi regime, had close access to Hitler and other leading Nazis, and his work was regarded as especially expressive of key elements of Nazi *Kunstpolitik*: Aryan racial superiority, German military power, and the link to classical antiquity. He enjoyed the full support of the regime, profited immensely from his status, and enjoyed unparalleled publicity from Goebbels's propaganda ministry. As the most successful and powerful art dealer in Germany, Haberstock served many leading Nazis as clients, was instrumental in the effort to "liquidate" so-called "degenerate" art, and profited both financially and professionally from the purging of modern art from public collections and from the plunder of Jewish-owned art abroad. Buchner held the coveted position of director of the Bavarian State Painting Collections. An ardent nationalist who at times opposed the Nazis' agenda for the arts, Buchner remained a party member and, over time, easily acclimated himself to the opportunities offered by the regime. Thus, he purchased works abroad at deflated prices, cooperated with the Gestapo in the seizure of Jewish-owned art, and in the later war years worked with the regime to safeguard plundered art.

These three leaders in the Nazi art world were faced with choices: to remain in Germany or work abroad; to work with the Nazis, to oppose them, or to retreat into an "inner emigration." All three chose to remain Germany to pursue their careers. Breker enjoyed tremendous fame, Haberstock profited immensely from the purchase of "aryanized" property and the sale of modern art abroad, and Buchner willingly participated in the exploitive acquisition of plundered and underpriced art for Germany's galleries. Not surprisingly, after Nazi Germany's collapse these men effectively rationalized the choices they made, with Breker claiming his work was undertaken in an international style that was not ideological, Haberstock maintaining that he simply operated as an effective businessman in the interests of the art world, and Buchner styling himself as a defender of art against the regime's more radical elements and the destruction of war. Finally, with respect to justice, all three men were designated merely "fellow-travelers" in denazification hearings and went on to enjoy prosperous and respected postwar careers.

Each of these three individuals demonstrated both the complexity and facility of choices made under the Nazis, and the ways in which such choices were rationalized. Moreover, as Petropoulos contends, these choices illustrate that the art world "cannot be separated from ethical considerations." "Theft," he argues, "was an important juncture on 'the twisted road to Auschwitz,'" and the profits reaped from such theft not only enriched the perpetrator, but also contributed to the impoverishment and dehumanization of the victim. Finally, these case studies remind us that the three individuals involved were neither wholly guilty nor wholly innocent–the complexity of their behavior placing them in the ambiguous "gray zone" of culpability. This is not a call for moral relativism, for this story requires both the historian's objectivity and the historian's judgment. Remembering, as Petropoulos concludes, "that the Nazis were not only among the most malevolent leaders in history, but also among those most focused on culture and cultural policy," we are reminded that neither the world of art nor the worlds of literature, music, and film could remain entirely apolitical. The "nexus of culture and barbarism," if not always obvious, was a characteristic feature of the regime and is undoubtedly the most cautionary element in the history of the arts under National Socialism.

Notes

1. Henry Picker, *Hitlers Tischgespräche im Führerhauptquartier* (Stuttgart: Seewald Verlag, 1983, 94-95).
2. Jeremy Noakes and Geoffrey Pridham, eds., *Nazism, 1919-1945: A Documentary Reader*, vol. 2 (Exeter: University of Exeter, 1984), 398–399.
3. See Ian Kershaw, *Hitler 1889-1936: Hubris* (New York: W.W. Norton, 1999), 21–22.
4. Adolf Hitler, *Mein Kampf* (New York: Reynal and Hitchcock, 1941), 354–355.
5. See Alan Steinweis, *Art, Ideology, and Economics in Nazi Germany: The Reich Chambers of Music, Theater, and the Visual Arts* (Chapel Hill: University of North Carolina Press, 1993), 1–6.
6. Quintin Hoare and Geoffrey Nowell Smith, eds., *Selections from the Prison Notebooks of Antonio Gramsci* (New York: International Publishers, 1973), 265.
7. Ibid.
8. See Appendix B.
9. See Appendix C.
10. See Steinweis, *Art, Ideology, and Economics in Nazi Germany*, 7–8, 38–44.
11. Ibid., 2.
12. See Michael Kater, *The Twisted Muse: Musicians and Their Music in the Third Reich* (New York: Oxford University Press, 1997), 4–6. See also Michael Kater, *Different Drummers: Jazz in the Culture of Nazi Germany* (New York: Oxford University Press, 1992).
13. Examples of these earlier views include most notably Peter Gay, *Weimar Culture: The Outsider as Insider* (New York: Harper and Row, 1968); and George L. Mosse, *Nazi Culture: Intellectual, Cultural, and Social Life in the Third Reich* (New York: Grosset and Dunlap, 1966).
14. See, for example, Michael Walter, *Hitler in der Oper: Deutsches Musikleben, 1919-1945* (Stuttgart: J. B. Metzler, 1995), 118.
15. Kater, *The Twisted Muse*, 6.
16. Michael Kater, *Composers of the Nazi Era: Eight Portraits* (New York: Oxford University Press, 2000), 273.
17. See Pamela Potter, *Most German of the Arts: Musicology and Society from the Weimar Republic to the End of Hitler's Reich* (New Haven: Yale University Press, 1998), xvii.
18. Primo Levi, *The Drowned and the Saved*, trans. Raymond Rosenthal (New York: Summit Books, 1988), 15.

Chapter One

Anti-Semitism and the Arts in Nazi Ideology and Policy

Alan E. Steinweis

On 18 April 1937, the great German novelist Thomas Mann delivered an address to a Jewish audience in Carnegie Hall in New York City. Mann was one of the few German cultural luminaries who had voluntarily chosen a life in exile rather than remain in Nazi Germany. The main focus of his speech was on the contribution of Jews to the cultural and intellectual life of Germany, and, more generally, Europe. The Jews, Mann asserted, had brought something special and different to European culture. Mann attempted to articulate what this difference was. "The Jews," he observed: "are called the people of the Book. We must be aware of all the sensitiveness, receptivity, spiritual maturity, knowledge of suffering, love of the spiritual which is here symbolically implied in the word Book in order properly to understand the debt of gratitude which especially in Germany the literary spirit owes to the Jews." But this was not all. Mann continued to explain that the unique cultural and intellectual perspective of the Jews in Germany had derived from their "Mediterranean-European-Oriental" nature, an element otherwise missing in German society. Over the many centuries of Jewish habitation in central Europe, the intellectual essence of the Jews had become "part and parcel of, altogether inalienable from German morals and culture." For this reason, Mann concluded, no genuinely cultured German could be an anti-Semite.[1]

What is striking is Mann's insistence that Jews were in some fundamental way different from other Germans. He regarded this difference as a positive thing, as a source of creativity, and he championed what has often been called the "German-Jewish symbiosis," a mutually beneficial interdependence between two distinct entities. In believing that Jews and Germans were essentially different from one another, Mann was very much a person of his times. Adherents of the Zionist movement also underscored the unique cultural, spiritual, and even racial characteristics of the Jews. In their eyes, both the persistence of anti-Semitism among Gentiles and the pursuit of a pure Jewish identity underscored the futility of pursuing a Jewish symbiosis with other cultures. And then there were the anti-Semites, for whom the preferred metaphor for describing the Jewish relationship with Gentiles was not symbiosis, but rather parasitism.

The notion of Jews as economic and cultural parasites was a fundamental tenet of Nazism. From the beginning of its existence as an organized movement, the Nazi Party had emphasized the need for an ethnic cleansing of German art and culture. In its founding document, the 25-point program of 1920, the party had called for the "legal prosecution of all those tendencies in art and literature which corrupt our national life, and the suppression of cultural events which violate this demand."[2] Between the Nazi party's inception and its seizure of power in 1933, its official newspaper, the *Völkischer Beobachter*, consistently devoted ample space to artistic and cultural criticism. Hitler's keen personal interest in the arts, which he repeatedly displayed throughout his political career, may well have reflected an effort to overcome personal failure as an artist during his Vienna days. During the Nazi *Kampfzeit*, the "era of struggle" before 1933, Hitler's speeches often emphasized the need for a new national art policy (*Kunstpolitik*). In his book *Mein Kampf* (1924–25), Hitler elaborated upon his conception of the relationship between art and a future National Socialist regime. "It is the business of the state," he wrote, "to prevent a people from being driven into the arms of spiritual madness" and to guarantee "the preservation of those original racial elements which bestow culture and create beauty and dignity of a higher mankind."[3] This racialist conception of culture remained a core principle in Hitler's worldview. Throughout his years in power, Hitler was actively involved in the details of cultural policy, even to the point where he decided personally on the ambiguous racial credentials of artists and entertainers.[4]

Other Nazi spokesmen frequently elaborated upon National Socialist cultural principles. Alfred Rosenberg, the party's chief of ideology, explained that the *völkisch* state had the responsibility to cultivate the healthy and to root out the decadent in the nation's cultural life: "There arises from the idea of a cultural community the duty to nurture culture.

Biologically as well as spiritually understood, this means that we have the duty above all to promote organic growth, to promote that which is inwardly strong and necessary to life, that which serves the values of Germans and their beauty ideal. At the same time, the community must keep as far away as possible any growth which is sick or inwardly foreign, and which does not act in the best interests of Germandom but in the interest of undermining the German being."[5] In the same vein, Joseph Goebbels, the Minister for Public Enlightenment and Propaganda (Reichsminister für Volksaufklärung und Propaganda), often articulated the differences between the National Socialist conception of culture and the "liberal" principles that had prevailed in Germany during the Weimar Republic. The cultural and spiritual welfare of the "people's community" (*Volksgemeinschaft*), Goebbels liked to emphasize, took priority over the rights of the individual artist. The liberal notion of "art for art's sake" was, therefore, inconsistent with the tenets of National Socialism. As Goebbels explained, "we have replaced individuality with *Volk* and individual people with *Volksgemeinschaft*." The state had not only the right but also the obligation to advance art in the interests of the *Volksgemeinschaft*. "Culture is the higher expression of the creative power of a nation," and the artist as a "giver of meaning" is "as indispensable to the state as those who provide its material existence."[6]

German culture, the Nazis claimed, had been contaminated by alien influences, particularly Jewish ones. According to the Nazi view, Jews, lacking their own country, lived parasitically off their host societies, nourishing themselves economically and culturally at the expense of others. Having assimilated into German society, so went the Nazi argument, Jews moved into positions of influence in the press, music, theater, the visual arts, and other fields of cultural endeavor. But the Nazi racist view of the world ruled out the possibility of full and genuine assimilation. Jews, the Nazis argued, would always think and act like Jews, no matter how much they might take on the external characteristics of Germans. According to this logic, Jews could never really pursue an authentically Germanic culture, but only contaminate that culture with their own innately Jewish sensibility. An important responsibility of a Nazi government would be to purge Jews and their cultural production from German society.

These ideas were not invented by the Nazis. They extend well back into the nineteenth century, having arisen as part of the anti-Semitic reaction against the emancipation of the Jews and their subsequent integration into the mainstream of German society.[7] Nineteenth-century Germany (and other countries as well) had seen two phases in the development of anti-Semitism. Initially, anti-Semitism had focused on the religious and cultural otherness of the Jews. The answer to the so-called Jewish Question would be found in religious conversion to Christianity and assimilation to German culture. In the late nineteenth century, however, with the rise of Social Darwinism and modern biological racism, anti-Semites in Germany and elsewhere began to advocate the exact opposite. They no longer saw the Jews as a religious, cultural, and social group, but rather as a race. Racist anti-Semitism (like racism more generally) assumed that the characteristics, behaviors, and values of the Jews were fixed and unchangeable. Neither religious conversion nor cultural assimilation would alter their essential Jewishness. Racist anti-Semites, therefore, regarded assimilation as a dangerous chimera, a process they believed would facilitate Jewish parasitism by allowing the Jews to disguise themselves as Germans. Nazism embodied the legacy of this tradition of racist and exclusionist, as opposed to assimilationist, anti-Semitism.

As racist anti-Semitism developed in the late nineteenth and early twentieth centuries, its exponents attempted to document the parasitical influence of assimilated Jewry over German art and culture. Among the most frequently cited texts was "Judaism in Music," an essay published in 1850 by the composer Richard Wagner.[8] Although the essay did not explicitly define the Jews as a race, it tended in that direction by linking supposedly Jewish musical traits to physical characteristics that were frequently ascribed to Jews. Wagner claimed that German music was a "worm-infested corpse" that had been taken over by Jews. Despite their attempts to sound German, in Wagner's opinion, Jews, in both their speech and their music, could not help but retain the sounds that were peculiar to their nature. Jews might imitate German musical styles, but in the end their compositions and performances would always bear the marks of their Jewish origins. Wagner's depiction of Jews as an alien contaminant in German culture became common currency in the increasingly racist anti-Semitic polemics of the late nineteenth century. This view was represented in many of the standard works of that emerging genre. It was present, most notably, in the writings of Wagner's son-in-law, Houston Stewart Chamberlain, whose book *The Foundations of the Nineteenth Century*, published in 1899, became a touchstone work for later racist right-wing political movements.

It should be emphasized that a racial interpretation of art was by no means limited to occasional rants by disgruntled aesthetes. It appeared increasingly in writings that purported to be grounded in scholarship. Among the most influential proponents of this ostensibly scientific approach were Richard Eichenauer, Paul Schultze-Naumburg, and Hans F. K. Günther. Eichenauer's book *Musik und Rasse* (Music and Race), published in 1932, echoed the central theme of Wagner's "Judaism in Music," but used a language that was much more informed by racial theory.[9] Eichenauer criticized Jewish composers such as Gustav Mahler for attempting to sound German, and attacked modernist composers of Jewish background, most important among them Arnold Schoenberg, for their corrosive influence on German music.

Schultze-Naumburg's book *Kunst und Rasse* (Art and Race), published in 1928, was a frontal assault on modernism in the visual arts.[10] Through the use of many illustrations, Schultze-Naumburg attempted to demonstrate the close resemblance between the physical appearance of mentally disabled and physiologically deformed people on the one hand, and the images contained in modern paintings on the other. Through this method he hoped to prove a causal link between racial degeneration and modern art. While his publications did not focus specifically on Jews, Schultze-Naumburg was active in the anti-Semitic Kampfbund für deutsche Kultur (Combat League for German Culture), which was a creation of the Nazi movement.

Hans F. K. Günther was a prolific author of works on the origins of the "Nordic" and other races. In his book on the Jewish race, *Rassenkunde des jüdischen Volkes* (Racial Characteristics of the Jewish People), published in 1930, Günther made extensive use of artistic evidence to underscore the racial differences between Jews and other Europeans.[11] Günther interpreted the cultural influence attained by Jews in Germany as an incursion of an alien "racial soul" from Asia Minor, where he believed the primary racial origin of the Jewish people could be found. In 1930, Günther received a professorship at the University of Jena, made possible by Nazi participation in a coalition government in the German state of Thuringia. This same government also appointed Schultze-Naumburg to direct the Academy of Architecture, Visual Arts, and Design in the city of Weimar.

Both of these appointments reflected the escalating intensity of the culture war that raged in Germany during the period from 1918 to 1933. Nazi resentment of Jewish influence in the arts was closely connected with an antimodernist aesthetic sensibility. Although artistic modernism had made important inroads in Germany before 1918, it was during the Weimar Republic that it emerged in its full force in literature, painting and sculpture, architecture, music, and theater. Many of the artistic innovations attracted the wrath of cultural conservatives spanning the right side of the political spectrum. They condemned artistic modernism as overly cerebral and international. It did not conform to their notion of authentic "Germanness." The Nazi critique was especially emphatic in its emphasis on racial decay as the underlying cause of aesthetic degeneration. The regulation of cultural production through censorship would not by itself suffice to set matters right. They believed that the underlying cause of artistic decay had to be addressed by removing Jews and other alien influences from German cultural life.

One must ask why the Nazi assertion of a connection between Jewry and certain artistic innovations was deemed credible by many Germans. It is undeniable that Jews, or at least persons of Jewish heritage, numbered among the most prominent exponents of artistic modernism in the early twentieth century. This truth should not be rejected by Jews simply because anti-Semites have exploited it. At the same time, we must recognize how the Nazis misrepresented this truth. In actuality, the vast majority of Jewish artists in Germany were rather traditional in their aesthetic outlook, but Nazi ideology could not accommodate this reality. The Nazis saw Jewish cultural influence in Germany as a destructive pincers. Aesthetically progressive Jews were seen as corrupting German culture from the outside, while artistically traditional Jews were doing the same from the inside. In the racist cultural logic of Nazism, the Jews were damned no matter what.

During their fight to attain power in Germany, the Nazis translated this dimension of anti-Semitism into a strategy for attracting and mobilizing followers.

In 1928, the party created the Combat League for German Culture as a vehicle for expanding the Nazi movement's appeal among culturally conservative members of Germany's educated middle class.[12] The Combat League's leader, Alfred Rosenberg, was a close associate of Hitler and the chief of ideology in the party. The Combat League's stated mission was to "defend the value of the German essence" in the "midst of present-day cultural decadence" by promoting every "authentically native expression of German cultural life." It hoped to educate Germans about the "connections between race, art, and science." It would highlight the work of German artists who had been "silenced" by the forces of decay. Among the enemies of the "German essence," the Combat League identified Jews, communists, modernists, feminists, and the exponents of "nigger jazz." Public lectures were relatively inexpensive and easy to organize, and therefore quickly became the most common form of Kampfbund function. Early lecturers included Othmar Spann, a well-known theorist of authoritarian corporatism, and Alfred Heuss, the editor of the prestigious *Zeitschrift für Musik* (Journal of Music). Most often, however, it was Rosenberg himself who appeared on the podium to denounce the cultural manifestations of Judaism, Marxism, liberalism, and feminism. The Combat League remained a small organization of only a couple of thousand members, but its high-profile condemnations of "degenerate" modernism probably reinforced the widespread perception of Jews as agents of cultural decay.

When the Nazis came to power in Germany in 1933, they possessed no blueprint or master plan for the purification of German culture, but their guiding principles and priorities were clear enough. The Nazi approach to cultural policy can be understood as a variation on its notorious eugenics program, which purported to nourish the healthy while weeding out the "unhealthy" and the "alien." Thus, Nazi cultural policy unfolded simultaneously on parallel tracks. On one track, artists and cultural products considered to be authentically Germanic enjoyed government support and patronage. Through programs that in some important ways resembled measures undertaken in the United States as part of the New Deal, the Nazi regime subsidized the artistic endeavors of Germans who were acceptable in both racial and political terms. On another track, the Nazi regime presided over a massive purge of the German art world, excluding those who were considered racially alien—mainly Jews—and prohibiting the performance or exhibition of "un-German" art, which by definition included everything created by Jews. The censorship of Jewish works was accomplished through a complex system of official monitoring, in which blacklists formed one important component.

Jews constituted the largest segment of those who were purged from German cultural life on ideological grounds. But it should be emphasized that they were not the only ones. The Nazi "purification" of the arts also involved the exclusion of communists, homosexuals, "Gypsies" (i.e., Roma and Sinti), and others who did not conform to the Nazi vision of a true Germanic culture by virtue of their race, their political affiliation, or their personal behavior.

About 8,000 Jews were purged from culturally related positions during the first several years of Nazi rule.[13] The purge occurred in phases. The first stage of the purge, carried out in 1933, took the form of a series of improvised emergency measures implemented in a quasi-revolutionary atmosphere, which by the end of the year had evolved into a more systematic, institutionalized effort. In the spring of 1933 Nazi officials relied on special police powers derived from the Law for the Protection of the People and the State (Reichstag Fire Decree) of 28 February 1933 to prohibit performances by several prominent Jewish artists and entertainers, citing as their justification the need to maintain public order. Among the most famous of the Jewish figures affected by these actions was the conductor Bruno Walter, who was prevented from performing in Leipzig and Berlin. Walter eventually went into exile.[14] Like other German Jewish artists and intellectuals who chose exile early on, Walter possessed the advantage of an international reputation that would virtually guarantee employment and a comfortable existence outside of Germany. Although the Walter case was, or should have been, instructive to other Jewish artists who remained in Germany, demonstrating that an international reputation offered little protection against a regime that was pledged to eradicate Jewish influence from German culture, the vast majority initially chose, or were compelled, to remain. Considerable as the psychological and practical barriers in the way of emigration may have been for all German Jews,[15] they may well have been even greater for artists and intellectuals, whose roots were deeply embedded in German culture, and for whom employment prospects seemed dismal in a world still mired in the Depression.

The institutionalization of the purge began with the Law for the Restoration of the Professional Civil Service of 7 April 1933. This law resulted in the dismissal of thousands of Jews from positions of public employment, including all positions in radio broadcasting and most positions in academies of the fine and performing arts, orchestras, theater companies, and museums. These civil service positions had offered good pay and job security; the material and psychological consequences of these dismissals were therefore considerable. Measured quantitatively, in some fields the law's impact on Jews was minimal. For example, in all of Germany there were only two Jewish musicologists employed in German higher education, owing not only to the small size of the musicology profession, but also to the traditional animus against Jews in that field.[16] But in other fields, particularly music and theater, the impact of the law was felt much more broadly.

Because the majority of German Jewish artists and intellectuals had been privately rather than publicly employed, their status remained unaffected by the civil service law of 7 April. The Nazis, therefore, needed to design a new mechanism through which the cultural purge of Jews could be made universal. This mechanism was created in the autumn of 1933 in the form of the Reich Chamber of Culture (Reichskulturkammer) and its subchambers for music, the visual arts, theater, literature, film, radio, and the press. A host of artistic unions and professional associations that had been active in the Weimar Republic, most of which had Jewish members, were forcibly integrated into the new organization. The Chamber of Culture operated under the supervision of Nazi propaganda minister Joseph Goebbels, who was among the more fanatical anti-Semites within the German leadership. Membership in the chamber was declared compulsory for the hundreds of thousands of Germans engaged in artistic and intellectual life. Growing out of a broader Nazi ideological goal that sought to reorganize the occupational structure of German society, the chamber was supposed to resemble the guilds of the middle ages, whose members would regulate and police their own occupations under the protective hand of the government.[17] During the Third Reich, the chamber served as the primary means through which the Nazi regime could pursue its dual-track policy toward the arts. Members of the chamber enjoyed a variety of protections and benefits, while persons who were excluded from the chamber were forbidden to engage in artistic activity professionally or in public.

One provision in the law establishing the chamber system was especially important to the regime's ability to expand the cultural purge. Paragraph 10 provided for refusing membership to any person who did "not possess the necessary reliability and aptitude for the practice of his activity."[18] Unlike the so-called "Aryan paragraphs" that were included in many other Nazi-era statutes, including the Civil Service Law, Paragraph 10 did not specifically employ racial definitions. But it was precisely the elasticity of the language that made Paragraph 10 a versatile weapon in the hands of the regime. The key word "reliability" could be interpreted flexibly so as to exclude from membership in the chambers not only persons who were considered racially alien, but also those who were deemed to be politically, artistically, or personally objectionable. Because of the compulsory nature of the chamber system, rejection of membership or expulsion was tantamount to cultural blacklisting. Early on, Goebbels made clear that membership in the chamber would not be open to Jews, and starting in early 1935, the chamber expelled Jews systematically.

With this new purge mechanism in place by the end of 1933, the regime now had at its disposal the technical and procedural means necessary to build on the dismissals that had ensued from the Civil

Service Law and to bring the cultural purge of Jews to completion. But this did not happen immediately. Over a year would pass before widespread, systematic use of Paragraph 10 against Jews would commence. The main reason for the delay was technical. Time was needed for members and potential members of the chambers to gather and submit documentation of their ancestry. Additional time was required for the bureaucratic processing of all this data, as well as for the preparation of lists of Jews who would be refused membership or expelled.

But the mountains of paperwork were not the only obstacle. There was also some disagreement within the leadership of the chambers about the speed and thoroughness of the purge. Some objections were based on principle, as was that of Richard Strauss, the famous composer who agreed to serve as president of the Chamber of Music. He was forced out of that position largely as a result of his opposition to the purge. Other objections were based more on pragmatic, and specifically economic, concerns. The Minister of Economics, Hjalmar Schacht, specifically feared that the application of Paragraph 10 to Jewish-owned publishing houses, art dealerships, and similar cultural enterprises might lead to the collapse of those businesses, which would have a negative impact on Germany's unemployment and balance of trade situations. After special provisions were made to allow such economically indispensable Jewish business operators to remain active (at least for a while), the mass expulsions of Jews from the chambers was initiated in early 1935. By the end of 1936 about 6,000 Jews had been purged from the chambers.[19]

The gradual nature of the culture purge conformed to a pattern common in other occupations from which Jews were excluded in the 1930s. Assessing this situation from our post–Holocaust perspective, the membership of several thousand Jews in the Chamber of Culture for a short time in the early and mid-1930s might seem like a trivial detail. But it may well have had a significant and tragic psychological consequence for some German Jews, contributing to false hopes about the possibility of preserving a more or less normal Jewish existence in Germany.

The creation of the Jüdischer Kulturbund (Jewish Cultural League) in 1933 was a factor further affecting the psychological accommodation of German Jews to their victimization by Nazi cultural policy.[20] Created by Jews with the assent of the regime, the cultural league sponsored and organized concerts, plays, and other events performed by Jews before exclusively Jewish audiences. The league provided employment for Jewish artists who had been dismissed from their positions, while at the same time carving out a space in which Jewish audience members could enjoy themselves and find respite from the mounting hardships of daily life in Nazi Germany. The Nazi regime exploited the existence of the league for its own purposes. It preferred to see Jewish artists working for money rather than living off the public dole, and it invoked the League to prove to foreign critics that the Jews were not being treated inhumanely. Finally, the creation of a ghettoized Jewish cultural space within Germany made perfect sense from the perspective of Nazi ideology. Cultural events mounted by the league were allowed to feature only works that had been composed or written by Jews. This would promote the cultural dissimilation of the Jews in Germany, undoing the damage supposedly created by past decades of Jewish cultural assimilation. From the Jewish point of view at the time, the league might well have cushioned the impact of cultural exclusion, but considered objectively, its most major consequence may have been to have lured some Jews into a false sense of security. Elizabeth Bab, the wife of a league official, later observed with the benefit of hindsight that among some Jews the league had nurtured the "fantasy that they could do themselves and their companions some good."[21]

A very small number of Jews, and larger numbers of so-called mixed-race persons (*Mischlinge*), were allowed to remain active in mainstream German cultural life beyond the conclusion of the major purge of 1935–1936.[22] These individuals were the recipients of what were known as "special dispensations," which in most cases had been issued for economic reasons, but in some instances were the result of favoritism or well-placed connections. In his diaries, which have now been published almost in their entirety, Minister for Public Enlightenment and Propaganda Joseph Goebbels referred to these *Mischlinge* and special cases repeatedly, always underscoring his desire to eliminate these residual racial contaminants within German cultural life.[23] That Goebbels could be so distracted by a few instances of ideological inconsistency is compelling evidence of his determination to address the "Jewish Question" in his own sphere of authority.[24]

The Nazi regime energetically attempted to legitimize its anti-Jewish cultural policies. It would not be an exaggeration to say that Nazi propaganda aimed at the general population was deeply obsessed by the supposed Jewish cultural domination of Germany. The extent of this obsession was reflected in a large, pseudoscholarly book, *Die Juden in Deutschland* (The Jews in Germany), published in 1935 by the Institut zum Studium der Judenfrage (Institute for the Study of the Jewish Question), a unit of the Ministry for Public Enlightenment and Propaganda.[25] The book contained chapters devoted to Jewish activities in the economy, politics, and other aspects of German life, yet fully half of the book's 400 pages were dedicated to documenting the "Jews as Administrators of German Culture." The book appeared at precisely the time that the Nazi purge of the Jews from the arts was in full swing.

Creating public support for the purge of Jews from German culture was also one of the basic purposes served by two high-profile exhibitions mounted by the regime. In 1937 the propaganda ministry organized a huge exhibition titled "Degenerate Art," which opened in Munich and then traveled to several other cities over the next three years. The paintings and sculptures featured in the exhibition had been removed from German art museums on account of their alleged decadent modernism. Although most of the objects in the exhibition had not been created by Jews, the accompanying text attempted to drive home the connection between cultural degeneracy and the Jewish race. Works by Marc Chagall, among other Jewish artists, were labeled as a "revelation of the Jewish racial soul." The exhibition frequently invoked the epithet of "Judeo-Bolshevism," this being the notion that Jews promoted radical Marxism as a means to promote the disintegration of German society.[26]

The "Degenerate Art" exhibition proved extremely popular; about two million visitors attended during the four months it was on view in Munich. We have no reliable way of assessing public responses to the exhibition. Ironically, the exhibition offered to admirers of modern art an opportunity to see works that had been censored. But for many (perhaps most) viewers, the exhibition fulfilled its intended purpose. The Sicherheitsdienst (Security Service), which monitored German public attitudes on a wide variety of issues, reported an overwhelmingly positive reception of the exhibition among the German public.[27] One young visitor, who later became a professor of art history in the United States, was convinced that most who attended the exhibition came away from it convinced that modern art had been a giant sham foisted onto German society by a conspiracy of art dealers, critics, and museum directors.[28] Even more anti-Semitic in content and tone was the exhibition "Degenerate Music," which accompanied the Reich Music Days, a national festival in Düsseldorf in 1938. The exhibition presented Jews as the enemies of German musical culture, emphasizing the Jewish role in promoting not only modern music but also jazz, which Nazism condemned for its alleged primitivism and its roots in African American culture.

How did non-Jewish Germans respond to the exclusion of Jews from cultural life and to their demonization through Nazi cultural propaganda? The Security Service reports on public opinion contain no hint of dissatisfaction on account of these measures.[29] Furthermore, the documentation of the Ministry for Public Enlightenment and Propaganda and the Reich Chamber of Culture, the two agencies most involved in implementing the purge, contains no evidence that the officials in charge were overly concerned with opposition to the measures; nor do the detailed diaries of Joseph Goebbels, who otherwise made numerous entries chronicling the process of cultural de-Judaization. There were, to be sure, isolated instances of opposition, perhaps the best known example of which was Wilhelm Furtwängler, the celebrated conductor of the Berlin Philharmonic, who objected to the removal of his Jewish musicians.[30] It is important that the risks faced by opponents of Nazi anti-Jewish measures not be underestimated. But we also know that the legal, bureaucratic, nonviolent measures taken against Jews during the 1930s generally met with widespread approval in German society, in which the belief that Jews had achieved too much influence was a matter of consensus.[31] Aside from the ideological factor of anti-Semitism, professional and economic opportunism also played an important role, as many Germans stood personally to profit from the purge of Jews from cultural life. Some German artists welcomed the elimination of Jewish competition, believing that it would enhance their chances for employment, promotion, and recognition.[32]

Some contemporary observers did not fail to recognize the tragic significance of this widespread acquiescence and complicity in the purge of Jews from German cultural life. In his Carnegie Hall speech of 18 April 1937, cited at the beginning of this essay, Thomas Mann condemned his German compatriots for their abysmal conduct. In their willingness to abandon their Jewish colleagues, and in their readiness to embrace the Nazi regime and its cultural policies, Mann lamented, German artists and intellectuals had "dishonored themselves and deserve nothing better than the pitiable role they now play under the lash of the rabble."

Notes

1. Thomas Mann, "The Jewish Martyrdom," *Opinion: A Journal of Jewish Life and Letters*, May 1937, 9–11.

2. Jeremy Noakes and Geoffrey Pridham, eds., *Nazism, 1919-1945: A Documentary Reader*, vol. 1 (Exeter: University of Exeter Press, 1983), 16.

3. Adolf Hitler, *Mein Kampf*, trans. Ralph Mannheim (Boston: Houghton Mifflin, 1943), 258–259, 391.

4. Details in Alan E. Steinweis, *Art, Ideology, and Economics in Nazi Germany: The Reich Chambers of Music, Theater, and the Visual Arts, 1933-1945* (Chapel Hill: University of North Carolina Press, 1993), 117–118.

5. Robert Pois, ed., *Race and Race History, and Other Essays by Alfred Rosenberg* (New York: Harper and Row, 1970), 163.

6. Quotations from speech delivered by Goebbels at the inauguration of the Reichskulturkammer on 15 November 1933, reprinted in Joseph Goebbels, *Goebbels-Reden*, vol. 1, ed. Helmut Heiber (Düsseldorf: Droste, 1971), 131–141.

7. For the nineteenth-century background to these ideas, several classic studies are still useful, the two most important of which are George L. Mosse, *The Crisis of German Ideology: Intellectual Origins of the Third Reich* (New York: Grosset and Dunlap, 1964); Fritz Stern, *The Politics of Cultural Despair: A Study in the Rise of the Germanic Ideology* (Berkeley: University of California Press, 1961; paperback ed. 1974).

8. Richard Wagner, "Judaism in Music," in *Richard Wagner: Stories and Essays*, ed. Charles Osborne (London: Owen, 1973), 23–39. The extent of Wagner's anti-Semitism, and that of his music, has been a matter of some controversy. See Jacob Katz, *The Darker Side of Genius: Richard Wagner's Antisemitism* (Hanover, NH: University Press of New England, 1986); Theodor W. Adorno, *In Search of Wagner*, trans. Rodney Livingstone (New York: Verso, 1981); Mark A. Weiner, *Wagner and the Anti-Semitic Imagination* (Lincoln: University of Nebraska Press, 1995); and, most recently, Na'ama Sheffi, *The Ring of Myths: The Israelis, Wagner, and the Nazis*, trans. Martha Grenzeback (Brighton: Sussex Academic Press, 2001).

9. Richard Eichenauer, *Musik und Rasse* (Munich: Lehmanns, 1932). For an analysis see Pamela Potter, *Most German of the Arts: Musicology and Society from the Weimar Republic to the End of Hitler's Reich* (New Haven: Yale University Press, 1998), 179–181.

10. Paul Schultze-Naumburg, *Kunst und Rasse* (Munich: Lehmanns, 1935).

11. Hans F. K. Günther, *Rassenkunde des jüdischen Volkes* (Munich: Lehmanns, 1930).

12. Alan E. Steinweis, "Weimar Culture and the Rise of National Socialism: The Kampfbund für deutsche Kultur," *Central European History* 24 (1991), 402–423.

13. Estimate based on census statistics of Jewish participation in cultural fields in 1933, and on Reich Chamber of Culture documentation concerning expulsions. For details see Steinweis, *Art, Ideology, and Economics*, 104–113.

14. On the Walter case see Michael H. Kater, *The Twisted Muse: Musicians and their Music in the Third Reich* (New York: Oxford University Press, 1997), 114–116, and Pamela M. Potter, "The Nazi 'Seizure' of the Berlin Philharmonic, or the Decline of a Bourgeois Musical Institution," in *National Socialist Cultural Policy*, ed. Glen R. Cuomo (New York: St. Martin's Press, 1995), 47–48.

15. Two key recent studies are Saul Friedländer, *Nazi Germany and the Jews: The Years of Persecution, 1933-1939* (New York: HarperCollins, 1997), and Marion Kaplan, *Between Dignity and Despair: Jewish Life in Nazi Germany* (New York: Oxford University Press, 1998).

16. See Potter, *Most German of the Arts.*

17. These issues are explored thoroughly in Steinweis, *Art, Ideology, and Economics,* 73–102.

18. The text of Paragraph 10 can be found in any one of several reference works and legal compendia published during the Nazi regime, two of the most useful of which are Hans Hinkel, *Handbuch der Reichskulturkammer* (Berlin: Deutscher Verlag für Politik und Wirtschaft, 1937), and Karl-Friedrich Schrieber, Alfred Metten, and Herbert Collatz, eds., *Das Recht der Reichskulturkammer: Sammlung der für den Kulturstand geltenden Gesetze und Verordnungen, der amtlichen Anordnungen und Bekanntmachungen der Reichskulturkammer und ihrer Einzelkammern.* 2 vols. (Berlin: de Gruyter, 1943).

19. For background on Schacht's impact on anti-Jewish policy see Uwe Dietrich Adam, *Judenpolitik im Dritten Reich* (Düsseldorf: Droste, 1972 and Königstein im Taunus: Athenäum, 1979), 88, 122–124. In his diaries Goebbels reacted bitterly against what he (incorrectly) deemed Schacht's protection of Jews. See *Die Tagebücher von Joseph Goebbels: Sämtliche Fragmente. Teil I: Aufzeichnungen 1924-1941*, vol. 3, ed. Elke Fröhlich (Munich: K. G. Saur, 1987), entry for 4 November 1937.

20. The most detailed study of the Kulturbund is Volker Dahm, "Kulturelles und geistiges Leben," in *Die Juden in Deutschland 1933-1945: Leben unter nationalsozialistischer Herrschaft,* ed. Wolfgang Benz (Munich: Beck, 1988), 75–267. On the Nazi official who supervised the Kulturbund see Alan E. Steinweis, "Hans Hinkel and German Jewry," *Leo Baeck Institute Yearbook* 38 (1993): 209–219.

21. Kaplan, *Between Dignity and Despair,* 42.

22. "In der Kammer tätige Voll-, Dreiviertel- u. Halbjuden," 1937, file on "Entjüdung der Einzelkammern," files of the Reichskulturkammer Zentrale, former Berlin Document Center (BDC) materials, Bundesarchiv (BA), Berlin.

23. *Die Tagebücher von Joseph Goebbels: Sämtliche Fragmente. Teil I*, vol. 2, entries for 4 September, 5 October 1935; vol. 3, entries for 5 May, 5 June, 2 July, 21 September, 9 October, 4 November, 24 November, 11 December, 15 December, 16 December 1937, 13 January, 9 February, 18 May, 27 July, 1938, 26 January 1939.

24. For a detailed discussion see Glenn R. Cuomo, "The Diaries of Joseph Goebbels as a Source for the Understanding of National Socialist Cultural Politics," in *National Socialist Cultural Policy,* ed. Cuomo, 197–245.

25. Institut zum Studium der Judenfrage, *Die Juden in Deutschland* (Munich: Eher, 1935). This institute should not be confused with the Research Department for the Jewish Question, an arm of Walter Frank's Reich Institute for History of the New Germany, or with Alfred Rosenberg's Institute for Research on the Jewish Question. Both of these units aspired to academically respectable anti-Semitic Jewish research in a way that the propaganda ministry's institute did not.

26. For a detailed reconstruction of the exhibition see Mario Andreas von Lüttichau, "Entartete Kunst, Munich 1937: A Reconstruction," in *"Degenerate Art": The Fate of the Avante-Garde in Nazi Germany*, ed. Stephanie Barron (New York: Los Angeles County Museum of Art/Harry Abrams, 1991), 45–81.

27. "Vierteljahreslagebericht 1939 des Sicherheitshauptamtes," in *Meldungen aus dem Reich: Die geheimen Lageberichte des Sicherheitsdienstes der SS, 1938-1945*, ed. Heinz Boberach, 17 vols. (Herrsching: Pawlak, 1984), vol. 2, 275–276.

28. Peter Guenther, "Three Days in Munich, July 1937," in Barron, *Degenerate Art*, 33–43.

29. The Security Service (SD) was not reluctant to report on public dissatisfaction about a wide range of other issues. It must, however, be pointed out that these reports begin in 1938, by which time the purge of Jews from the cultural fields had been largely completed.

30. Kater, *The Twisted Muse*, 196–198.

31. The distinction between the German public's approval of legal and orderly anti-Semitism and its discomfort with violence targeted at Jews is a theme developed in the following works: David Bankier, *The Germans and the Final Solution: Public Opinion under Nazism* (Oxford: B. Blackwell, 1992); Ian Kershaw, *Popular Opinion and Political Dissent in the Third Reich: Bavaria 1933-1945* (Oxford: Clarendon Press, 1983); Robert Gellately, *The Gestapo and German Society: Enforcing Racial Policy, 1933-1945* (Oxford: Oxford University Press, 1990).

32. For an analysis of this dimension of the response see Ernst Piper, "Nationalsozialistische Kulturpolitk und ihre Profiteure: Das Beispiel München," in *"Niemand war dabei und keiner hat's gewusst": Die deutsche Öffentlichkeit und die Judenverfolgung 1933-1945*, ed. Jörg Wollenberg (Munich: Piper, 1989), 129–157.

Chapter Two

THE IMPACT OF AMERICAN POPULAR CULTURE ON GERMAN YOUTH

Michael H. Kater

CLASSIC, LONG-ENTRENCHED VIEWS of National Socialism and the totalitarian Third Reich hold that Hitler's polity was a streamlined monolith, unbreakable and having a well-defined beginning and ending, with strong codes for the collective life of society, tolerating neither exceptions nor any contradictions.[1] For many years, rigid models such as these blocked more differentiated interpretations. These could have resulted in the recognition of more brittle societal textures, greater fluidity in the development of pre-Nazi to Nazi phenomena and, as an important matter of timing in defining the end of the Third Reich, skepticism regarding the artificial construct "Zero Hour" (Stunde Null). According to the traditional historiographical lore, "Zero Hour" in May 1945 was to have marked a genuine chasm between the old era of dictatorial oppression and a new one characterized by rejuvenated democracy, to be accompanied by its customary civic liberties and duties. As the concept of "Zero Hour" is increasingly being demolished today, and not just in political terms,[2] such doubts come at the end of a long line of queries over the years regarding the alleged homogeneity of National Socialism and the Third Reich as self-contained entities, consistently sustained by their own logic, however depraved.

In the mid 1960s, David Schoenbaum outlined multiple processes of social transformation in the Nazi Reich, shaking at its roots a very Nazi thesis of a single, predefined, social revolution and asking penetrating questions about the role of Nazism as a vanguard of modernity.[3] Not yet five years later, Reinhard Bollmus wrote of the Social Darwinism of Nazi institutions programmed to cannibalize each other (if not for Hitler's ultimate decision-making), thereby alluding to constant flux, even turmoil—anything but stasis—in the twelve years of Nazi organizational rule.[4] Parallel to and beyond Bollmus's work, Hans Mommsen produced evidence of structural incoherence, hence negating the dynamics, and in the final analysis the efficacy, of Nazi rule.[5] Radicalization of gubernatorial processes, of which Mommsen has written in his later works, extend and complement his earlier theories about the many inconsistencies of Nazi administration, without conclusively settling the issue of its efficiency. In more recent years, led by Ian Kershaw, there has been discussion about a constant dialectic between the subjects and their rulers, in particular Hitler himself, whose increasing reign of terror was abetted by processes within the German populace that worked "towards the Führer," thereby assuring his essential functions until the end.[6] That Hitler's persona as omnipotent tyrant may have depended on the willing interaction with his citizen clientele is a view far removed from the early exegeses of Nazi historiography, as is the derivative thesis that, because of this willingness, Hitler needed fewer policemen than commonly prescribed in manuals for police states, and that he received gratuitous backing by countless little would-be Hitlers.[7]

More flexible models of Hitlerian governance such as these might explain why, in an allegedly rigid and immutable neo-Germanic structure such as the Third Reich after January 1933, certain phenomena from the liberal-democratic Weimar era, although officially not allowed, penetrated the dictatorship seemingly easily and undetected, at least until the watershed of World War II. They might also account for almost ritualistic affinities that less than bona-fide members of Nazi society had for things patently non-German, such as elements of American popular culture, embellished and driven, to some extent, by U.S.-type mass-consumerist phenomena. This essay will attempt to trace the pre-Nazi origins of such often cultist commodities as U.S.-style films, certain brands of popular music derived from them, as well as jazz and the swing dance, and their peculiar attraction for youth. Positing that in their intrinsic modernism the original (German) locus of these cultural articles was the pre-Nazi and American-influenced Weimar Republic, this essay considers why these genres, as byproducts of modernism, were allowed to cross over into an illiberal Third Reich. As it turned out, they were carried by many of the Reich's younger subjects, who did astonishingly well in espousing them and moving them a stretch or two even into the war period, although at ever greater risk to themselves.

Images of America that influenced adolescents in the Third Reich ultimately derived from German-American relations in the Weimar Republic. To an appreciable extent, that republic's modernity was determined by phenomena originating across the Atlantic. It was because these were perceived as modern and as a potential vehicle of open disagreement with the rulers that young people under Hitler were attracted to them.

American-derived modernity in Weimar society had two sides. One was the technical, expressing itself through the rationalization of production processes and the normification and standardization of products. The catchword "Taylorism" stood for those; it heralded a broader consumer culture.[8] The other side was political and cultural; to the extent that mass democracy was introduced, popular, mass culture made inroads at the lower end of the societal spectrum. At the higher end, this modernity manifested itself in aesthetic movements such as the Bauhaus (which counted among its members the American painter Lyonel Feininger), in ambitious stage works such as Ernst Kreneks *Jonny spielt auf* (1927) or Kurt Weill and Paul Hindemith's *Der Lindberghflug* (1929), and perhaps in a few high-quality films. American myths became the quintessential "symbol of modernity," wrote Detlev Peukert.[9]

It is the popular culture current that interests us most here. Its essential ingredient was film. Film, as a U.S. invention, significantly born of the original technical processes mentioned above, did develop a strong indigenous German quality and spawned the Universum Film-Aktiengesellschaft (Ufa) of Berlin, soon one of the world's leading motion-picture companies.[10] Nonetheless, by 1925 U.S. films constituted 60 percent of all films shown in Germany. American trends led the way, not only in terms of technical progress (rationalization, automation, mechanization—the characteristics of the city), but also with respect to human role models. During the silent-movie era that lasted until ca. 1928, Charlie Chaplin became an icon; German actors patterned themselves on U.S. exemplars. With the introduction of the "talkies" in the late 1920s, American actors such as Al Jolson predominated. Films had an egalitarian effect befitting a new democracy; huge movie cinemas were built in all the major German cities, inviting a broadly representative segment of the population and imparting hitherto unknown "modern" images and values, that of the grotesque (Chaplin, Harold Lloyd), quick rhythmic motion, stereotypical happy endings à la Hollywood, and bold fashion ideas.[11]

Some of this fashion was personified by a new type of liberated woman, or liberated as she was imagined to be in the United States: young, independent, self-secure, clothes-conscious, with slender limbs and bobbed hair, and potentially capable of mastering a film role. In 1925, Fritz Giese described "das Girl" as an American archetype jumping out of the new consumer staple, the U.S. film, and into the lap of enthusiastic audiences via German cinema screens. But more importantly, she was the model of the emancipated Weimar-republican young woman.[12]

Yet another strong element of U.S. feature films was music, especially after Al Jolson crooned "Sonny Boy" in the classic flick *The Singing Fool*, which in February 1928 drew crowds of 300,000 in Berlin alone. The recording of this song sold 12 million copies in short order, and it formed the basis for much of the popular and jazz music that was performed in Germany thereafter.[13]

Never far removed from film or film music, jazz in particular was popularized in Germany by visiting American bands that sometimes played, à la Paul Whiteman, in a style purists found repulsive, but also by the developing German radio network, especially after 1930. In June of that year, Hans Blüthner, a sales apprentice not yet twenty years old, was listening to "Negermusik" on Berlin's radio station Funkstunde. This was a program by the U.S. orchestra leader Sam Wooding, who featured "St. Louis Blues" by W.C. Handy, and "Love Me or Leave Me" by Kahn-Donaldson.[14] The African American revue dancer Josephine Baker, intermittently based in Paris, toured Germany, exemplifying a curious mixture of sex and commercialized jazz, with which she intrigued Harry Graf Kessler, the champion of modernist art and theater.[15] Jazz, however badly performed or represented by visiting American artists and, increasingly, by German dance-band musicians, became so great a hallmark of modernism in Weimar Germany that, naturally, the emblematic Bauhaus had to have its own jazz band.[16] Initially, those dance band musicians had taken their cue from the American standard by interpreting the art more as an act of vaudeville cacophony, which usually resulted from ignorance of the original style and a lack of musical skills. Hence, during the early stages of German jazz it was common for the drummer to play the clown and produce merely noise rather than a pulse on his drums; indeed, in those days the entire drum set was called "the jazz."[17]

Even as German jazz was maturing and becoming more credible, it retained its proximity to current pop tunes and its epigonal qualities to the point that both American and German experts were relentless in their criticism.[18] However, by 1928 Bernhard Sekles, the director of the Hoch'sche Konservatorium in Frankfurt, had founded a jazz class scheduled for cellist Matyas Seiber, who wished to educate German music students in jazz technique, even though some critics cynically dismissed it as a mere exercise in the arts and crafts.[19] At the end of the Weimar Republic, the young German pianist Georg Haentzschel, who in 1942 would compose the film music for the Nazi hit *Baron Münchhausen*, had learned how to perform jazz like the best of his American peers. He knew his harmony and prided himself on being able to play block chords, with locked or crossed hands. "People thought I was an American," he claimed, "because from the outset my piano-playing was conceived in that way."[20]

To the extent that official relations between Germany and the United States were improving after the end of World War I, interpersonal exchanges were increasing between groups and individuals from both countries. German engineers, for instance, studied rationalization procedures in American factories and chain stores.[21] These exchanges occurred most notably among youth and at the level of higher education. Armed with their strong dollars, young Americans, including some jazz musicians, crossed the Atlantic to Germany, often by way of London or Paris. They were warmly received by an enlightened, democratic-minded German public. Conversely, German university students in need of money and experience sailed for the United States as "work students" who would be employed in a U.S. factory and, upon their return home, would spread favorable news about the land of unlimited opportunities. The very institution of the work student was copied from the U.S., and was making important headway in the German university student population. In 1930, the United States established the Carl Schurz Memorial Foundation with the aim of fostering cultural relations between both countries. It aided the influx of American study groups into Germany.[22]

Opposition to these currents emanated mainly from the political right: the more right-wing the party or lobby, the stronger the protest.[23] Against the background of a lost world war, for which U.S. President Woodrow Wilson and his Fourteen Points were blamed, various foreign-political and economic arguments were used to discredit the United States, its Wall Street, its technological progress, and its modernist "American" ideas. Within this framework, common targets in politics were the Versailles Treaty of 1919, the Dawes Plan of 1924, and the Young Plan of 1929.[24]

Ideologically, an assortment of ultraconservative interest groups combated *Amerikanismus* as the epitome of the despised Weimar modernism. American films, the new ideal of an emancipated woman coupled with a more enlightened sexuality, popular music and jazz, and new-society dance fads such as the shimmy, foxtrot, and one-step were vilified. The attackers were members of the paramilitary Freikorps, patriotic youth groups, bigoted women's leagues, and the established media of culture such as the journal *Die Musik* or the tabloid *Süddeutsche Monatshefte*, the brainchild of the converted and anti-Semitic Jew Paul Nikolaus Cossmann. Cossmann's close friend, the composer Hans Pfitzner, also raged against American excrescences in his writings. Throughout, these phenomena were called into question on racial grounds because of their close identification with the despised Negroes and Jews, and were said to permeate all of what might masquerade as culture in America.[25]

Leading Nazis were the chief antagonists. They kept hammering away at Weimar culture as a derivative of the culture of American Jews, blacks, and licentious "girl" types. In their negative evaluation of African American phenomena, they allowed themselves to be guided by the pseudoscientific research of German anthropologists and eugenicists such as Ernst Haeckel, Alfred Ploetz, Eugen Fischer, and Fritz Lenz, who claimed to be able to prove the Negroes' inferiority.[26]

Hence, Hans Schemm, a Nazi Party leader from Bayreuth, spoke out publicly against the former Weimar Reichswehr Minister Gustav Noske, against the Jewish confidence men Barmat, Sklarek, and Kutisker, who were seen as responsible for widespread financial scandals, and against jazz, equating all with "moral degeneration."[27] Hugo Rasch, an active member of the Nazi storm troopers (SA) who was also a music critic, condemned Sekles and Seiber's efforts at the Frankfurt conservatory, writing that nowadays it was not impossible for a theme from Richard Wagner's *Tannhäuser* to be grunted by "blue Negro lips" or turned into a foxtrot. With reference to Krenek's *Jonny spielt auf,* Rasch warned of that "piece of Negro in America — the slave who broke the chain. Preserve your holiest possession: German culture, German art!"[28] Joseph Goebbels, who later would control most of the culture establishment in the Third Reich, felt that the U.S. vocal group "The Revelers" was issuing "crap," and labeled the plot of Jolson's *The Singing Fool* "terrible New York sentimental kitsch."[29] Goebbels' rival for control of German culture, Alfred Rosenberg, polemicized against what he called "nigger culture" more than any other Nazi because, fanatic that he was, he was also in charge of several publication outlets, including the Nazi Party's daily, *Völkischer Beobachter*.[30] When, in January of 1930, Wilhelm Frick, the newly appointed Minister of the Interior of Nazi-ruled Thuringia, proscribed the "smut and dirt in literature, Negro and jazz culture, abortion epidemic and degenerate art, corruption and the foes of National Socialism," Rosenberg applauded the loudest.[31]

In this context, it is interesting to scrutinize Adolf Hitler's attitudes. He was ambivalent. On the one hand, he admired the expansive United States, which had evidently understood how to secure enough *Leben–raum* for its inhabitants. On a continent assumedly populated by a plurality of "Aryan" types, he liked the way American leaders practiced racial segregation and insisted on the prohibition of alcohol. Above all, he was impressed by the signs of U.S. technological progress, notably assembly-line production, airplanes, railways, and automobiles. Hence, he admired Henry Ford, who had also written a pamphlet against international Jewry that Hitler had read in German translation and respected. In it, there was a statement about Jewish Hollywood films "reeking of sexual smut, preoccupying themselves ever more with criminal activities."[32]

About American Jews, Hitler could not have agreed more. In his opinion, they had been behind Woodrow Wilson's ill-advised actions concerning Germany's defeat in World War I and its ignominious republican metamorphosis. The same Jews, in an alliance with Negroes, were currently seeking to deprave German youth through dance, jazz, and sexual permissiveness.[33]

These views became entrenched after Hitler assumed the chancellorship in January 1933. Although he continued his old prejudices against the United States (official relations between the two countries soured incrementally until America's entry into the war in December 1941), he grudgingly kept up his admiration for selected U.S. specialties. This tendency was supported by representatives of both countries, such as Reichsbank President Hjalmar Schacht, who, during a trip to America in the early years of the regime, tried to put the best face on the Third Reich. As ever, the Germans were at pains to stress their blood ties with Americans of "Aryan" background, and many Americans even came to believe that Germany had been treated unjustly at Versailles. Typical among them was Martha Dodd, the young daughter of U.S. Ambassador William Dodd, who had taken his doctorate in American history at Leipzig and spoke fluent German. Martha sought the company of important German men such as Gestapo chief Rudolf Diels, empathized with the Nazis' law-and-order mentality, and was eager to meet Hitler. On the other hand, many Germans saw in Roosevelt a sort of strongman because of his New Deal, which suggested parallels to the Führer's policies.[34]

This had both economic and related psychological effects. Economically, it encouraged the broad consumerist trend already under way in the Weimar Republic, a trend noticeably influenced by American mass-produced goods and production and marketing techniques. For example, American cars such as Packard, Cadillac, or Chevrolet (the Dodds drove a "Chevy," setting one example) became quite common. So did Coca-Cola, U.S.-type electric household items such as refrigerators and coffee makers, and upscale radios, notably a certain powerful Blaupunkt model. Notwithstanding his grudges against Washington, Hitler, because of his conception of socialism, was able to appreciate the success of mass consumption in the United States. He wanted this material prosperity for the greatest number of people in his Reich, and not only to pacify them.[35]

The psychological implications of this are obvious. As long as official dogma was not violated, Hitler did not wish to offend his subjects needlessly by forbidding them to enjoy sophisticated Blaupunkt receivers, even if they were listening to American stations on shortwave. He allowed for a certain freedom of expression in the media, for instance in magazines like *Westermanns Monatshefte* or *Koralle*, and in film. Sometimes he even enjoyed watching American films such as *The Grapes of Wrath*. He found the step-dancing of Eleanor Powell and Fred Astaire in revue films, or film musicals, aesthetically pleasing and conducive to discipline, as in the military.[36]

Well into World War II, Germans under thirty were able to take advantage of Hitler's limited permissiveness. This was so because three particular phenomena managed to thrive, with varying degrees of openness, under the broader umbrella of a comparatively tolerant mass consumer culture that affected or appealed to the young. These were German-American exchanges, films, and popular music, particularly danceable jazz music.

Until December 1941, exchanges could take the form of mutual visits and written correspondence. Because of increasing prosperity after 1933, more and more Germans were traveling to America.[37] Among them, members of the younger generation tended to be in the majority because their knowledge of English usually was better (after 1935, that language was more widely taught in the schools). In 1938, American studies became an integral part of English language classes in *Gymnasien* (high schools), while in the universities, *Amerikanistik* developed as a discipline.[38] Hence, organized student exchanges on both sides were becoming more common, with Americans favoring Heidelberg and Germans the greater New York or Boston areas.[39] Nor did the work student phenomenon disappear; one of the more prominent young German academics who returned from extended work in a Ford plant as a convinced pro-American was Prince Louis Ferdinand von Hohenzollern, the grandson of the last Kaiser. "He drank, danced, thought and acted like many Americans," observed Martha Dodd.[40] Other young Germans, sufficiently fascinated by American popular culture to venture on a journey to New York, included medical student Hans Korseck of Berlin who also played professional jazz guitar (earning his crossing in that manner), Robert Vogel, the young heir to a Hamburg shipping fortune, and Carlo Bohländer, a Frankfurt lad of more modest means. Each spent some time in New York watching films, tasting typically American foods, and submerging himself in the new swing culture.[41] Of special interest today is an extended correspondence conducted in the years before the war by Leipzig dental technician and jazz fan Kurt Michaelis, born in 1913, with an unemployed young man in California, as well as with a young Jewish dentist in New York. The California drifter, Ross Russell, who later became an agent and one of the chief biographers of saxophonist Charlie "Yardbird" Parker, was trying his luck as a freelance crime reporter. In November 1937, for instance, Russell wrote to Michaelis about a Los Angeles multiple sex murder case, which reportedly led to the first use of California's gas chamber.[42] This was the stuff of which Hollywood detective movies were made, and it naturally caught Michaelis's imagination.

One of the constants in these German-American youth exchanges was film, especially film as musical. In the Third Reich, the movie theaters were increasingly packed with young people.[43] The two versions of *Broadway Melody* (1936 and 1938), both with Eleanor Powell, captured this enthusiasm like no other film. A third version, made in 1939–1940 and starring Powell and Astaire, undoubtedly was seen by Hitler but no longer shown publicly. Powell came across as alluringly attractive, in many aspects fitting the chorus "girl" image of the Weimar Republic: "cat eyes, tooth-paste smile, and silk-stocking legs, elastic as drum sticks," as the singer Evelyn Künneke recalls. Künneke, then using the stage name "Evelyn King," was modeling herself on American idols.[44] Margot Hielscher, at the time on the verge of her own movie career, remembers that "there was no saving me" after she had seen the premiere of the film at Berlin's Marmorhaus theater as a student.[45] For a Düsseldorf teenager and her *Gymnasium* classmates, Eleanor Powell was nothing less than God, and one young Hamburg shop clerk saw Powell in *Broadway Melody* as well as in *Rosalie*, with Nelson Eddy (1937), in which Powell stepped her famous "Drum Dance" on a giant drum.[46] Apart from the dancing, Powell's character in *Broadway Melody* (1936), the singer Irene Foster, impressed these German girls for two reasons: first, she got her rich and famous man in a Hollywood-type happy ending, but second, and even more importantly, Foster came from provincial Albany to rise to stardom in New York. This double leitmotif of professional and social advancement, being American, democratic, and modern at the same time, was something with which intelligent and not yet completely indoctrinated young women in Nazi Germany could identify.[47] Songs from Powell's films, such as "You Are My Lucky Star" and "I've Got a Feelin' You're Foolin'," sung by Powell herself or co-stars such as Frances Langford and a young Judy Garland, were marketed in Germany by Brunswick and Electrola, and were cherished by those teenage girls and their boyfriends.[48]

Young Germans flocked to many other American films, a good number of them interspersed with music and dance, such as *Dancing Lady* (1933), *Born to Dance* (1936), and *On the Avenue* (1937). Child star Shirley Temple made such a successful appearance on the German silver screen that the Nazis sought to create their own prototype, embodied by one Carmen Lahrmann, who also tried to step-dance, but was a dismal failure. Joan Crawford and Clark Gable, who starred in *Dancing Lady*, became idols for Germany's young, and they remained largely unmatched by indigenous and more homespun actors such as Lilian Harvey and Willy Fritsch. The names of Marlene Dietrich and Greta Garbo returned to the German collective consciousness, but now as Americanized personae.[49] Neither Hitler nor the overlord of the German movie industry, Joseph Goebbels, missed these films. Goebbels tried to use *Gone With the Wind* with Vivien Leigh (1939) to seduce German starlets in his private studio.[50] Goebbels was impressed by U.S. film production, about which he confessed as late as 1942 that "the Americans know how to take their relatively small store of culture and turn it into something that is usable in our times, by modernizing techniques of representation."[51]

More often than not, the music in American music-oriented films was inspired by big-band, jazz, or swing, sometimes pronouncedly so, as in Shirley Temple's *Rebecca of Sunnybrook Farm* (1938), a 20th Century Fox film featuring the Raymond Scott Quintet.[52] Despite the Nazi regime's attempts at repression or at least modulation, U.S.-style jazz remained a fixture of the German entertainment industry and held special pride of place among many of Germany's young. This peculiarity was less obvious than, but directly parallel to, the American film craze in prewar Nazi Germany. There were important jazz clubs in Düsseldorf, Münster,

Hamburg, Berlin, Frankfurt, and Leipzig. Berlin and Hamburg served as hubs for live jazz performances, increasingly given by well-qualified German musicians in night clubs, ballrooms, and concert halls.[53]

Thus, Theo Hoeren, a sixteen-year-old German pianist belonging to the Düsseldorf jazz club, was already performing in public in 1938 and trying to sound like a genuine American. After World War II, he chose to emigrate to Oregon, where he played jazz in piano bars.[54] The Leipzig group of fans that had congregated around Kurt Michaelis organized "Blue Mondays" to the sound of jazz records, many of them American originals featuring the latest swing.[55] In January 1936 economics student Dietrich Schulz, who earlier had founded a small jazz club in Königsberg, was engaged by the recording company Deutsche Grammophon to deliver a learned public lecture on American and British jazz in Berlin, with sound samples from Brunswick records by Fletcher Henderson, Duke Ellington, Jack Teagarden, and Teddy Wilson. Schulz repeated this in March and April, this time including songs from *Broadway Melody*.[56] As he explained later in his doctoral dissertation on the record industry, because of a complicated network of international recording companies, including German ones, Deutsche Grammophon owned the German rights for the U.S. label Brunswick.[57] Original American jazz records, even those by Jewish artists, stayed around in Germany well into the war, when young Wehrmacht soldiers could buy or barter for them in Nazi-occupied territories.[58] In the autumn of 1942, even in the girls' section of one Hitler Youth brigade, interest centered less on "whether Bach or Chopin had been the greater genius" than on popular hits and "American dances."[59]

Even though we still do not know for sure how many Hollywood films the German authorities allowed into their local cinemas, it is certain that the halcyon days of American (music) films in the Reich ended some time before World War II, as xenophobic Nazis came to exert greater control over this aspect of cultural policy.[60] This must be seen in the context of deteriorating relations between Berlin and Washington, which shored up all the existing, if sometimes veiled or latent, prejudices by National Socialists against Americans and *Amerikanismus*. These frictions were exacerbated after the beginning of Hitler's war with Great Britain, a nation traditionally friendly with the United States.[61] From this vantage point, the openness after 1933 discussed above was really the exception to the rule.

As in the Weimar Republic, many of these negative German perceptions were based on racist distortions. As such, particularly in so far as they involved popular culture, though not only then, they also affected German youth. Official Nazi views regarded African Americans and Jews as corrosive elements and, in the tightly circumscribed subculture of youth, a threat to dissenting young Germans' enjoyment of their favorite pastimes: films, jazz, swing dance, and sensually attractive fashions.

Early in the Third Reich there was an official policy with the object of discrediting American Jews through vituperative press releases and the smuggling of subversive literature into the United States. Germany's consul general in New York, Karl Otto Kiep, who later turned against the regime and was murdered as a resistance fighter, paid thousands of dollars to pro-German Americans in 1933 so that they would publish anti-Semitic diatribes. These actions led to an anti-German trade boycott backed by the American Jewish Congress.[62] By summer 1936, when Hitler slighted the Americans by refusing to acknowledge black athletes such as Jesse Owens at the Olympic games,[63] Germany had already embarked on a hate campaign against blacks. They were portrayed as conspiring with American Jews to corrupt the entertainment industry in the U.S. and, by extension, in Germany, and it was claimed that they knowingly caused gangsterism, social degeneracy, and unrest.[64] Things deteriorated further after the *Kristallnacht* pogrom in November 1938, when Jewish stores were ransacked and synagogues torched.[65] The theme of social subversion by American Jews was driven home once more in the German propaganda film *Der ewige Jude* (The Eternal Jew), 1940, which purported to show the Jews, otherwise likened to rats, as they corrupted New York, especially Wall Street.[66]

In Nazi dogma, the stereotypical combination of anything African American and Jewish led to the condemnation of both U.S. blacks *and* American Jews, as well as the entire spectrum of American culture. When the black U.S. *Lieder* and opera singer Marian Anderson wished to undertake a concert tour of Germany in 1935, Reich authorities prevented her, and Nazi invectives against her lasted for years.[67] More meaningful for German youth was that black jazz musicians such as Coleman Hawkins and Duke Ellington, who were on tour in other parts of Europe at the time, were kept from performing in Germany.[68] For entrenched Nazis, and at the peril of some of Germany's young, the alleged connivance between blacks and Jews in the creation and marketing of jazz and music for swing dancing became an article of faith. Thus, *Der SA-Mann*, the tabloid of the storm troopers, defined jazz as "nigger music painted over by Jews;" swing dancing, explained the tabloid, was the product of a "negroid dance culture," reminiscent of the Weimar-republican period dominated by Jewish corruption, and fit only for the inmates of madhouses.[69] On the first day of World War II, the Nazis proclaimed a ban on, among others, the song "Swing for Sale," co-written by the Jewish resident in the United States, Charlie Chaplin, and distributed in Germany by the Odeon recording firm, as well as "Caravan," co-written by Duke Ellington and marketed by Brunswick.[70] By this time, the image of the American woman, with painted lips and fingernails, long flowing hair, sexually suggestive tight pants or skirts (as one had observed them in U.S.-imported films) was already effectively being discredited. Instead of "das Girl" ideal, the Nazis espoused the Hitler Youth model of young women, "all in a uniform folk costume and proud and tanned and healthy, one beside the other."[71]

After Germany's declaration of war on the United States on 11 December 1941, the situation deteriorated completely as the Nazi regime embarked on an unrestrained anti-American propaganda campaign. Attacks on the various symbolisms of an allegedly evil American empire were now intensified. In stereotypical fashion, the Jews were singled out as the root cause of all the problems; Roosevelt himself was said to be the progeny of Jews.[72] Next to the Jews, blacks were identified as a source of moral depravity, chronic lack of culture, and social misery. Hitler himself said that, measured in terms of its "spiritual attitude," America constituted a "half-Jewish and Negro society."[73] Nazi propaganda placed particular emphasis on the high degree of moral and social decrepitude of American youth, for which promiscuous girls, the product of a disastrous women's emancipation over the decades, were made especially responsible.[74] More than ever, *Amerikanismus*, filling in for the alleged lack of culture in the United States, was made synonymous with Hollywood films, swing dance, and jazz, the essence of immorality.[75] The Nazis were going to drive home their point. A few days after 11 December 1941, they made a propaganda film, *Rund um die Freiheitsstatue*, which negatively portrayed swing, sexy fashion, jazz, and other American abominations. Goebbels showed it to Hitler in early 1942, and Hitler was pleased.[76] So were many young German men and women in the large cities who went to see the film, not to learn about American ills, but to catch the rare and precious snippets of swing dance and jazz.[77]

At the height of World War II, Germany's youth became the true victims of the Nazis' relentless witch-hunt against anything American, certainly as far as popular culture was concerned. It is true that this affected only certain youths, among them those who, despite official propaganda, kept themselves attuned to U.S. currents, particularly fashion, films, mass-consumer paraphernalia such as Coca-Cola, and easily defined popular music. Although there was a lack of consensus within the Nazi regime, active resistance from these quarters may be discounted, for no tokens of a rebellious youth culture were sufficient to generate the will among juveniles to overthrow Hitlerian rule. Yet it is significant that the main environment for these popular-culture predilections was to be found in large, anonymous cities that were potentially more alienated from National Socialism, rather than in provincial towns or the countryside, which historically had been breeding grounds for the Nazi movement.[78] In September 1942, the Hitler Youth leadership singled out the cities of Berlin, Hamburg, Dresden, Frankfurt, Essen, and Munich as critical venues to be watched.[79]

As long as American films were still being shown in Germany, they were important to these youths. In Hamburg, this occurred at the Waterloo cinema near the Dammtor railway station; often Axel Springer, of later media empire fame, was the projectionist.[80] An attractive young ladies' man, he was a fan of American jazz and swing, and so were his closest Hamburg associates. Even though U.S. jazz records were officially taboo in Germany, along with everything else American, they made the rounds in clandestine jazz clubs in Berlin, Breslau, Leipzig, Frankfurt, Kiel, and other cities.[81] Several youths were clever enough to manufacture copies of precious records with special machinery and distribute them among friends.[82] Some of that music could also be listened to on enemy propaganda stations such as the British-based Soldatensender Calais; imported Dutch and Belgian bands played it, as did home-grown German bands from time to time, even if the quality was often poor.[83] American jazz sounds, the opposite of the German marching beat, meant the first step toward "a positive identification with the Americans;" for Peter Wapnewski, later a professor of German literature, jazz possessed "the magical allure of 'Negro music'."[84]

Those young men and women who loved to listen to jazz were apt to engage in the "swing dance" as a unique form of socialization, especially in Hamburg, where adherents to the cult, usually from the upper strata of society, were appropriately known as "Swings." The archetype of this dance—the Lindy Hop—naturally was American. In Hamburg, people indulged in it at private parties in the sumptuous homes of the city's patriciate as well as publicly in, for example, the Curio-Haus near the Dammtor station in February and March 1940, when the Gestapo put a stop to it. The police went by a report from a Hitler Youth observer, who had written in disbelief: "Sometimes two boys would dance with one girl, sometimes several pairs formed a circle, with everybody linking arms and hopping around, clapping their hands and rolling the backs of their heads against one another, in which stooped position, upper torsos hanging down and wild hair in the face, they were almost on their knees, with both legs kicking."[85]

These Swings were dressed expensively and ostentatiously, with much of their fashion reminiscent of American styles in the movies. This was especially true of the girls, for whom long, shiny hair, lipstick, silk stockings, and tightly fitting skirts or pants to show off hourglass figures were *de rigueur*. This is how many Hollywood actresses looked. Some girls even wore red fingernail polish and dyed their hair blond. Often, a carefully draped trench coat was the finishing touch to a casually elegant appearance.[86] This was, of course, a function of the adolescent mating ritual; "Swing boys" liked sexy "Swing girls."[87] The boys, too, sported long hair and trench coats, along with crepe-soled shoes and a star-spangled-banner pin on their glen-checked jackets. An American newspaper, neatly folded, might be carried under one's arm.[88]

Such cult objects were not reserved solely for the swing youth of north German cities. They could be observed among equally jazz-obsessed boys and girls in Frankfurt or in Leipzig and, in variation, among members of lower-class gangs who tended to be Marxist-influenced, such as the "Navajos," "Kittelbach," or "Edelweiss" Pirates of the Rhineland. Kittelbach Pirates liked American cowboy pants, and Edelweiss Pirates bore nicknames such as "Texas-Jack" or "Alaska-Bill." In Celle, northeast of Hannover, there was an Al Capone-Bande in early 1943. Led by a juvenile "mulatto" called Flasbart, the group accosted innocent citizens in the town's center under the cover of darkness. Juveniles in Pomerania preferred to pattern criminal activities such as break-ins on "American models," doubtless inspired by Hollywood gangster films.[89]

In 1941 in the Bavarian countryside, an eighteen-year-old milk maid was found to have had sexual intercourse with a black French prisoner-of-war, whose attention she had caught after speaking to him in English. It was then revealed that the girl had been with relatives in the United States in peacetime and had apparently developed a preference for black men.[90] U.S.-influenced German juveniles easily made the connection between an openly expressed sexuality and *Amerikanismus*, and their Nazi superiors exaggerated this connection in their imagination, motivated, as they were, by extreme prurience.[91] To the extent that a strong sensual quality adhered to Hollywood films, swing music and the swing dance, accentuated as in the Hamburg case by sensuously provocative clothing, the majority of these dissenting youths employed a more liberated sexual lifestyle as an additional means of expressing their uniqueness. Still, the projection of unrestricted sex as a key manifestation of the admired American way of life was as ahistoric and unreal as many of the American movies themselves, amounting, essentially, to a misunderstanding even of the "Girl" culture.

In contrast to what the regime's leaders liked to think, these misconceptions did not translate into a collective promiscuous mentality or into what the Nazis often described as "orgies." In the large-city cliques, a freer view of sex usually meant monogamous relationships characterized, to be sure, by full sexual activity much earlier in the lives of these adolescents than was common in German society at large. It also meant that partners could be changed more rapidly, sometimes stretching the monogamy to its limits. Inga Madlung from Hamburg explains that "the steady friend was often replaced," and that she was "always in love, sometimes for four weeks, sometimes for four months." "These were solid relationships, as we have them today," remembers Robert Vogel, "naturally, there were also some one-night-stand situations, this was known beforehand."[92] Edelweiss Pirates in Duisburg are said to have practiced more licentious forms of "free love" involving the assignment of girls to individual demanding males, while groups in Wuppertal organized "lotteries" for changing nightly adventures.[93]

Greater sexual freedom, like other imagined tokens of the American opposite, was cherished until the end of the war, even against all odds. During the finale, the increasing proximity of the Americans at the fronts was welcomed. Pro-American youths conscripted into the Wehrmacht sought out jazz on powerful army receivers and even talked in English to the enemy from within armored cars.[94] As Rolf Schörken has recorded, Hitler Youth boys who were servicing the artillery as " flak helpers" (*Flakhelfer*) ran to the crash sites of U.S. fighter planes to have a first-hand look at these "great guys with God knows what unheard-of haircuts and casual uniforms."[95] For them, "military and material superiority, unlimited possibilities, generosity, a loose life style (jazz) blend into one another to create curiosity and a sense of attraction."[96]

The Nazi leaders struck back, but not in unison because, as was characteristic for the regime, too many agencies were involved. But there was consensus among them that they had to make examples of American-inspired infractions, of the loudest and most raucously dissenting cohorts of jazz lovers and Swings. Thus, from the end of 1937 to the spring of 1939, various municipal governments prohibited the swing dance, with Hamburg pronouncing its own ban in June of 1939. Significantly, parallel to those communal decrees, Nazi Party agencies such as the University Student Leadership of Württemberg followed suit, demonstrating that the swing menace was conceived as a national, not merely a local, phenomenon.[97] It was not quite a year later that the Gestapo, in collaboration with the Hitler Youth, decided to take action against Swings in their unofficial headquarters, Hamburg, by disrupting the Curio-Haus fête of 2 March 1940 and detaining, overnight, the majority of the 408 participants.[98] Not only in Hamburg, but all over Germany, Hitler Youth area commanders now started employing special controls to check what kinds of films boys and girls were frequenting.[99] In Hamburg, *Gymnasium* students known to be active Swings were beginning to be dismissed from their classes by school authorities, while the Gestapo and SS began a wave of arrests. The police also became active in Frankfurt, where jazz-loving members of the so-called Harlem Club had been hotting it up. This kind of behavior was defined as "offensive to the state."[100]

Then, in January 1942, SS and Gestapo chief Heinrich Himmler decided to "take drastic measures, in a fundamental and brutal manner." Spurred by Hitler Youth leader Artur Axmann, he instructed his deputy Reinhard Heydrich to dispatch the worst Swing leaders to a concentration camp, for a term of up to three years. They should receive beatings and be prohibited from ever studying at institutions of higher learning.[101] Until then, during the first Hamburg dragnets, a total of 138 arrests had been made (93 young men and 45 women), most for only a few weeks and without concentration camp internment. It had been taken for granted, however, that swing-dance and jazz infractions would be merely stepping stones to far more serious crimes. Repeated attempts to re-socialize the offenders within the Nazi *Volksgemeinschaft* had failed, and they were now looked upon as heroes and martyrs by their still free-roaming peers.[102]

By the time of Himmler's order, no more than perhaps half a dozen Hamburg youths had been interned in concentration camps.[103] But these numbers increased significantly during 1942 and 1943, especially as more and more girls were indicted on expressed charges of "promiscuity." These developments must be viewed in the wider context of an intensification of the penal process for German adolescents. This was encouraged by Himmler's police forces in conjunction with the Hitler Youth leadership and had the tacit approval of many municipal school administrations, but also faced the lukewarm objections of the traditional and more immobile judiciary. The salient characteristics of this trend were a departure from more conventional methods of punishment, such as limited reform or jail terms, in favor of the extrajudicial and quintessentially fascist institutions of the concentration camps under exclusive Gestapo and SS control, and terms of indefinite confinement.[104] For the youthful Hamburg suspects, these camps turned out to be Fuhlsbüttel, Neuengamme, Ravensbrück, and the new, brutal, "youth protection camps" (*Jugendschutzlager*) of Uckermark (for girls), and Moringen (for boys).

In the summer of 1942, Jutta Madlung and her younger sister Inga, on the threshold of their twenties and both charming and attractive, were consigned to the Ravensbrück concentration camp in Mecklenburg. They had been known to engage freely in sex and to entertain Hamburg Swing friends with stunning imitations of the American Andrews Sisters, whose records they owned. Inga Madlung, who already suffered from tunnel vision, was deliberately blinded by a sadistic SS physician who forced her to stare, for days, at the sun. When she was released, the once willowy girl was unrecognizable for the weight she had gained because of a chemical she had been forced to ingest to curb an allegedly vast sexual appetite. Both sisters were interned with Ulla Nielsen, who had to endure the advances of lecherous SS guards, and with Ingeborg Jarms and Verena Kerber after they had spent months in Fuhlsbüttel concentration camp. Later, Eva Petersen, a Hamburg Protestant with a Jewish mother, also arrived. One day, Eva was put on a freight train to Auschwitz, and was never seen again.[105]

In July 1942, Nielsen's friend Helga Rönn, at eighteen the very picture of an "Aryan" girl, whose life goal so far had been to win an American-style beauty contest or to become a film star, was placed in Uckermark, a concentration camp for minors near Ravensbrück. Uckermark, "in a beautiful landscape setting," as SS-Colonel Paul Werner allowed, had been founded only in June. As for Rönn, she had confessed to having participated in Swing celebrations in the suite of two wealthy Persian brothers who, undoubtedly for sexual finesse, had outfitted their rooms with mirrors.[106] Rönn was joined in Uckermark by Eva Rademacher, Elfriede Schneider, and Erna Brehm. Along with the other youthful inmates, they were weighed down by onerous chores such as felling trees and converting swamp into topsoil. They were beaten by SS guards and mauled by watchdogs; their diet consisted of watery soup and bread. From this, they developed dysentery; from wearing clogs, they had bruised feet. Health care was administered by SS physicians from Ravensbrück, but it was health care only in name. Elfriede Schneider remembers: "The camp commander was worse than the Devil, she was Satan incarnate."[107]

Since August 1940, Uckermark's equivalent for boys had been Moringen, near the university town of Göttingen.[108] In April 1942, when Nazi social workers described it as "primitive but clean," the camp housed 489 inmates between the ages of sixteen and twenty, among them "gypsies," boys of partially Jewish lineage, and "two Negro bastards." By July 1944, the inmate population had almost doubled.[109] The ratio of SS guards to inmates always was 1 to 10, extremely high compared even to ordinary concentration camps. The captive boys were considered incorrigible and hence slated, by the Social-Darwinist standard of the regime, for elimination, preferably through hard work, "euthanasia" in insane asylums, or in some cases through exposure at military fronts. There were provisions for transfer to adult concentration camps once the boys had come of age. The daily regimen was extremely severe, with back-breaking work in outlying fields, on the Autobahn, or with heavy machinery. Punitive sports, aggravated confinement, beatings, and food withdrawal were common; like their female peers in Uckermark, these inmates had to struggle with debilitating footwear. As early as the summer of 1942, nutrition had deteriorated to the point where the boys were susceptible to the slightest infection; four had died of malnutrition. Overall, conditions were so bad that by July 1944 forty-one boys had died, three of them as suicides and one while trying to escape. There were thirteen more deaths by May 1945.[110]

Günter Discher, who was said to have provided half of Hamburg with original jazz and swing records from Nazi-occupied Europe, was taken to Moringen in chains. "Work shifts were a catastrophe," he says. After the war, he was classified as fully disabled, barely surviving operations on his stomach, eyes, and a hernia.[111] Inmate Heiner Fey, like Discher, was a Swing from Hamburg. After his liberation, he lived only until 1961, when he succumbed to ill health.[112] Next to Fey was Heinz Lord, who, having lived through the sinking of the Nazi concentration camp ship Kap Arcona in 1945, went to the land of his love, America, to practice medicine. Dr. Lord, then a surgeon, died in Chicago in February 1961 at the age of forty-three from a heart ailment, the chronic aftereffect of maltreatment at the hands of xenophobic Nazi fanatics.[113]

The significance of American popular culture for German society after World War I lies in its potential as an additional catalyst of the modernism that was sweeping the country in the 1920s and early 1930s. Core elements of this modernism did not originate with the United States but were indigenously German, as were the paintings of Expressionists like Otto Dix and George Grosz, or the serious music of Arnold Schoenberg and Paul Hindemith. Some of this modern culture, such as the art of Grosz, was finding its way to America, as had more traditional art forms, such as high literature or classical music, for decades.[114] The novels of Thomas Mann, for instance, were published in the U.S. by Alfred A. Knopf. Within the genre of serious music, Elisabeth Rethberg, a soprano originally anchored at the Saxon capital of Dresden, moved to join the Metropolitan Opera in 1922. The Berlin-born conductor Bruno Walter became a regular guest of the New York Philharmonic.[115] It is important to note that the cultural commodities of artists like Grosz, Mann, Rethberg, and Walter were consumed by older people rather than the young, in Germany and the U.S, alike.

Products of American popular culture such as jazz, certain dances, and films—film as musical, in particular—arrived in Germany and furthered the modernism that was already under way before 1918. This occurred in lock-step with the influx of a broader material consumer culture, aspects of which also hailed from the United States. Cultural modernism and the fruits of an advanced mass consumer culture came to hold a peculiar appeal for people in their teens and early twenties who, in the republic, belonged among the future trendsetters, if not necessarily future leaders, of a very narrow *avant garde*. In contradistinction to older persons, these young people tended to be believers in the new democracy that had been championed by U.S. President Woodrow Wilson after World War I, as a mutual interaction developed between democratic politics on the one side and cultural modernism and mass consumerism on the other. It is fair to say that if republican democracy had prevailed beyond January 1933, these new forces would have been strengthened, and their American popular-art ingredients might have become ever more important. In 1932, a youthful, democratic-minded German citizen with a wide tolerance for innovation and culture might have counted the U.S. cultural and mass-consumerist influences as positives, along with ideas about democracy and the generous economic aid that Germany had been receiving from the U.S. Without the specter of right-wing conservatism and fascism, and in the absence of a terrible economic depression, Germany might have been on the threshold of beneficent democracy, logically accompanied by further experiments in modernism, of which American-based derivatives would have been a prominent part.

This was not to be. Although the National Socialists expressed an interest in certain technical aspects of U.S.-style modernism such as Taylorism in the non-cultural sphere, and, in the cultural one, advances in the production of color films, after January 1933 they rejected mass consumerism as ardently as they denounced what American popular culture intrinsically stood for. They correctly identified the latter's manifestations with freedom and democracy, and mistrusted its creative agents out of racist bigotry, condemning them as black or Jewish by ethnic origins. From its vantage point, the Nazi regime had to be wary of alien forces that could capture the imagination of its youth, since recruits of the Thousand-Year-Reich, to safeguard its longevity, required an upbringing and education unsullied by pernicious foreign influences. Because they could not be immediately neutralized, American popular culture and some of its consumer byproducts, such as Coca-Cola, continued to beguile a significant part of Germany's young until the start of World War II in September 1939. This took place, however, under the careful watch of Nazi regime leaders who, in that phase, still preferred pacification by persuasion to Gestapo-type coercion. Thus, identifiable examples of U.S.-type popular culture with consumerist dimensions survived from the Weimar Republic into the early years of the Nazi regime. But after September 1939, against the backdrop of global war, Hitler's government became more oppressive because, it believed, its self-preservation was at stake. Moreover, after war with the United States began in December 1941, political pressures visibly increased against "aberrant" minorities who, the regime concluded, were stepping out of line. By May 1945, young German swing dancers, jazz fans, and U.S. film buffs had been all but snuffed out in a brutal campaign.

Yet the pro-American trend, once begun in the 1920s, was merely driven underground rather than stopped. After Nazi capitulation and the arrival of American soldiers, American popular culture along with its materialist, consumerist manifestations slowly regained a foothold in a soon-to-be democratized Germany. Helped along by young adults such as Heinz Lord and Peter Wapnewski, older and already familiar forms of popular entertainment became part of a new mass culture in Germany, symbolized, beyond the avant-garde art of jazz, by rock'n roll and western films.[116] Mass consumption, chewing gum, and jeans came in their wake. It would take new waves of anti-Americanism to counter those trends—this time in democratic, not politically totalitarian, circumstances, and always short of defeat.

Notes

1. Karl Dietrich Bracher, *The German Dictatorship: The Origins, Structure and Effects of National Socialism* (New York: Praeger, 1972). From a Marxist perspective, see Franz Neumann, *Behemoth: The Structure and Practice of National Socialism, 1933-1944* (New York: Harper Torchbooks, 1966).

2. The latest and thus far most instructive example of this is Steven P. Remy, *The Heidelberg Myth: The Nazification and Denazification of a German University* (Cambridge: Harvard University Press, 2002). See also Michael H. Kater, *Composers of the Nazi Era: Eight Portraits* (New York: Oxford University Press, 2000), 264–284.

3. David Schoenbaum, *Hitler's Social Revolution: Class and Status in Nazi Germany, 1933-1939* (Garden City: Doubleday, 1967).

4. Reinhard Bollmus, *Das Amt Rosenberg und seine Gegner: Zum Machtkampf im nationalsozialistischen Herrschaftssystem* (Stuttgart: Deutsche Verlags-Anstalt, 1970).

5. See Christian Jansen et al., eds., *Von der Aufgabe der Freiheit: Politische Verantwortung und bürgerliche Gesellschaft im 19. und 20. Jahrhundert: Festschrift für Hans Mommsen* (Berlin: Akademie Verlag, 1995), 736–743.

6. Ian Kershaw, *Hitler, 1889-1936: Hubris* (New York: Norton, 1999), and *Hitler, 1936-1945: Nemesis* (New York: Norton, 2000).

7. Robert Gellately, *The Gestapo and German Society: Enforcing Racial Policy, 1933-1945* (Oxford: Oxford University Press, 1990), and *Backing Hitler: Consent and Coercion in Nazi Germany* (New York: Oxford University Press, 2002).

8. Mary Nolan, *Visions of Modernity: American Business and the Modernization of Germany* (New York: Oxford University Press, 1994), 17–107.

9. Detlev Peukert, *Die Weimarer Republik: Krisenjahre der klassischen Moderne* (Frankfurt: Suhrkamp, 1987), 178–181 (quote 180); Arnold Sywottek, "The Americanization of Everyday Life? Early Trends in Consumer and Leisure-Time Behavior," in *America and the Shaping of German Society, 1945-1955,* ed. Michael Ermarth (Providence: Berg Publishers, 1993), 134–135; Anton Kaes, "Mass Culture and Modernity: Notes Toward a Social History of Early American and German Cinema," in *America and the Germans: An Assessment of a Three-Hundred-Year History,* eds. Frank Trommler and Joseph McVeigh, 2 vols. (Philadelphia: University of Pennsylvania Press, 1985), vol. 2, 323–325; Peter Gay, *Weimar Culture: The Outsider as Insider* (New York: Harper and Row, 1968).

10. Siegfried Kracauer, *From Caligari to Hitler: A Psychological History of the German Film* (Princeton: Princeton University Press, 1974); Klaus Kreimeier, *The Ufa Story: A History of Germany's Greatest Film Company, 1918-1945* (New York: Hill and Wang, 1996).

11. Philipp Gassert, *Amerika im Dritten Reich: Ideologie, Propaganda und Volksmeinung, 1933-1945* (Stuttgart: Steiner Verlag, 1997), 60; Thomas J. Saunders, *Hollywood in Berlin: American Cinema and Weimar Germany* (Berkeley: University of California Press, 1994), esp. 51–144; Kaes, "Mass Culture," 326–328; Monika Sperr, ed., *Das grosse Schlager-Buch: Deutscher Schlager, 1800-Heute* (Munich: Rogner und Bernhard, 1978), 117.

12. Fritz Giese, *Girlkultur: Vergleiche zwischen amerikanischem und europäischem Rhythmus und Lebensgefühl* (Munich: Delphin-Verlag, 1925), e.g. 9–18, 51–61, 137–141.

13. Sperr, *Das grosse Schlager-Buch*, 117.
14. Blüthner diary of broadcasts, 17 June 1930 (copy in author's archive); Karl Christian Führer, "A Medium of Modernity? Broadcasting in Weimar Germany, 1923–1943," *Journal of Modern History* 69, no. 4 (1997): 722–753.
15. Clarence Lusane, *Hitler's Black Victims: The Historical Experiences of Afro-Germans, European Blacks, Africans, and African Americans in the Nazi Era* (New York: Routledge, 2002), 180–181, 235–237; Tamara Barzantny, *Harry Graf Kessler und das Theater: Autor, Mäzen, Initiator, 1900-1933* (Cologne: Böhlau, 2002), 246–251.
16. Kaes, "Mass Culture," 324–325; Hans M. Wingler, *The Bauhaus: Weimar, Dessau, Berlin, Chicago* (Cambridge: MIT Press, 1986), 485.
17. See the telling examples in *Der Artist*, 13 March and 8 May 1925, 16 November 1928, 22 January 1932; Astrid Eichstedt and Bernd Polster, *Wie die Wilden: Tänze auf der Höhe ihrer Zeit* (Berlin: Rotbuch, 1985), 49.
18. See Kurt Pabst in *Der Artist*, 23 October 1931, and Michael Danzi, *American Musician in Germany, 1924-1939: Memoirs of the Jazz, Entertainment, and Movie World During the Weimar Republic and the Nazi Era—and in the United States as Told to Rainer E. Lotz* (Schmitten: N. Ruecker, 1986), 25. See also Michael H. Kater, "The Jazz Experience in Weimar Germany," *German History* 6, no. 2 (1988): 152.
19. Matyas Seiber, "Jazz-Instrumente, Jazz-Klang und neue Musik," *Melos* 9 (1930): 122–26; Theodor W. Adorno in *Die Musik* 21 (1929): 625; Adorno, "Kleiner Zitatenschatz," *Melos* 24 (1932): 738.
20. Georg Haentzschel in recorded interview with author, Köln-Mühlheim, 1 October 1988 (audiotape in author's archive).
21. Nolan, *Visions of Modernity*, 18–19, 25, 27, 29.
22. Gerhard L. Weinberg, "From Confrontation to Cooperation: Germany and the United States, 1933–1949," in *America and the Germans*, ed. Trommler and McVeigh, vol. 2, 45; Stephen Duggan, *A Professor at Large* (New York: Macmillan, 1943), 172–173; Georg Michaelis, "Selbsthilfe: Sinn des Werkstudententums," *Deutsche Allgemeine Zeitung*, 25 December 1923; Carl Duisberg, "Die Wirtschaftshilfe der deutschen Studentenschaft und der deutsche Werkstudent," *Der Arbeitgeber*, 15 March 1924; "Geschäftsbericht der 'Wirtschaftshilfe der deutschen Studentenschaft'," in Reinhold Schairer et al., *Die Wirtschaftshilfe der deutschen Studentenschaft, 1923-1925: Geschäftsberichte der "Wirtschaftshilfe der deutschen Studentenschaft e.V." und der "Darlehnskasse der deutschen Studentenschaft e.V." über die Geschäftsjahre 1923-1925* (Leipzig: Quelle and Meyer, 1925), 43, 71; Ferdinand Graf von Degenfeld-Schonburg, *Geist und Wirtschaft: Betrachtungen über die Aussichten der deutschen Akademiker* (Tübingen: Mohr, 1927), 66.
23. Generally, see Klaus Schwabe, "Anti-Americanism within the German Right, 1917–1933," *Amerikastudien: American Studies* 21, no. 1 (1976): 89–107.
24. Ibid. For an assault on Wilson's Fourteen Points, see Adolf Halfeld, *Amerika und der Amerikanismus* (Jena: E. Diederichs, 1927), 55. As an example of a combined attack against the Young Plan and Wall Street, in this case by the Nazi Secondary-Student League, see [Polizei-Direktion München], "Der Nationalsozialismus und die Schule," [1931], Staatsarchiv München, Pol. Dir. München/6841.

25. Herbert Johannes Gigler, "Der Verfall der Musik," *Die Musik* 17 (1925): 358; Werner Müller, "Begegnung mit der Hitler-Jugend," *Die Kommenden*, 10 May 1929, 218; "Satzungen des Deutschen Frauenordens," [2 May 1929], Staatsarchiv Bremen, 4/65-II/A/9/a/13; Guida Diehl, *Die Deutsche Frau und der Nationalsozialismus* (Eisenach: Neuland-Verlag, 1933), 66; Kurt Hutten, *Kulturbolschewismus: Eine deutsche Schicksalsfrage* (Stuttgart: Kohlhammer, 1932), 12–15, 29, 84–87; Ernst von Salomon, *Die Geächteten: Roman* (Reinbek: Rowohlt, 1968; [1929]), 32; Friedrich Hussong, *"Kurfürstendamm": Zur Kulturgeschichte des Zwischenreichs* (Berlin: Scherl, n.d.), 7; Hans Pfitzner, *Gesammelte Schriften*, 3 vols. (Augsburg: Benno Filser, 1926–29), vol. 1, 113–120, vol. 3, 309–310; Gassert, *Amerika*, 60; Kater, *Composers of the Nazi Era*, 148–150.

26. Eugen Fischer, *Die Rehobother Bastards und das Bastardierungsproblem beim Menschen: Anthropologische und ethnographische Studien am Rehobother Bastardvolk in Deutsch-Südwest-Afrika, ausgeführt mit Unterstützung der Kgl. preuss. Akademie der Wissenschaften* (Jena: Fischer, 1913), 296; Eugen Fischer, "Spezielle Anthropologie: Rassenlehre," in Eugen Fischer et al., *Anthropologie* (Leipzig: B.G. Teubner, 1923), 189–190, 193–194; Fritz Lenz, "Die krankhaften Erbanlagen," in Erwin Baur et al., *Menschliche Erblichkeitslehre und Rassenhygiene* (Munich: J.F. Lehmann, 1921), 288–289. For a critical analysis, see Hans-Walter Schmuhl, *Rassenhygiene, Nationalsozialismus, Euthanasie: Von der Verhütung zur Vernichtung "lebensunwerten Lebens," 1890-1945* (Göttingen: Vandenhoeck und Ruprecht, 1987), 69.

27. This was according to the Hanover police president's memorandum of 27 January 1930. Niedersächsisches Hauptstaatsarchiv Hannover, Hann. 122a/XI/79.

28. Hugo Rasch, "König Jazz," *Allgemeine Musikzeitung* 57 (1930): 932; Kater, *Composers of the Nazi Era*, 232.

29. *Die Tagebücher von Joseph Goebbels: Sämtliche Fragmente. Teil I: Aufzeichnungen 1924-1941*, vol. 1, ed. Elke Fröhlich (Munich: K. G. Saur, 1987), entries for 1 and 2 September.

30. *Mitteilungen des Kampfbundes für deutsche Kultur* 1 (1929): 98, 119–127; ibid. 2 (1930): 43; ibid. 3 (1932): 62–63, 67; Alfred Rosenberg, *Der Sumpf: Querschnitte durch das "Geistes"-Leben der November-Demokratie* (Munich: Eher Nachf., 1930), 23–36, 87–89 (quote 23); Alfred Rosenberg, *Der Mythus des 20. Jahrhunderts: Eine Wertung der seelisch-geistigen Gestaltenkämpfe unserer Zeit* (Munich: Hoheneichen-Verlag, 1934; [1930]), 501, 673; *Völkischer Beobachter*, e.g., 21 October 1930.

31. "Dr. Frick, Reichsminister des Innern," undated pamphlet, published by Hauptamt Ordnungspolizei, Bundesarchiv, Aussenstelle Berlin, personal file Wilhelm Frick (quote); *Mitteilungen des Kampfbundes für deutsche Kultur* 2 (1930): 36–38.

32. Gerhard L. Weinberg, ed., *Hitlers Zweites Buch: Ein Dokument aus dem Jahr 1928* (Stuttgart: Deutsche Verlags-Anstalt, 1961), 123–125; Henry Ford, *Der internationale Jude*, 2 vols. (Leipzig: Hammer, 1922), vol. 2, 54 (quote); Ernst Hanfstaengl, *Zwischen Weissem und Braunem Haus: Memoiren eines politischen Aussenseiters* (Munich: Piper Verlag, 1970), 46–47; Gassert, *Amerika*, 98, 101; Detlef Junker, "The Continuity of Ambivalence: German Views of America, 1933–1945," in *Transatlantic Images and Perceptions: Germany and America Since 1776*, ed. David E. Barclay and Elisabeth Glaser-Schmidt (Cambridge: Cambridge University Press, 1997), 249–251. See also Nolan, *Visions of Modernity*, 34.

33. Hitler's remarks in Eberhard Jäckel, ed., *Hitler: Sämtliche Aufzeichnungen, 1905-1924* (Stuttgart: Deutsche Verlags-Anstalt, 1980), 265, 565–566; Schwabe, "Anti-Americanism," 99; Gassert, *Amerika*, 100.

34. Otto Lohr, "Wehrhaftes Deutschtum in den Vereinigten Staaten," *Der Auslandsdeutsche* 19 (1936): 394; Duggan, *Professor*, 180; Martha Dodd, *Through Embassy Eyes* (New York: Harcourt Brace, 1939), 37–38, 42, 63; William E. Dodd, Jr., and Martha Dodd, eds., *Ambassador Dodd's Diary, 1933-1938* (New York: Harcourt Brace, 1941), 4; Alton Frye, *Nazi Germany and the American Hemisphere, 1933-1941* (New Haven: Yale University Press, 1967), 60; Sywottek, "Americanization," 136.

35. Dodd, *Through Embassy Eyes*, 17, 28; James V. Compton, *The Swastika and the Eagle: Hitler, the United States, and the Origins of World War II* (Boston: Houghton Mifflin, 1967), 19; Hans Dieter Schäfer, *Das gespaltene Bewusstsein: Über deutsche Kultur und Lebenswirklichkeit, 1933-1945*, 2nd ed. (Munich: Hanser, 1982), 118–120, 122, 127; Junker,"Continuity," 256.

36. Evelyn Künneke, *Sing, Evelyn, Sing: Revue eines Lebens* (Reinbek: Rowohlt Taschenbuch, 1985), 39–40; Compton, *Swastika*, 19; Michael H. Kater, *Different Drummers: Jazz in the Culture of Nazi Germany* (New York: Oxford University Press, 1992), 46–47; Junker, "Continuity," 253.

37. Schäfer, *Bewusstsein*, 121; Gassert, *Amerika*, 142–144.

38. Schäfer, *Bewusstsein*, 126; Gassert, *Amerika*, 118, 132.

39. Duggan, *Professor*, 176; Gassert, *Amerika*, 139–141; Remy, *Heidelberg Myth*, 8–9.

40. Dodd, *Through Embassy Eyes*, 68 (quote), 264.

41. *Die Unterhaltungsmusik*, 28 February 1940, 177–78; author's recorded interviews with Robert Vogel, Hamburg, 21 June 1988, and Carlo Bohländer, Frankfurt, 7 June 1987 (audiotapes in author's archive).

42. Ross Russell to Kurt [Michaelis], 10 November 1937 (photocopy in author's archive); Kater, *Different Drummers*, 79–80. See also Ross Russell, *Bird Lives! The High Life and Hard Times of Charlie (Yardbird) Parker* (New York: Charterhouse, 1973).

43. David Welch, *Propaganda and the German Cinema, 1933-1945* (Oxford: Clarendon Press, 1983), 217–218.

44. Künneke, *Sing*, 34, 37.

45. Author's recorded interview with Margot Hielscher, Munich, 4 June 1988 (audiotape in author's archive).

46. Author's recorded interviews with Leonore Boas, Cappenberg, 22 June 1988, and Hanne-Lore Evers-Frauboes, Hamburg, 18 June 1988 (audiotapes in author's archive).

47. Karsten Witte, "Gehemmte Schaulust: Momente des deutschen Revuefilms," in *Wir tanzen um die Welt: Deutsche Revuefilme, 1933-1945* ed. Helga Belach (Munich: Hanser, 1979), 24; Adelheid von Saldern, "The Hidden History of Mass Culture," *International Labor and Working-Class History* 37 (spring 1990): 32–40.

48. Author's recorded interviews with Margot Hielscher, Munich, 4 June 1988, and with Herbert Koleczek, Rüdesheim/Rhein, 25 June 1988 (audiotapes in author's archive); *Skizzen* (June/July 1938), 20; German Brunswick record catalogs for March and April 1936, and April 1938 (photocopies in author's archive).

49. Schäfer, *Bewusstsein*, 129–132; Klaus Krüger, "Wir machen Musik: Tanzorchester im Dritten Reich," in *"Swing Heil": Jazz im Nationalsozialismus*, ed. Bernd Polster (Berlin: Transit, 1989), 64–65; Historisches Museum Frankfurt am Main, ed., *Jugend im nationalsozialistischen Frankfurt: Ausstellungsdokumentation, Zeitzeugenerinnerungen, Publikum* (Frankfurt: Historisches Museum Frankfurt am Main, 1987), 113; Gassert, *Amerika*, 164–166.

50. Author's recorded interview with Margot Hielscher, Munich, 4 June 1988 (audiotape in author's archive).

51. *Die Tagebücher von Joseph Goebbels, Teil II: Diktate, 1941-1945*, ed. Elke Frölich, 16 vols. (Munich: K. G. Saur, 1993–1996) (hereafter *TGII*), vol. 4, entry for 3 May 1942. See also Michael H. Kater, "Film as an Object of Reflection in the Goebbels Diaries: Series II," *Central European History* 33, no.3 (2000): 391–414.

52. *Fox auf 78* 6 (fall 1988): 9.

53. For the overall picture, see Kater, *Different Drummers*.

54. Werner van Alphen, "Bei Toni gab es immer guten Jazz," *Düsseldorfer Nachrichten*, 9 October 1965.

55. Michaelis memorandum for author, 19 March 1990 (author's archive).

56. Announcements for "Brunswick-Schallplatten-Abend" in Berlin for 20 January, 5 March and 2 April 1936 (photocopies in author's archive); Kater, *Different Drummers*, 72.

57. Dietrich Schulz-Köhn, *Die Schallplatte auf dem Weltmarkt* (Berlin: Hans Triltsch, 1940), 91.

58. "Musikalische Feldpost," 24 September, early January 1942, and early April 1942 (photocopies in author's archive).

59. Melita Maschmann, *Fazit: Kein Rechtfertigungsversuch*, 5th ed. (Stuttgart: Deutsche Verlags-Anstalt, 1964), 132, 134. Note that Chopin was at that time thought by leading Nazis to have had German roots and training. See Michael H. Kater, *The Twisted Muse: Musicians and their Music in the Third Reich* (New York: Oxford University Press, 1997), 155.

60. Heinz Boberach, ed., *Meldungen aus dem Reich 1938-1945: Die geheimen Lageberichte des Sicherheitsdienstes der SS, 1938-1945*, 17 vols. (Herrsching: Pawlak, 1984), vol. 3 (10 January 1940), 631; vol. 4 (8 April 1940), 970–971, (23 May 1940), 1168; Gassert, *Amerika*, 167–174.

61. See, inter alia, Elisabeth Noelle, "Das Geschichtsbild der Amerikaner," *Das Reich*, 18 May 1941; Colin Ross, *Unser Amerika: Der deutsche Anteil an den Vereinigten Staaten* (Leipzig: F.A. Brockhaus, 1936); Adolf Halfeld, *USA. greift in die Welt*, 5th ed. (Hamburg: Broschek und Co., 1941); Dodd, *Through Embassy Eyes*, 36, 39; Duggan, *Professor*, 177–78; Fritz Wiedemann, *Der Mann der Feldherr werden wollte: Erlebnisse und Erfahrungen des Vorgesetzten Hitlers im 1. Weltkrieg und seines späteren persönlichen Adjutanten* (Velbert: Blick und Bild Verlag, 1964), 214–215; Frye, *Nazi Germany*, 46, 58, 62, 80–82, 87–88, 94, 100, 132, 135, 138, 145, 148–149, 152–153, 155, 161, 163, 177, 179; Compton, *Swastika*, 11–12, 14, 20, 21; Gassert, *Amerika*, 133, 136, 235, 240, 309–310.

62. Frye, *Nazi Germany*, 34, 44–45, 48, 51, 53, 55; Annedore Leber, ed., *Das Gewissen steht auf: 64 Lebensbilder aus dem deutschen Widerstand, 1933-1945* (Berlin: Mosaik Verlag, 1960), 143–144.

63. On the Olympics, see Dodd, *Through Embassy Eyes*, 211–212; Frye, *Nazi Germany*, 61; Arnd Krüger, *Die Olympischen Spiele 1936 und die Weltmeinung: Ihre aussenpolitische Bedeutung unter Berücksichtigung der USA* (Berlin: Bartels and Wirnitz, 1972), 147–148, 197.

64. On the latter charge, see "Deutsche Arbeitsgemeinschaft für Volksgesundung e.V.: Mitteilungen," 2 April 1936, Bundesarchiv Koblenz (hereafter BAK), R56I/114; *Ziel und Weg* 6 (1936): 316–318; Ross, *Unser Amerika*, 280–285; Halfeld, *USA. greift in die Welt*, 181–186; Manfred Sell, *Die schwarze Völkerwanderung: Der Einbruch des Negers in die Kulturwelt* (Vienna: Wilhelm Frick Verlag, 1940), 218, 271–272; Boberach, *Meldungen aus dem Reich* 7, (23 June 1941): 2430; Gassert, *Amerika*, 240–241.

65. Frye, *Nazi Germany*, 89.

66. Boberach, *Meldungen aus dem Reich* 6 (20 Jan. 1941): 1917–1918; Francis Courtade and Pierre Cadars, *Geschichte des Films im Dritten Reich* (Munich: Carl Hanser, 1975), 193–194.

67. Konzertdirektion C. Ebner to Reich propaganda ministry, 27 March 1935; Reich propaganda ministry to Konzertdirektion C. Ebner, 9 April 1935, BAK, R55/1177; *Das Deutsche Podium*, 3 April 1936, 4; *Ziel und Weg* 9 (1939): 453.

68. Edward Kennedy Ellington, *Music is My Mistress* (New York: Doubleday, 1973), 151; Kees Wouters, "Krieg dem Jazz! Holland vor und während der Nazi-Besetzung," in Polster, *"Swing Heil"*, 175.

69. *Der SA.-Mann*, 26 February 1938 (1st quote); ibid., 19 February 1938 (2nd quote). In the same vein, see Georg Seywald, "Jazz im neuen Deutschland?," *Die Scholle* 10 (1934): 348–349; "Buhu, es ist zum Weinen," *Das Schwarze Korps*, 25 November 1937; "Dann lieber gleich wieder in den Urwald!," *Stuttgarter NS-Kurier*, 7 January 1939; Karl Blessinger, "Zur Frage der Unterhaltungsmusik," *Die Musik* 35 (1942): 67–69.

70. "Beilage zu den amtlichen Mitteilungen der Reichsmusikkammer," 1 Sept. 1939, BAK, RD33/2–2.

71. Cf. the juxtaposition of both types in the Nazi film *Der verlorene Sohn* (1934) in Eric Rentschler, *The Ministry of Illusion: Nazi Cinema and its Afterlife* (Cambridge, MA: Harvard University Press, 1996), 78–79, 87; president of the Reich Chamber of Music, Professor Peter Raabe, in *Die Unterhaltungsmusik*, 26 October 1939, 1405; Gassert, *Amerika*, 235; Maria Kramarz, *Dies Mädel ist Hanne-später bist Du es* (Berlin-Lichterfelde: Junge Generation Verlag, 1937), 113 (quote). On the Hitler Youth model, see Michael H. Kater, *Hitler Youth* (Cambridge: Harvard University Press, 2004), 73–85.

72. Joseph Goebbels, "Aus Gottes eigenem Land," *Das Reich*, 9 Aug. 1942; Giselher Wirsing, *Der masslose Kontinent: Roosevelts Kampf um die Weltherrschaft* (Jena: Eugen Diederichs Verlag, 1943), 61–62, 65, 67, 85, 99–109, 146–150, 165–168, 210–213, 220–228, 261–262, 335, 426–429; "Die Gefahr des Amerikanismus," *Das Schwarze Korps*, 16 March 1944; Compton, *Swastika*, 22–23.

73. Doc. 88 (7 Jan. 1942), in Werner Jochmann, ed., *Monologe im Führerhauptquartier, 1941-1944: Adolf Hitler, Die Aufzeichnungen Heinrich Heims*, (Hamburg: A. Knaus, 1980), 184 (quote); Wirsing, *Der masslose Kontinent*, 96–97, 163–164, 174, 422–423, 430; "Negersoldaten gesucht! Onkel Toms Urenkel als Kanonenfutter für das Sternenbanner," *Koralle*, 20 August 1944, 228–229.

74. "Jugendmoral in Amerika: Im Schatten der Kriegskonjunktur," *Das Reich*, 30 May 1943; "USA.-Kinder sind verwildert! Ein Kriegsproblem im Lande Roosevelts," *Berliner Illustrierte Zeitung*, 1944, no. 37, BAK, R22/1165; Wirsing, *Der masslose Kontinent*, 77, 79, 167, 216; Gassert, *Amerika*, 359.

75. Joseph Goebbels, "Aus Gottes eigenem Land," *Das Reich*, 9 Aug. 1942; "Der neueste Modeirrsinn Anglo-Amerikas," *Der Mittag*, 17 August 1942; Carl Hannemann, "Der Jazz als Kampfmittel des Judentums und des Amerikanismus," *Musik in Jugend und Volk* 6 (1943): 57–59; "Der 'magische Trompeter'," *Stettiner General-Anzeiger*, 26 July 1943; J. Mayerhofer, "Liebe und Ehe," *SS-Leitheft* 9, no. 8 (1943): 17; *Das Podium der Unterhaltungsmusik*, 16 Sept. 1943, 165; *Amerikanismus: Eine Weltgefahr*, ed. Der Reichsführer SS, SS-Hauptamt [Berlin, 1943], 24–37; [Herbert Gerigk], "Gift bleibt Gift," *Das Schwarze Korps*, 27 July 1944. Critically, see Gassert, *Amerika*, 323, 354–357.

76. *TGII*, vol. 3, entry for 10 February 1942.

77. Interview with Günther Lust in Polster, *"Swing Heil,"* 166; Werner Burkhardt, "Musik der Stunde Null (II)," *Zeitmagazin*, 18 November 1983, 42.

78. On this last aspect, see Jürgen Falter and Michael H. Kater, "Wähler und Mitglieder der NSDAP: Neue Forschungsergebnisse zur Soziographie des Nationalsozialismus, 1925 bis 1933," *Geschichte und Gesellschaft* 19, no. 2 (1993): 155–177.

79. Appendix to Reichsjugendführung - Personalamt - Überwachung, "Cliquen- und Bandenbildung unter Jugendlichen," Berlin, September 1942, BAK, R22/1177.

80. Ibid.; author's recorded interview with Hans Engel, Mamaroneck, 5 March 1988 (audiotape in author's archive); Wege memorandum, Gestapo Hamburg, 9 September 1941, Staatsarchiv Hamburg (SAH hereafter), Amtsgericht Hamburg, Abtlg. Vormundschaftswesen, 115XI, R1886, 1653 Rönn; entry for 12 April 1940 in Willi A. Boelcke, ed., *Kriegspropaganda, 1939-1941: Geheime Ministerkonferenzen im Reichspropagandaministerium* (Stuttgart: Deutsche Verlags-Anstalt, 1966), 318; Arno Klönne, *Jugend im Dritten Reich: Die Hitler-Jugend und ihre Gegner: Dokumente und Analysen* (Düsseldorf: Diederichs, 1982), 238; Kater, *Different Drummers*, 155.

81. Georg E. Krämer to author, Kirschweiler, 10 May 1999 (author's archive); author's recorded interviews with Herbert Koleczek, Rüdesheim, 25 June 1988, Hanne-Lore Evers-Frauboes, Hamburg, 18 June 1988, and Robert Vogel, Hamburg, 21 June 1988 (audiotapes in author's archive); Uwe Storjohann, "In Hinkeformation hinterher: Swing-Jugend an der Bismarck-Schule," in *"Die Fahne hoch": Schulpolitik und Schulalltag in Hamburg unterm Hakenkreuz*, ed. Reiner Lehberger and Hans-Peter de Lorent (Hamburg: Ergebnisse Verlag, 1986), 402.

82. Author's recorded interview with Herbert Koleczek, Rüdesheim, 25 June 1988 (audiotape in author's archive); proceedings against Wilhelm Diedrich and Wilhelm Karl Heinrich, 18 October 1941; proceedings against Wolfgang Richen, 21 October 1941, SAH, Oberschulbehörde VI, 2FVIII/a2/40/1.

83. Entry for 4 April 1944 in Klaus Granzow, *Tagebuch eines Hitlerjungen, 1943-1945* (Bremen: C. Schüneniann, 1965), 85–86; Cornelia Rühlig and Jürgen Steen, eds., *Walter: [geb.] 1926 [gefallen] 1945 an der Ostfront: Leben und Lebensbedingungen eines Frankfurter Jungen im III. Reich* (Frankfurt: am Main: Amt für Wissenschaft und Kunst der Stadt Frankfurt am Main, 1983), 118; Historisches Museum Frankfurt am Main, *Jugend im nationalsozialistischen Frankfurt*, 298; Rolf Schörken,

Luftwaffenhelfer und Drittes Reich: Die Entstehung eines politischen Bewusstseins, 2nd
ed. (Stuttgart: Klett-Cotta, 1985), 156.

84. Author's recorded interviews with Hans Engel, Mamaroneck, 5 March 1988,
(audiotape in author's archive); Hans-Joachim Scheel to author, Mississauga, 7
April 1988 (author's archive); Schörken, *Luftwaffenhelfer,* 157, 159 (1st quote);
Peter Wapnewski in Marcel Reich-Ranicki, ed., *Schulzeit im Dritten Reich: Erinnerungen deutscher Schriftsteller* (Munich: Deutsche Taschenbuch Verlag, 1984),
101 (2nd quote).

85. "Beilage zu den amtlichen Mitteilungen der Reichsmusikkammer," 1 September
1939, BAK, RD33/2-2; Schult to Kohlmeyer, 8 February 1940; "Bericht über eine
Veranstaltung am 2.3.40 im Curio-Haus," Nygaard to Kohlmeyer, 6 March 1940,
SAH, Jugendbehörde I/343c; Sozialverwaltung Hamburg to Amtsgericht Hamburg, 3 January 1942, SAH, Amtsgericht Hamburg, Abtlg. Vormundschaftswesen,
115XI, R1886, 1653 Rönn; Prinzhorn memorandum, 12 December 1942, SAH,
Oberschulbehörde VI, 2FVIII/a2/40/1.

86. Transcript of Inga Madlung-Sheldon interview for the British video series, "Swing
under the Swastika," Yorkshire Television, London, 1988 (photocopy in author's
archive); author's recorded interview with Hanne-Lore Evers-Frauboes, Hamburg,
18 June 1988 (audiotape in author's archive); "Musikalische Feldpost," September
1941 (photocopy in author's archive); "Bericht über eine Veranstaltung am 2.3.40
im Curio-Haus," SAH, Jugendbehörde I/343c; Gelehrtenschule des Johanneums
[Hamburg] to Landesunterrichtsbehörde, [20 November 1940] (photocopy in
author's archive); Sass memorandum, 22 March 1943, SAH, Oberschulbehörde VI,
2FVIII/a2/5/1; Historisches Museum, *Jugend im nationalsozialistischen Frankfurt,*
114–117; Rainer Pohl, "'Das gesunde Volksempfinden ist gegen Dad und Jo': Zur
Verfolung der Hamburger 'Swing-Jugend' im Zweiten Weltkrieg," in *Verachtet—
verfolgt—vernichtet: Zu den "vergessenen" Opfern des NS-Regimes,* ed. Wolfgang
Ayass, Klaus Frahm, and Elke Alperstedt (Hamburg: VSA-Verlag, 1986), 21.

87. Author's recorded interviews with Hans-Joachim Scheel, Mississauga, 29 March
1988, and Robert Vogel, Hamburg, 21 June 1988 (audiotapes in author's archive).

88. Author's recorded interview with Hans Engel, Mamaroneck, 5 Mar. 1988
(audiotape in author's archive); Nygaard to Kohlmeyer, 6 March 1940, SAH,
Jugendbehörde I/343c; Gestapo Hamburg memorandum, 13 October 1941,
SAH, Oberschulbehörde VI, 2FVIII/a2/40/1; Ursula Prückner and Axel Waldhier,
"Verweigerung—Opposition—Widerstand: Einblicke in das Leben dreier Nicht-
Faschisten," in *"Ohne uns hätten sie das gar nicht machen können": Nazi-Zeit und
Nachkrieg in Altona und Ottensen,* ed. Brigitte Abramowski et al. (Hamburg: VSA-
Verlag, 1985), 68; Ursula Prückner, "Wilde Jahre: Begegnungen mit Hamburger
Swings," in Polster, *"Swing Heil,"* 227.

89. "Auszug aus dem Lagebericht des GenStA. Celle," 1 February 1943; "Tagesmeldung
des GenStA in Stettin," 18 Feb. 1943, both in BAK, R22/1177; Historisches
Museum, *Jugend im nationalsozialistischen Frankfurt,* 298; Matthias von Hellfeld,
*Edelweisspiraten in Köln: Jugendrebellion gegen das 3. Reich: Das Beispiel Köln-
Ehrenfeld,* 2nd ed. (Cologne: Pahl-Rugenstein, 1983), 22, 30; Alfons Kenkmann,
*Wilde Jugend: Lebenswelt grossstädischer Jugendlicher zwischen Weltwirtschaftskrise,
Nationalsozialismus und Währungsreform* (Essen: Klartext, 1996), 190.

90. Protokoll, Jugendgericht München, 3 October 1941, Archiv, Rechtshistorisches
Institut der Universität Lüneburg, 6.1.2 (Munich).

91. For examples of this prurience see Gestapo Hamburg, Wege protocol, 9 September 1941; Sozialverwaltung Hamburg to Amtsgericht Hamburg, 3 Jan. 1942, both in SAH, Amtsgericht Hamburg, Abtlg. Vormundschaftswesen, 115XI, R1886, 1653 Rönn; Prinzhorn memorandum, 12 December 1942, SAH, Oberschubehörde VI, 2FVIII/a2/40/1.

92. Author's recorded interviews with Inga Madlung-Sheldon, London, 9 May 1988 (1st quote) and Robert Vogel, Hamburg, 21 June 1988 (2nd quote); see also recorded interviews with Hans Engel, Mamaroneck, 5 March 1988, Hans-Joachim Scheel, Mississauga, 29 March 1988, and Hanne-Lore Evers-Frauboes, Hamburg, 18 June 1988 (audiotapes in author's archive); Scheel to author, 7 April 1988 (author's archive).

93. Albath, "Bericht der Stapo-Leitstelle Düsseldorf: Wilde Jugendgruppen—Edel-weisspiraten," [1943], BAK, R22/1177.

94. Author's recorded interviews with Gerd Peter Pick, Toronto, 10 July 1987, and Hans-Joachim Scheel, Mississauga, 29 March 1988 (audiotapes in author's archive); Dieter Borkowski, *Wer weiss, ob wir uns wiedersehen: Erinnerungen an eine Berliner Jugend* (Frankfurt am Main: S. Fischer, 1980), 161.

95. Schörken, *Luftwaffenhelfer*, 142–143.

96. Ibid., 211.

97. Gau Essen u. Düsseldorf, Fachschaft Tanz in der Reichstheaterkammer, Fach-gruppe II, to Weinhaus "Bei Toni" (Düsseldorf), 24 November 1937 (photocopy in author's archive); Thorsten Müller, "Feindliche Bewegung," in *That's Jazz: Der Sound des 20. Jahrhunderts: Eine Ausstellung der Stadt Darmstadt ... 29. Mai bis 28. August 1988*, ed. Institut Mathildenhöhe Darmstadt (Darmstadt: Roetherdruck, 1988), 383; *Die Unterhaltungsmusik*, 19 May 1939, 689; 6 July 1939, 906; Uwe Dietrich Adam, *Hochschule und Nationalsozialismus: Die Universität Tübingen im Dritten Reich* (Tübingen: Mohr, 1977), 114.

98. Memorandum, Hitler-Jugend, Gebiet Hamburg, 12 March 1940, SAH, Jugend-behörde I/343c; recorded interview with Hanne-Lore Evers-Frauboes, Hamburg, 18 June 1988 (audiotape in author's archive).

99. See, e.g., Reithmayr, work report regarding activities of HJ-Streifendienst in HJ-Bann Allgäu, for October 1940, Staatsarchiv Neustadt an der Donau, EAP/221-b-20/9.

100. Thede to Puttfarken, 26 October 1940, SAH, Oberschulbehörde VI, 2FVIII/a2/3/1; Bürger to Züge, 3 December 1940, SAH, Oberschulbehörde VI, 2FVIII/a2/3/2; Gestapo Hamburg to Gemeindeverwaltung Hamburg, 13 Novem-ber 1940; Gelehrtenschule des Johanneums to Landesunterrichtsbehörde, [19 November 1940], and to Hitler-Jugend Hamburg, 27 November 1940; "Ver-zeichnis der Schüler und Schülerinnen der Schulen der Hansestadt Hamburg, die wegen staatsabträglichen Verhaltens bestraft worden sind," n.d., all appended to Henze to Hintze, 29 June 1942 (quote) (photocopies in author's archive); HJ-Ban-nführer Knopp, "Kriminalität und Gefährung der Jugend: Lagebericht bis zum Stande vom 1. Januar 1941," in *Jugendkriminalität und Jugendopposition im NS-Staat: Ein sozialgeschichtliches Dokument*, ed. Arno Klönne (Münster: Lit, 1981), 136–138; Wege memorandum, 9 September 1941, SAH, Amtsgericht Hamburg, Abtlg. Vormundschaftswesen, 115XI, R1886, 1653 Rönn.

101. Axmann to Himmler, 8 January 1942 (quote); Himmler to Axmann, 26 January 1942, and to Heydrich, 26 Jan. 1942, BAK, NS19/Neu 219.

102. Kruse memorandum, [January 1942], BAK, NL/289.

103. Ibid.

104. See Gauss to Amtsgerichtspräsident Breslau, 23 January 1943; Kaltenbrunner to Sicherheitspolizei and SD et al., 25 October 1944, BA, R22/1177; Jörg Wolff, *Jugendliche vor Gericht im Dritten Reich: Nationalsozialistische Strafrechtspolitik und Justizalltag* (Munich: C.H. Beck, 1992), esp. 33–34, 67–69, 112, 181; Kater, *Hitler Youth*, 113–166.

105. Author's recorded interviews with Inga Madlung-Sheldon, London, 9 May 1988, and Ursula Nielsen-Rönn, Hamburg, 20 June 1988 (audiotapes in author's archive); Kater, *Different Drummers*, 159–160, 190–192. On the Andrews Sisters, see Hans Christoph Worbs, *Der Schlager: Bestandsaufnahme, Analyse, Dokumentation: Ein Leitfaden* (Bremen: C. Schünemann, 1963), 211.

106. Author's recorded interview with Inga Madlung-Sheldon, London, 9 May 1988, and Ursula Nielsen-Rönn, Hamburg, 20 June 1988 (audiotapes in author's archive); Grell memorandum, 17 December 1941; Grell memorandum, 14 July 1942; Landesjugendamt Hamburg to Vormundschaftsgericht Hamburg, 1 Feb. 1943, all in SAH, Amtsgericht Hamburg, Abtlg. Vormundschaftswesen, 115XI, R1886, 1653 Rönn; Paul Werner, "Die Einweisung in die polizeilichen Jugendschutzlager," *Deutsches Jugendrecht* 4 (1943): 97 (quote).

107. Michael Hepp, "Vorhof zur Hölle: Mädchen im 'Jugendschutzlager' Uckermark," in *Opfer und Täterinnen: Frauenbiographien des Nationalsozialismus*, ed. Angelika Ebbinghaus (Nördlingen: F. Greno, 1987), 191–216 (quote 211).

108. See "Unterbringung in polizeilichen Jugendschutzlagern," 27 Apr. 1944, BAK, R22/1191.

109. Kümmerlein and Eichler, "Reisebericht über die Besichtigung des polizeilichen Jugendschutzlagers Moringen," [April 1942], BAK, R22/1176 (quotes); Heermann to Oberlandesgerichtspräsident Hamm, 31 July 1944, BAK, R22/1191.

110. Ibid.; "Auszug aus dem Lagebericht des OLGPräs. in Kassel," 2 August 1944; Werner to Kümmerlein, 6 September 1944, BAK, R22/1191; Werner, "Die Einweisung," 95–103; Martin Guse et al., "Das Jugendschutzlager Moringen—Ein Jugendkonzentrationslager," in *Soziale Arbeit und Faschismus: Volkspflege und Pädagogik im Nationalsozialismus*, ed. Hans-Uwe Otto and Heinz Sühnker (Bielefeld: KT-Verlag, 1986), 333–334; Hannah Vogt, ed., *KZ Moringen: Männerlager, Frauenlager, Jugendschutzlager* (Göttingen: Steidl, 1983), 55; Wolf-Dieter Haardt, "'Was denn, hier—in Moringen?! Die Suche nach einem vergessenen KZ," in *Die vergessenen KZs? Gedenkstätten für die Opfer des NS-Terrors in der Bundesrepublik*, ed. Detlef Garbe (Bornheim-Merten: Lamuv, 1983), 104.

111. Interview with Discher in Polster, *"Swing Heil"*, 164.

112. Prückner and Waldhier, "Verweigerung," 63.

113. Hermann Kater, *Politiker und Ärzte: 600 Kurzbiographien und Portraits*, 3rd. ed. (Hamelin: C.W. Niemeyer, 1968), 213.

114. M. Kay Flavell, *George Grosz: A Biography* (New Haven: Yale University Press 1988), 72–105.

115. Alain Paris, *Lexikon der Interpreten klassischer Musik im 20. Jahrhundert* (Munich: Deutscher Taschenbuch Verlag, 1992), 597; Erik Ryding and Rebecca Pechefsky, *Bruno Walter: A World Elsewhere* (New Haven: Yale University Press 2001).

116. Maria Höhn, *GIs and Fräuleins: The German-American Encounter in 1950s West Germany* (Chapel Hill: University of North Carolina Press, 2002); Uta G. Poiger, *Jazz, Rock, and Rebels: Cold War Politics and American Culture in a Divided Germany* (Berkeley: University of California Press, 2000).

Chapter Three

THE LEGACY OF NAZI CINEMA: *TRIUMPH OF THE WILL* AND *JEW SÜSS* REVISITED

Eric Rentschler

THE FEATURE FILMS AS WELL AS THE DOCUMENTARIES, newsreels, and short subjects produced in Germany during the Third Reich continue to circulate and resonate. Nonetheless, their undeniable presence is neither self-understood nor fully comprehended. What is their rightful place? Do they belong in the garbage pile of history? Or, with the passing of time, do they now warrant less impassioned and more measured consideration? To reject—and with what justification? To redeem—and at what cost? In any event, these examples of mass media deserve our renewed reflection, particularly because they have become an integral part of contemporary culture. What does the continuing unreeling of these sights and sounds tell us about our own world and its own interests and investments? How do and how should these artifacts from the past speak in the present, if they are to speak at all?

These are, to be sure, large questions; only a much lengthier consideration might yield full answers. In the hope of coming to some initial conclusions, I would like to bear these concerns in mind while focusing on arguably the two most influential and well-known propaganda films produced during the Third Reich, Leni Riefenstahl's *Triumph des Willens* (Triumph of the Will), 1935, and Veit Harlan's *Jud Süss* (Jew Süss), 1940.

The Discipline of Distraction

The Third Reich produced very few feature-length propaganda films, i.e., works that overtly meant to convince or convert, to sway public opinion, or to mobilize collective action. They included: movement films, or the so-called *Bewegungsfilme,* such as *Hitlerjunge Quex* (Hitler Youth Quex), 1933, *Hans Westmar,* 1933, and *SA-Mann Brand,* 1933; "Heim ins Reich" productions that showed Germans abroad on dangerous ground (and in many cases celebrated a safe return passage), such as *Flüchtlinge* (Fugitives), 1933, *Friesennot* (Frisians in Peril), 1934, *Der verlorene Sohn* (The Prodigal Son), 1934, and *Heimkehr* (Homecoming), 1941; *Triumph des Willens* (Triumph of the Will), 1934, the Nazi Party's definitive self-portrait; hate films, be they anti-Semitic, anti-Slavic, or anti-English; apologias for "euthanasia" such as *Opfer der Vergangenheit* (Victims of the Past), 1937, and *Ich klage an* (I Accuse), 1942; desperate films of the last hour ("Durchhaltefilme") such as *Kolberg* (1945) and the never-completed *Das Leben geht weiter* (Life Goes On).

The vast majority of films made during the Nazi era, however, were not overtly political. Generic productions, very similar in their outlines to Hollywood's formulas, figured prominently in the Third Reich; they constituted 941 of its 1,094 feature films.[1] That is not to say, however, that they were not political. Popular films and movie stars were put to use, mobilized to bolster the Nazi state and to legitimate the Hitler regime. The Ministry for Public Enlightenment and Propaganda, under the leadership of Joseph Goebbels, wanted films that could be both commercially viable and politically valuable. To be sure, there were a variety of appeals and a nuanced division of labor between heavy hands and light touches; not every film was doing the same thing at the same time. Likewise, films did not exist in isolation but functioned with other media (especially the press and radio) to fit into wider campaigns. Indeed, the use value of cinema was not limited to the screen: films were an important part of public life and of Germany's sense of national identity and its international standing as an advanced state. In that regard, the film world offered a powerful political weapon.

Minister Goebbels studiously made sure that popular audiences distinguished between what was political and what was non-political. This reflected his belief that seemingly non-political films could become even more effective as political tools than the overtly tendentious productions. At the very least, feature films were affirmative and rarely resistant; they offered a semblance of a better life, confirming that everyday life in Germany was normal and in step with the modern world. These offerings also demonstrated that the Nazi government was generous and indulgent, even *au courant* and hip.

Genre films were infused with political meanings in various ways: within the film narratives; in tales of errant desire that had to be punished, or of unruly femininity that posed a threat and had to be neutralized; and in dramas that showed how group solidarity persevered despite the most imposing challenges. Another narrative strategy was to articulate dissatisfaction and forbidden longing, to indulge it initially (but only to a point) before revealing the error of such sentiments, and then to punish and/or convert the characters who harbored these feelings, be they rebels who ultimately submit to authority or authoritarian personalities whose aggression transmutes into subservience. In this way, films provided object lessons. Political meaning could also be found in the style and form of films, the manner in which they molded human bodies and human activities. This was evident, for example, in the mass ornaments of the revue film, in this cinema's generally constrained body language, and in the lack of nudity or erotic excess.[2] Finally, the political existed outside of the film in terms of what reviewers chose to single out for attention and emphasis. Movie stars often figured within current events and popular films became part of wider political discussions.

Goebbels maintained that the most effective propaganda worked subtly. He granted cinema a central role in a concerted attempt to occupy private space and alternative possibility, giving people an illusion of free choice and room to move. In short, he cultivated distraction as a form of mass discipline. Cinema's promises of freedom became all the more compelling as ways to fetter the dreamer and, quite literally, to create a captive audience. What is essential about Nazi films is not so much their explicit propaganda, but the manner in which they gave shape to reality and promulgated a worldview through the means of audio-visual fantasy ware.

Hitler's Imagined Community

A celluloid account of the 1934 Nazi Party Congress, Leni Riefenstahl's *Triumph of the Will* remains the most influential artifact of the Third Reich and arguably the most often quoted film ever made. How well we know these sights and sounds; how familiar they appear to us. The production constitutes Nazi Germany's ultimate self-advertisement, the sanctification of its leader and his new order by an army of cinematographers and technicians. Despite National Socialism's legacy of murder and destruction, the film remains quite visible today and continues to resonate strongly, be it in excerpts on the History Channel, classroom presentations in high schools and universities, reprises at film festivals, or closed screenings for right-wing radicals.

To portray, as the trade paper *Kinematograph* put it, "the authentic face of the new Germany,"[3] Riefenstahl claimed that she did nothing more than bear witness. "Everything in it is true…. It is history. A pure historical film."[4] This was, of course, hardly the case. The director carefully choreographed what she filmed and painstakingly refined what her cameras recorded, letting two priorities guide her: "The first is the skeleton, the construction, the architecture. The second is a sense of rhythm."[5]

The National Socialist German Workers Party "Congress of Unity and Strength" took place in Nuremberg from 4 to 10 September 1934. Riefenstahl's filmic endeavor, which runs a little under two hours, transformed the seven days of the congress into a three-and-a-half day drama, imbuing the gathering with an epic dimension.[6] Nimbly juggling chronology, Riefenstahl condensed more than 130,000 meters of film footage to a final cut of 3,109. She animated speakers and mobilized events so that they might appear far more striking and compelling than their counterparts in reality.

The grandiose production enacted the party's desire to legitimate its power and appeal strongly to the masses so as to consolidate Hitler's regime. In reproducing an event, the film gave rise to further reproductions. Screenings throughout Germany studiously sought to recreate the spirit and spectacle of Nuremberg, putting party dignitaries on display in gala local premieres. Riefenstahl's film offered prospects of German strength and greatness in keeping with the designs of the Nazi party and its visionary leader. As a reviewer in the *Film-Kurier* observed, "Germany has assembled before Hitler, for Hitler, in Hitler."[7]

Indeed, Hitler's presence occupies one-third of the running time, and his speeches constitute one-fifth of the sound and two-thirds of the dialogue.[8] At those moments when the camera withholds Hitler's image, a tension arises about where he has gone and when he might reappear.[9] His look invigorates his people; he mesmerizes women and children, he seems to sway buildings and statues, he even catches the attention of a house cat. Repeatedly, Hitler's body assumes a luminous aspect and an auratic force. We see a halo on his head and a ray of light in his hand.

Orchestrating his own political legend, Hitler played a poet-priest whose idealized dream of Germany had, by dint of an act of will, become real. Indeed, the Nuremberg rally might be thought of as a literalized incarnation of Expressionism in which a messianic new man creates the world in his own vision. "The statesman is also an artist," Goebbels submits in his autobiographical novel of 1929, *Michael*. "For him, the people represent nothing different than what the stone represents for the sculptor…. Politics is the plastic art of the state, just as painting is the plastic art of color…. To form a people out of the masses, and a state out of the people, this has always been the deepest sense of a true politics."[10] Under fascism, as Walter Benjamin observed in 1936, political relations take on aesthetic shapes.[11]

Among the formal emphases in Riefenstahl's film, the most prominent surely is the precisely aligned rows of soldiers that we see repeatedly, often from a great distance in overhead vistas. The fastidiously ordered lines of these hundreds and thousands of followers take us back to the staged masses of Expressionist dramas by Ernst Toller and Georg Kaiser. They also bring to mind Siegfried Kracauer's 1927 essay on the "mass ornament" ("Ornament der Masse"), which commented on a troupe of precision dancers, the Tiller Girls, whose performances featured "an immense number of parallel lines, the goal being to train the broadest mass of people in order to create a pattern of undreamed-of dimensions."[12] The mass ornaments of Nuremberg mean to dazzle and enthrall the viewer with what Karsten Witte has called their "extreme perspectives of extreme uniformity."[13] Riefenstahl had learned from the crowd scenes of Fritz Lang's *Metropolis* and Sergei Eisenstein's *Battleship Potemkin* as well as from Busby Berkeley's kaleidoscopic swirls of bodies in motion. Party propagandists insisted nonetheless that there was something culturally singular about Riefenstahl's monumentalism. The massed minions of Nuremberg become a privileged formation in a cinematic spectacle, performed before rows of cinema audiences who in their own right constitute mass ornaments. The Nazis took the mythical potential of an abstract shape, infused it with a collective meaning, and enlisted it in the creation of an imagined people's community, a *Volksgemeinschaft*.

This imagined community was also imaginary. Despite Riefenstahl's claims to verisimilitude, her film showed little regard for reality or history and nonetheless presented itself as the definitive version of the rally. The party maintained sole ownership and exclusive rights over all representations of the proceedings, strictly forbidding the screening of materials taken there by any other cameras, whether silent or sound films, 35 or 16mm, until 30 November 1935.

When Riefenstahl passed away in September 2003 at the age of 101, *Triumph of the Will* continued, as it had for decades, to spark debate in the multitude of obituaries. A critical approach, in keeping with the premises of Susan Sontag's "Fascinating Fascism," castigates Riefenstahl for her enthusiastic glorification of Hitler and his new order.[14] A redemptive persuasion, sympathetic to the director's claims of political innocence, holds that the film is a consummate work of art that provided an objective record of the rally. A third school would have us distinguish between the bad politics of the Nazi party and the aesthetic virtues of a cinematic hallmark. A fourth reading, a pop appropriation, praises Riefenstahl for having crafted a spectacular fantasy of emotional agitation and erotic abandon. Without question, her shots of sculpted bodies and fine-featured physiognomies have exercised a considerable influence on modern visual culture's definition of glamour, from Bruce Weber's photographs of beautiful bodies to the gorgeous poses in advertisements for designers like Calvin Klein and Ralph Lauren.

Riefenstahl's self-image, elaborated in her bestselling memoir and Ray Müller's 1993 three-hour documentary *Die Macht der Bilder-Leni Riefenstahl* (*The Wonderful, Horrible Life of Leni Riefenstahl*) was that of a professional and an artist. When commentators drew attention to the political ramifications of *Triumph of the Will*, Riefenstahl insisted that she had remained deferent to the event, to its sites and its participants. Confronted with Susan Sontag's intervention, she told Ray Müller that she had no idea what fascist aesthetics might mean. At the same time, the director prided herself on her artistic impetus, on her consummate ability to transform mundane reality into cinematic poetry. Indeed, there is a decided disparity between her status as a careful observer and an active shaper. In one perspective she is deferent, in the other she is dynamic. In her defense she averred that she simply captured what was there without any ideological prejudice or political incentive; thus she had no need to assume moral responsibility, for these were things larger than herself over which she had no control. On the other hand, she spoke of herself as a self-conscious artist and argued that she was above all guided by her formal interest and stylistic resolve—and certainly not by the priorities of the propaganda ministry. And, she asked, does not the artist have the right to transcend reality? When reflecting on *Triumph of the Will*, Riefenstahl alternately assumed the position of author and denied it. Hers was a strategic and fluid position that sought to elude the grasp of anyone who wanted to take her to task for having worked with the Nazis.

Beyond Riefenstahl's embattled public image, there remains something both persistent and insistent about our own mass media's obsession with Riefenstahl and her iconography, particularly since the 1970s. As a guest of honor at the 1974 Telluride Film Festival in Colorado, the artist rejoiced: "It's like before the war. They like me." Andy Warhol invited her to his factory; her photographs of Mick and Bianca Jagger appeared in the glossy magazine *Interview*. Jagger claimed to have seen *Triumph of the Will* dozens of times and admitted that he had borrowed from it for his own concerts. Riefenstahl, in this light, gained appeal as the artist-director who had created a superstar's enabling act. Hitler, according to David Bowie, "wasn't a politician, he was a media artist. The way he worked his audiences! The girls got all hot and sweaty and the guys wished they were up there where he was. The world won't ever see his like again. He made the whole country into his own stage show." The British group Roxy Music, while seeking to cleanse her work of its fascist associations, appropriated quotes from her films. Stephen Spielberg repeatedly spoke about how much he would like to meet her. His colleague, Francis Ford Coppola, also described himself as a great admirer. The final sequence of George Lucas's *Star Wars* fondly recalls the closing scene from *Triumph of the Will.* "I know that Lucas and Spielberg and many others think very highly of me," Riefenstahl observed. "I don't come across the prejudices in America that I do in Germany." In 1977 there were reports of a Leni Riefenstahl fan club in Los Angeles whose members wore t-shirts bearing her face. A German rock group called itself Reifenstahl. In the 1990s she was acclaimed by the art world in Japan and photographed by Helmut Newton wearing the latest Versace fashions. Thea Dorn's *Marleni* premiered in Hamburg in November 1998, a play (also adapted for the radio) in which Riefenstahl appears at the aging Dietrich's Paris apartment and proposes a collaboration on "my last, my first, my greatest film." On 3 March 1998 Riefenstahl was among the guests of honor at a celebration of *Time* Magazine's 75th anniversary at Radio City Music Hall, the "party of the century" whose luminaries included Bill Clinton, Mikhail Gorbachev, Norman Mailer, Elie Wiesel, Bill Gates, and many Hollywood stars whose pictures had graced the cover of *Time* during the last three-quarters of a century. The only other German representative was Claudia Schiffer. Although at first extremely nervous, Riefenstahl said she was relieved and elated when she received a standing ovation.[15]

Less smitten observers maintain that those who blithely quote Nazi images do so at the risk of trivializing the historical past. Worse yet, critics complain, such mediated memories often uncritically reproduce and in fact even willfully celebrate the seductive appeal of fascist aesthetics. Take, for instance, the "teaser" for the compilation film *Michael Jackson: History 2* (1997), which puts on display the regalia, uniforms, and mass ornaments of the Nuremberg rally, and in which, quite literally, the rock star becomes hallowed as *der Führer*. The video recycles and recodes signifiers of fascism and totalitarianism, be they Italian, Soviet, or German highlights from the offerings of the 1937 Paris World Fair's Exhibition. They become the impressive trappings of a personality's obsessive and impressive cult. Michael Jackson is an uncritical poacher who draws on powerful images and images of power in order to create a self-aggrandizing spectacle that demonstrates just how powerful, and hence cool, he is. These appropriations take place without irony or distance, without any sense (save that Jackson refrains from using swastikas) that such borrowings might be problematic or irresponsible in light of the suffering, violence, and murder that are inextricable parts of their historical legacy. Nazi sights and sounds have become props and costumes in our own society of spectacle.

A flattering self-image of an omnipotent dictator and a proud nation, *Triumph of the Will* provided a hagiographical portrait in the guise of a documentary record. Working on the cutting edge of cinematic modernism, Riefenstahl instrumentalized advanced tools of sight and sound in ways that have indelibly marked the subsequent history of the mass media. Many of her innovations anticipated things that we now take for granted, for example, sound bites, simulations, or political conventions staged for television cameras. The mass ornaments of Nuremberg, the building blocks of Hitler's imagined community, have become refunctionalized in Super Bowl halftimes and Olympic opening ceremonies. They also serve as the prototypes for demonstrations of political consensus in times of crisis, e.g., human flags and Hands Across America. In our mediated "brave new world," current events do not simply take place; they are often scripted and staged, and always synthesized. An elaborate technical apparatus, from lights, cameras, sound recorders, editing bays, and special effects to projectors, screens, and monitors, determines what we see of the world and how we experience history. For all that separates us from Hitler and the Nazis, *Triumph of the Will* retains a poignant and disturbing prescience.

Mass Culture and Mass Murder

Triumph of the Will blends idealized images of German strength and beauty with Nazi designs for living, thus commingling mass culture and mass propaganda. Can we, however, go a step further and link Nazi mass culture with Nazi mass murder? What is the relationship between *Jew Süss* and the subsequent deportations to the death camps and the ensuing Shoah? How might we account for Nazi hate films like Veit Harlan's *Jew Süss*, and how should we treat them?

Even to this day, *Jew Süss* may not be screened publicly in the Federal Republic of Germany. Government policy stipulates that any showing must take place within a controlled setting and be accompanied by the commentary of a specialist as well as followed by a general discussion. Nonetheless, like the infamous 1940 feature-length documentary, *Der ewige Jude* (The Eternal Jew), *Jew Süss* circulates in North America and throughout the world in unauthorized versions, even though the legal rights are held by Transit-Film in Munich. As even a rudimentary search on the Internet confirms, both titles can be purchased from a spectrum of vendors, ranging from legitimate sources such as International Historic Films in Chicago to any number of radical right-wing and neo-Nazi outlets. *The Eternal Jew* is advertised, for instance, in *The Spotlight Magazine*, the organ of a wealthy anti-Semitic organization.

Opinons remain fiercely divided about the proper status of *Jew Süss*, Nazi Germany's most influential anti-Semitic feature film. There are those who argue that making the film accessible can further the cause of public enlightenment. If one sequesters this work, does one not (unwittingly or not) repress the memory and reality of racial hatred in the Third Reich? Do we not stand to learn much about the workings of Nazi pathology by comprehending representations that reflect its anxieties and phobias? Is this film not a crucial historical artifact? A counter-argument speaks in the name of the dignity of the dead, wondering how anyone could possibly justify the display of defiled and brutalized people.[16] Should we not show sensitivity for those individuals who were abused by Nazi cameras? When the Jews enter Stuttgart in Harlan's film, for instance, we are actually seeing Jewish extras who were coerced to perform. The synagogue sequence, likewise, is an act of desecration; it was shot in occupied Prague with Jewish citizens acting under Nazi orders. Beyond that, a grave fear abides that the film, if made public, might not only be misunderstood, but also blatantly misused. Indeed, there is evidence that *Jew Süss* and *The Eternal Jew* have been employed to foster prejudice and hatred; in some radical circles, in fact, they enjoy the status of cult films.

The discourse of *Jew Süss* was neither exceptional nor novel in a society that was no stranger to anti-Semitic sentiment, having long been an active site of racist legislation and violence. The rhetoric of Nazi hate films was hardly original; rather, it drew on longstanding stereotypes that reinforced pre-existing public beliefs. From the late 19th century and into the 1920s, anti-Semitic discourse presented the Jew as a bloodsucker and an intruder who lives at the cost and peril of its hosts. Paul de Lagarde, a famous Orientalist, compared Jews with bacteria that bring pestilence. In *Der Mythos des 20. Jahrhunderts* (The Myth of the Twentieth Century), 1930, Alfred Rosenberg pictured Jews as the anti-race (*Gegenrasse*), which is to say as negativity incarnate. In these representations, the Jew appears as a parasite who attacks and contaminates the body of a nation (*Volkskörper*), and whose very existence threatens the well-being of the German people (*Volk*).[17]

The German audiences that took in *Jew Süss* when it premiered in September 1940 knew of the Nuremberg Laws. They had experienced the *Kristallnacht* and were aware of the many other harsh measures their government had taken against German Jewish citizens. They had read *Mein Kampf* and had heard Hitler speak frankly and forcefully about his desire to eliminate the Jewish people from German life. Starting in September 1941, all Jewish citizens in Germany aged six or older would be required to wear a yellow star. During that same month, experimental gassings with Zyklon-B would take place at Auschwitz. And in October 1941, the mass deportation of Jews to the east from the German Reich would commence.

Veit Harlan's film depicts how a mercenary Jew, a conniver and a con man, infiltrates the court of Württemberg and endangers the Swabian citizenry. Couching the narrative in an eighteenth-century setting and taking liberties with the facts of history, Harlan fashioned strong images of a powerful and negative presence. In constructing a malevolent other, Nazi propagandists insisted that they were serving the public good by revealing the Jew's true face. Fritz Hippler's *The Eternal Jew* was advertised as a factual account with no faked or simulated scenes; the camera, it was said, simply showed ghetto Jews as they really existed. Hippler, to be sure, had manipulated his materials, inserting feature films as if they were documentary footage, simulating scenes, and staging shots in jails with Jews held under duress. Many of the faces we see are of individuals who will die in Nazi camps.[18] The creators of *The*

Eternal Jew maintained that they offered an x-ray view that revealed the true face behind the mask of the assimilated Jew. The dissolve became the technical means by which the spectator could see things for what they really are, the formal capacity that allows the viewer to scrutinize the Jew's transformative powers. This visual aid permits one to recognize the awful truth, to glimpse the Kaftan Jew and enemy of the state behind the visage of what appears to be a normal citizen.

The dissolves in *Jew Süss*, in the same way, show the intruder's agile transformation from ghetto denizen to courtly presence. *Jew Süss* creates a collective scapegoat in keeping with Nazi stereotypes. Strikingly, this curious construction reflects how Nazi ideology could only define an ideal self in terms of a negative image. In presenting the devil incarnate, the propagandists projected their own darker impulses onto an abject other. Süss, like the redeemer of the Aryan nation, is an idealist who acts in the name of a utopian vision. Just like the man who wrote *Mein Kampf,* the leader of the Jews makes his designs known from the beginning and has no doubt that his cause will triumph. As did Hitler, he preys on a conflicted state run by a weak leader, choosing an opportune moment to make his move, insisting on an enabling decree that grants him unlimited powers, and opening the gates for his previously proscribed comrades. Like Hitler, Süss undermines the opposition, creates a private militia, and employs secret police. Even in his demise, Süss rehearses the future fate of his German double. His final words, "I was nothing more than the faithful servant of my sovereign!," chillingly anticipate the pronouncements of condemned Nazi leaders at the Nuremberg trials who claimed that they were only following orders.

The film rewrites history; in that regard, it is typical and in keeping with most historical films, from *Birth of a Nation* to *Braveheart, Rob Roy,* and *The Passion of the Christ.* Less well-known, however, is the way Harlan's production plagiarizes and recodes film history. Note, for instance, the director's unabashed theft and subversion of the conclusion of the English film *Jew Süss* of 1934, directed by Lothar Mendes and starring Conrad Veidt (both emigrants who had fled Hitler). Harlan takes the winter setting and dark mood of the execution scene and reverses the dynamics of identification. In Mendes' final sequence, we see a martyr who is violated by the Germans and mourned by his own people, dying with dignity while his fellow Jews bemoan the injustice, a tableau of suffering followed by an appeal for a better and more peaceful world.

What, to restate my question, did Nazi mass propaganda and mass culture have to do with Nazi mass murder? What was different and radical about *Jew Süss* was its overt call to action. At the time of the film's production, the Wannsee Conference had not yet transpired and the "Jewish Question" had not been resolved. The possible alternatives under consideration–extermination or expulsion–are literally enacted in the film's double conclusion: Süss is brutally executed, and all Jews in Stuttgart are forced to leave the city. *Jew Süss* reinforced and built on well-known racial stereotypes, and it did so with hurtful intent. As propaganda, it not only confirmed existing prejudices; it agitated, militated, and called for action. The film culminates in an act of violence that is shown as appropriate, fair, and necessary; likewise, it is explicitly presented as an object lesson for future generations, so that, as the film's final words decree, they and their children's children can "be spared much pain and suffering." As a communal judgment, it appealed to the German audiences that watched and applauded the film. Propaganda official Fritz Hippler, director of *The Eternal Jew*, spoke of the film's final scene as a happy ending.[19] Anti-Semitic hatred assumed narrative force and dramatic necessity. At the level of form, style, and structure, the film was meant to be convincing and, at the same time, entertaining. It engaged audiences by dint of its appeal to both collective prejudices about Jews and popular expectations about movies. It offered an ideological solution along with a stirring evening in the dark. People watched this tale of horror in the belief that they were partaking of a narrative based on historical fact. The conclusion of this movie anticipated another historical fact and a tale of horror: the Nazi state's industrialized murder of millions.

A single film, to be sure, could not and did not determine the fate of the Jews in Germany and occupied Europe. This one film nonetheless constituted a central contribution within a much larger concerted endeavor. The Nazi leaders attached great importance to the production's success; they initiated, guided, and supported it. After the festive premiere in Berlin, Joseph Goebbels praised the production as "a quite grand and genial achievement. An anti-Semitic film as we could only wish one to be." This film, he would later note, "is in fact a new program. It proves that films can affect and inflame feelings in keeping with our own views."[20] Inordinately lucrative, this political entertainment film was the biggest box office hit of the 1939-40 season. One of three people in Germany, some 20.3 million viewers, had seen it by 1943. It was also a big success at the Venice Film Festival and a blockbuster in Vichy France. The Nazis granted the film a privileged status within their larger project of racist genocide: it served as something of a plebiscite, as its rousing success confirmed government hopes that there would be enthusiasm for their future anti-Jewish measures.

Jew Süss is an essential historical document, in terms of both what it intended to show and what it actually manifests. The film culminates in an act of collective violence, which is what it intended to present and justify. Like *The Eternal Jew*, it also took recourse to violence in its execution. In that sense, it not only prepared but also constituted in its own right an act of Nazi aggression. For this reason, *Jew Süss* and *The Eternal Jew* maintain a special status. Even if we carefully attend to their stylistic ploys and their formal workings, as we well should, we do not do so in the name of film appreciation but rather to study them as artifacts from the past, indeed, as testimonies in need of historical judgment. They need special treatment; not to grant them that treatment runs the risk of promoting misunderstanding, insensitivity, and misinformation.

The Continuing Allure of Nazi Attractions

What is at issue when audio-visual artifacts from Nazi culture continue to circulate in our own times? Responses to this question remain markedly divided. A moralistic position insists that the postmodern citation of the Nazi past is irresponsible and serves to erode our sense of history. Militant adherents of this persuasion would, in fact, forbid such borrowings in the name of a larger responsibility to the victims of Hitler's Germany and to the horrific consequences of Nazi violence. This approach is one of taboo and proscription; it is fearful and cautious, fulsome and apodictic. Are there not, one might wonder, ways to re-present this past that are not irresponsible, such as critical citation and analytical retrospection? Are all aspects of the Nazi legacy out of bounds?

A diametrically opposed, "anything-goes" position counters that these images are being used by a different culture and at a different time, which is to say that they cease to serve a Nazi cause when they are recontextualized. For that reason, we can free these signifiers from their historical calling and dispose over them playfully and irreverently, or any way we wish. Their meanings are not fixed; they can be manipulated and deconstructed. This approach is permissive and indulgent. It wonders: Where is the problem? Or it demands of those who protest: What is your problem? The past is past and these images no longer bear those past meanings, it claims. But, as one might respond, does being chic necessarily mean being cavalier about history, especially when this history brought immense tragedy and suffering to the lives of so many people? What does it mean that the allure of fascism plays on a fantasy of force, submission, and domination, especially when we know that this fantasy had a historical base? Right-wing groups today in Germany as elsewhere consciously revive these signifiers with an unabashed political impulse; in so doing, they are serious, not playful.

Why, to return to my initial question, do film productions from the Third Reich continue to intrigue us today? In his essay, "Silhouette City: Hitler, Manson, and the Millennium" (1989), Don DeLillo addresses himself to the continuing allure of the Nazis. There is something in us, he argues, "that creates a need to know the worst about ourselves." As thinking creatures, we sometimes think to the limits. If we imagine the worst, we try to imagine the purest example of what could be the worst. The Nazis obsess us because "they were masters of extremity. They not only imagined the worst; they did it. They engineered a level of pain and death that takes us to the end of self-knowledge." They were masters of destruction, violence, and ruin. They were also steeped in the uses of power and discipline. They found ways to make people surrender their minds and their persons. The Germans capitulated *en masse* to what they regarded as a master being. In this regard, DeLillo goes on, the Nazis "make us uneasy about ourselves, our occasional blind obedience to authority, our willingness to abandon ourselves to a strong personality"[21]—and, I would also insist, about our dependence on the mass media and our susceptibility to mediated stimuli.

Life in Germany under Hitler was not just violence and terror. Rather, the Nazis also cultivated a form of psychological engineering, channeling irrational impulses, unconscious thoughts, and regressive feelings, providing their followers with "an escape from conflict and a direct route to earthly rapture and salvation" by unburdening them of free will, choice, and responsibility.[22] The strength and secret power of Nazi propaganda, T. W. Adorno observed, may well have been that it simply took its audiences for what they really were: children of modernity and consumers of a standardized mass culture.[23] The radical extension of the American entertainment industry envisioned by Goebbels wanted to distract and occupy its audiences so fully that they became unable to think beyond or outside of its parameters. Attempting to coordinate thoughts and feelings, the Ministry for Public Enlightenment and Propaganda sought the systematic stylization of human subjectivity and collective will through sophisticated technology and modern fantasy ware. Under the aegis of the Nazis, mass propaganda, mass culture, and mass murder ultimately could become of a piece.

Notes

1. Gerd Albrecht, *Nationalsozialistische Filmpolitik* (Stuttgart: Enke, 1969), 96–97.
2. See Karsten Witte, "Visual Pleasure Inhibited: Aspects of the German Revue Film," trans. J. D. Steakley and Gabriele Hoover, *New German Critique* 24–25 (fall/winter 1981–1982): 238–263.
3. "*Triumph des Willens*," *Kinematograph*, 26 September 1934.
4. From her interview with Michel Delahaye, "Leni et le loup. Entretien avec Leni Riefenstahl," *Cahiers du Cinéma* 170 (September 1965): 42–63. Translated by Rose Kaplin and reprinted in *Interviews with Film Directors*, ed. Andrew Sarris (New York: Avon, 1967), 460.
5. Ibid., 461.
6. See Martin Loiperdinger, *Rituale der Mobilmachung: Der Parteitagsfilm "Triumph des Willens" von Leni Riefenstahl* (Opladen: Leske und Budrich, 1987), 63–67.
7. "Triumph über die Herzen–'*Triumph des Willens*.'" Festvorstellung des Weihefilms im Beisein des Führers," *Film-Kurier*, 29 March 1935.
8. Loiperdinger, *Rituale der Mobilmachung*, 68.
9. See Stephan Neale's analysis of the film's patterns of alternations in "*Triumph of the Will*: Notes on Documentary and Spectacle," *Screen* 20, no. 1 (1979): 63–86.
10. Joseph Goebbels, *Michael*, trans. Joachim Neugroschel (New York: Amok, 1987), 21.
11. Walter Benjamin, "The Work of Art in the Age of Mechanical Reproduction," in Walter Benjamin, *Illuminations*, trans. Harry Zohn (New York: Schocken, 1969), 250–251.
12. Siegfried Kracauer, "The Mass Ornament," in *The Mass Ornament: Weimar Essays*, ed. Thomas Y. Levin (Cambridge: Harvard University Press, 1995), 77.
13. Witte, "Visual Pleasures Inhibited," 262.
14. Susan Sontag, "Fascinating Fascism," in Susan Sontag, *Under the Sign of Saturn* (New York: Vintage, 1981), 71–105.
15. These examples are taken from the comprehensive account of Riefenstahl's comeback in Jürgen Trimborn, *Riefenstahl: Eine deutsche Karriere. Biographie* (Berlin: Aufbau, 2002), 475–505.
16. See Rebecca Lieb, "Nazi Hate Movies Continue to Ignite Fierce Passions," *New York Times*, 4 August 1991.
17. See, for instance, Walter Liek, *Der Anteil des Judentums am Zusammenbruch Deutschlands* (Munich: Lehmanns, 1924).
18. See Yizhak Ahren, Stig Hornshøj-Møller, and Christoph B. Melchers, "*Der ewige Jude*": *Wie Goebbels hetzte* (Aachen: Alano, 1990); also Ilan Avisar, "The Historical Significance of *Der ewige Jude*," *Historical Journal of Film, Radio and Television* 13, no. 3 (1993): 363–365.
19. Fritz Hippler, *Betrachtungen zum Filmschaffen* (Berlin: Hesses, 1942), 107.

20. As quoted in Klaus Kanzog, *"Staatspolitisch besonders wertvoll": Ein Handbuch zu 30 deutschen Spielfilme der Jahre 1934 bis 1945* (Munich: Schaudig und Ledig, 1994), 220.

21. Don DeLillo, "Silhouette City: Hitler, Manson and the Millennium," in *White Noise: Text and Criticism*, ed. Mark Osteen (New York: Viking, 1998), 345.

22. Ibid., 346.

23. T. W. Adorno, "Freudian Theory and the Pattern of Fascist Propaganda," in *The Essential Frankfurt School Reader*, ed. Andrew Arato and Eike Gebhardt (New York: Urizen, 1978), 134.

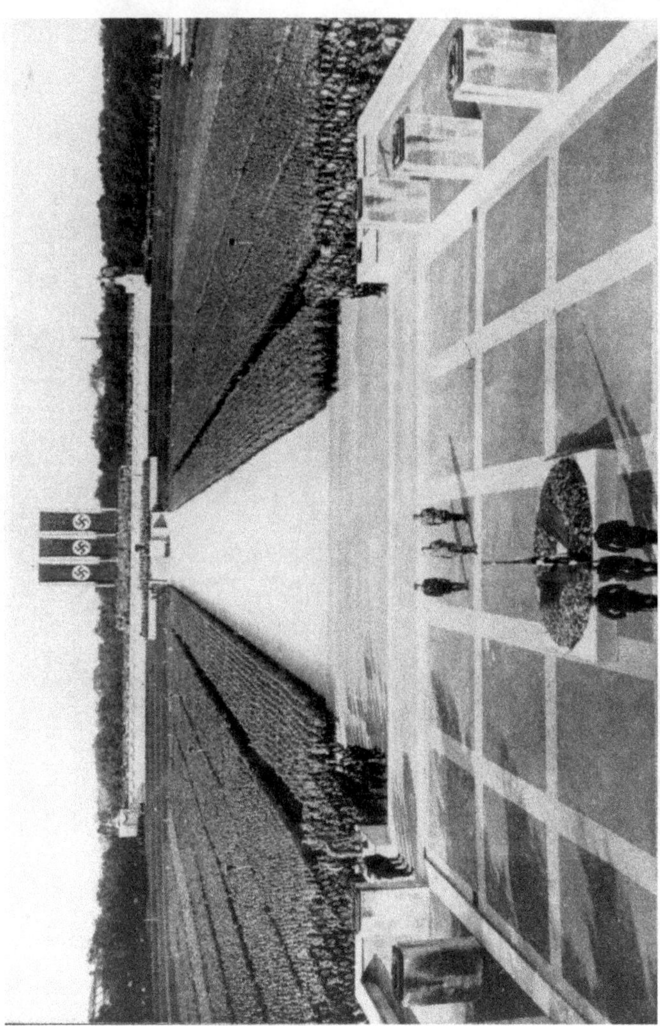

FIGURE 3.1: Scene from the Nazi Party Rally in Nuremberg in 1935, from the film *Triumph of the Will* (*Triumph des Willens*)
Directed by Leni Riefenstahl   September 1935
Source: Filmmuseum Berlin—Stiftung Deutsche Kinemathek

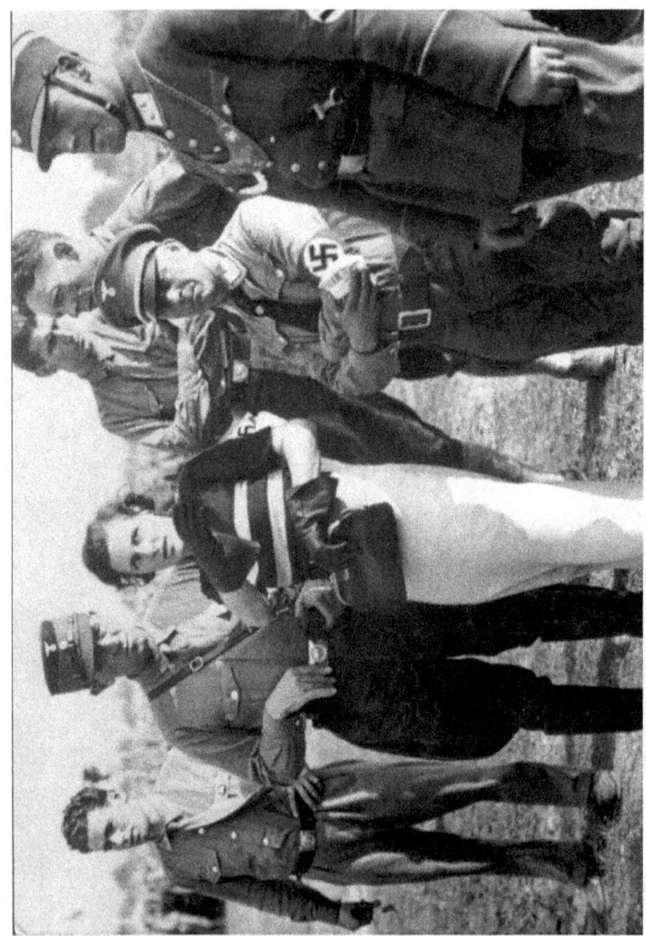

FIGURE 3.2. Leni Riefenstahl, director of the film *Triumph of the Will* (*Triumph des Willens*), at the Nuremberg Nazi Party Rally, accompanied by Nazi officials   September 1935
Source: Filmmuseum Berlin—Stiftung Deutsche Kinemathek

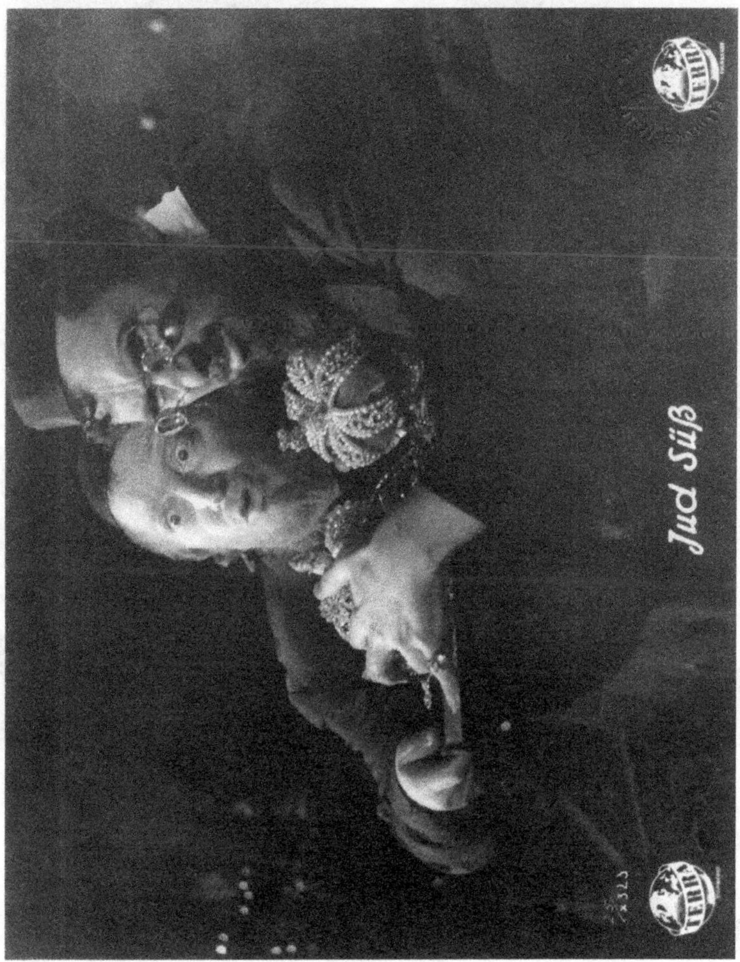

FIGURE 3.3. Scene from the film *Jew Süß* (*Jud Süß*)
Directed by Veit Harlan   1940
Source: Filmmuseum Berlin—Stiftung Deutsche Kinemathek

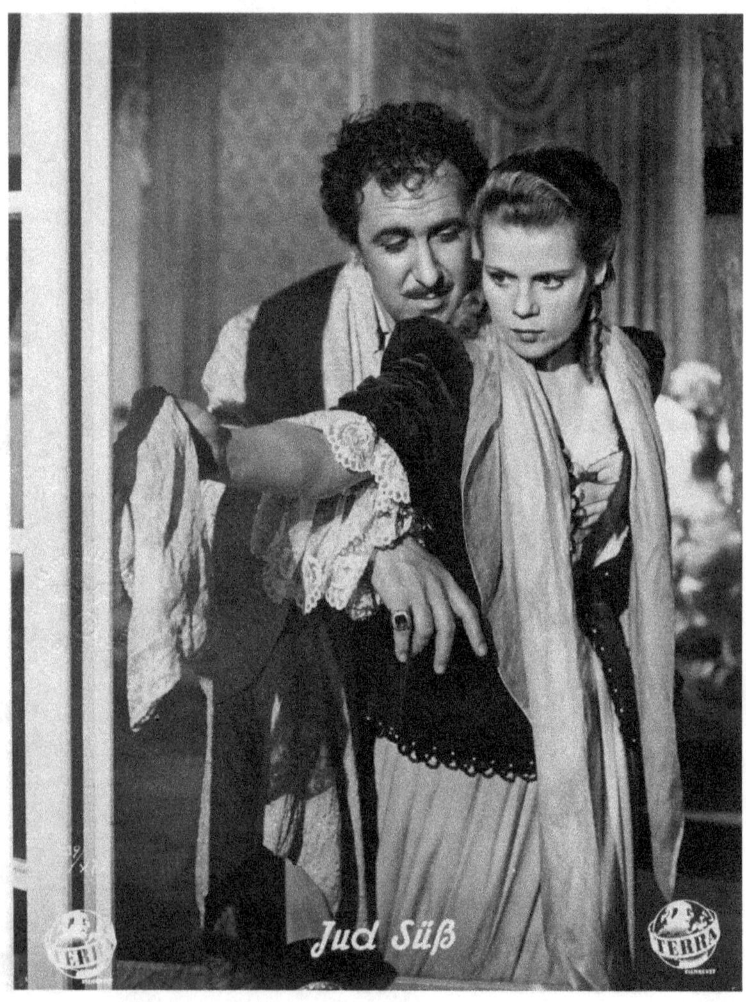

FIGURE 3.4. Scene from the film *Jew Süß* (*Jud Süß*)
Directed by Veit Harlan
1940
Source: Filmmuseum Berlin—Stiftung Deutsche Kinemathek

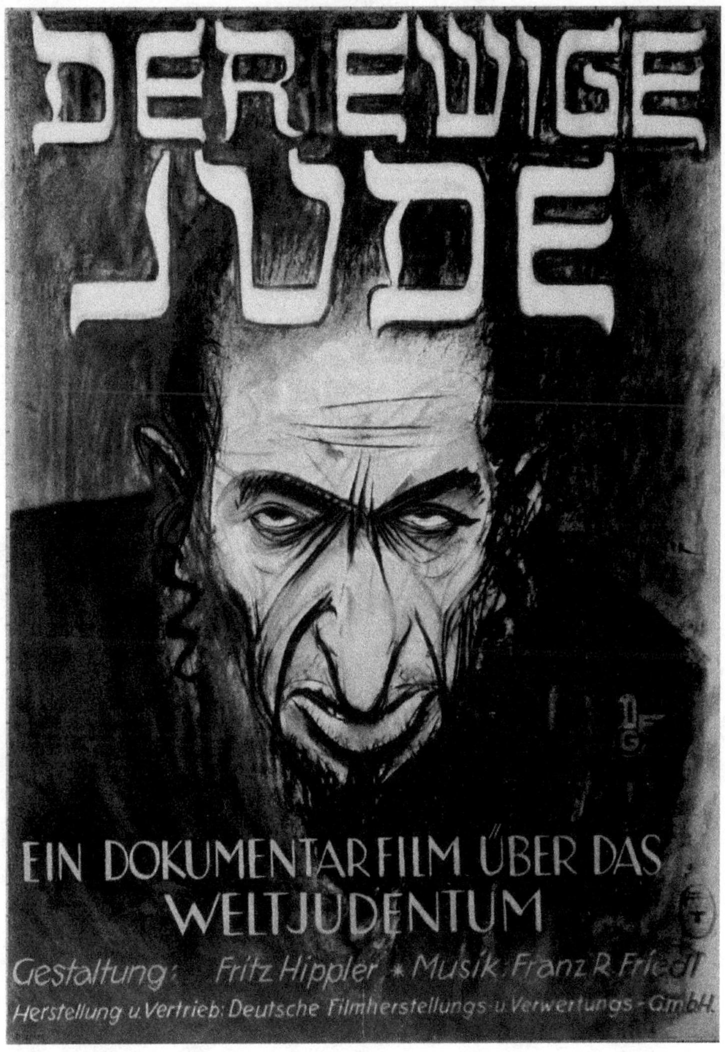

FIGURE 3.5. Advertising poster for the film *The Eternal Jew* (*Der ewige Jude*)
Directed by Fritz Hippler
1940
Source: Museum für Deutsche Geschichte, via the United States Holocaust Memorial
Museum

Chapter Four

MUSIC IN THE THIRD REICH:
THE COMPLEX TASK OF "GERMANIZATION"

Pamela M. Potter

IN NOVEMBER 1936, THE NAZI PROPAGANDA minister Joseph Goebbels made the following announcement in front of a convocation of the Reich Chamber of Culture:

> We now have German theater, German film, German press, German literature, German art, German music and German radio. The charge that was often made against us that it would be impossible to remove the Jews from artistic and cultural life because there were too many of them and that we would not be able to fill all of the vacant positions has been stunningly disproven [applause]. This change in personnel, organization, and direction proceeded without any friction or disruption. And at no other time in Germany have German artists been so revered, and German art so desired and respected as it is today.[1]

What had happened in those first few years of the Third Reich that could allow Goebbels to gloat over such "achievements?" Goebbels seemed quite confident in proclaiming that Jews had been successfully removed from participation in German cultural life, and by mentioning the state of "German" arts and media in the same breath, he implied that there was a connection between the attainment of these two separate goals. It is probably true that by the end of 1936 a radicalization of cultural policy had led to a significant reduction in the number of Jews practicing their professions.[2] But to what extent had the art, film, music, and theater of the Third Reich been changed so as to render them distinctively "German?" Goebbels's juxtaposition of ideas might lead to the assumption that one task, the "Germanization" of the arts and media, would be (or already had been) easily accomplished as a result of a second task, the elimination of Jewish personnel. Yet it is important to understand that this project of Germanization was far more complicated than Goebbels led his audience to believe. He actually conflated two very different projects, one of them being well underway, but the other far more difficult and, at least in the case of music, arguably impossible to achieve. To speak of the Germanization of music in the Third Reich requires a clear distinction between these two tasks: the Germanization of music personnel and the Germanization of the music itself. The first task was carried out with great zeal and, unfortunately, great success, while the second task proved far more difficult or even completely unfeasible.

Yet Goebbels's boisterous claims still resonate today. Knowing all too well of the musical "brain gain" enjoyed in the United States and Britain as a result of Nazi terror,[3] as well as the tragic losses of some great musical talents whose works are only now emerging from their silence,[4] it is easy to believe that musical life in Nazi Germany was transformed, even "Germanized," along both tracks as implied by Goebbels. Many today still assume that because the Nazis drove so many talented Jews in the music world out of Germany, this expulsion must have had dire consequences for the nature of the musical experience in Germany thereafter. Many assume that quality suffered, progress stagnated, and artistic freedom ceased. Before we can truly understand the complexities lying behind Goebbels's report, however, we must analyze and, in some cases, discard these assumptions. Only then can we evaluate the music that was actually produced and consumed, and ask whether musical life in Nazi Germany was really all that different from concurrent situations in other countries, or even all that different from what preceded and followed the Nazi episode within Germany.

Music in the Third Reich: Some Common Myths

Here, in condensed form, are three recurring myths about music in the Third Reich that need to be deconstructed. Preconceived notions like these have tended to obstruct an honest assessment of musical life during the Third Reich. They are not systematically gathered here from specific sources, but rather approximate the types of responses I often encounter when I tell people about my work.

Myth #1: Hitler made all Germans listen to Wagner.

The first problem with this statement is Hitler; the second is Wagner. In what capacity would Hitler have dictated the listening requirements of all, or even of any, citizens of the Reich? Historians have long debated the role of Hitler, but one can reasonably assume that he was not in the business of micromanaging musical repertoire. Many historians hold that Hitler functioned most effectively as a symbol of authority, filling the perceived power vacuum of the Weimar years and creating an illusion of central authority and ideology. Yet there is also reason to believe that he deliberately kept himself at arm's length from actual policy-making in order to uphold his popular appeal and deflect any public dissatisfaction toward those government and party agencies issuing the relevant measures, prompting such expressions of disapproval as "if only the Führer knew!" With respect to music, if Hitler had any notions beyond his preference for Wagner, he seldom made them known. In what was probably his most extensive public pronouncement on music, a speech at the 1938 Nuremberg party rally, Hitler not only refrained from naming any musical styles or genres, but also stated forthrightly that music cannot and should not serve any political agenda, and that musicians should be guided by their own sense of beauty and expressiveness alone rather than by any strict rules.[5]

As for the Wagner question, it may come as a surprise to learn that the Wagner mania in Germany was on the decline long before 1933. Stagings of Wagner's works in German opera houses fell off dramatically after 1926, lagging far behind productions of operas by Verdi, Puccini, Mozart, and Lortzing; attendance at the Bayreuth festival had also dropped. During the Nazi years, certain Wagner "hits" were excerpted and used as background music for the propaganda films of Leni Riefenstahl, newsreels, and radio announcements, but these gestures did not prompt interest in Wagner's complex music.[6] To the extent that Hitler did get involved in musical matters, it was mainly in his role as benefactor of the Bayreuth festival. An avid Wagnerian since his youth, he had been an honored guest at Bayreuth since the 1920s. After he became chancellor, he channeled large sums of money to Bayreuth to keep the festival running,[7] and during the war he averted its closure by opening the Bayreuth performances of *Die Meistersinger* to soldiers.[8] The Nazis exploited this opera more than any other by Wagner. In 1933, it was part of the Day of Potsdam celebrations, and the Bayreuth performances was broadcast with a message by Goebbels'. In this address he maintained that the present state of the

German nation provided the only atmosphere in which Wagner could ever be fully appreciated. He credited Hitler with giving Bayreuth the importance it deserved by honoring it with his presence.[9] The work was then staged at the Nuremberg party rally from 1935 on. Thus, if Hitler forced anyone to listen to Wagner, it was the soldiers invited to the "Kriegsfestspiele" (wartime festival) at Bayreuth and the party loyal assembled in his entourage at Nuremberg, none of whom had much choice in the matter.

Myth #2: Everyone was forced to listen to military marches.

It is true that the military and paramilitary organizations of the Third Reich had their own organized musical activities, many of which were intended to counteract the growing influence of popular music and to encourage the use of military marches for ceremonial functions. The Wehrmacht, as well as the SA, SS, youth groups, and other amateur musicians, were urged to take up brass instruments and participate in mass gatherings such as the Reich party rallies in the hope that the brass sound would inspire amateurs to emulate military music and serve as an "antidote" to the "misuse" of brass in jazz bands.[10] But even these organizations could not have tolerated a steady diet of band music. They also promoted the use of the organ, which was even featured in the Nuremberg party rally of 1936 and at the official memorial ceremony for World War I veterans in 1938.[11] Furthermore, the SA, SS, and Hitler Youth organized their own orchestras and chamber groups that gave public concerts of new and standard repertoire, while the Waffen-SS and the Wehrmacht ran their own music conservatories[12] and the youth organizations cultivated an appreciation of the music of the early German masters.

Beyond this rather circumscribed promotion of military music, no one was really forced to listen to or play anything in particular. The very nature of music production and consumption was such that it would have been impossible, in the twelve years of the Third Reich, to organize and implement supervision of all the professional, amateur, educational, devotional, public, and private music activities throughout the Reich, especially with much more ambitious economic, social, and administrative overhauls taking a higher priority. Even radio broadcasts, which had been under government control before the Nazis came to power, had to bend to the will of the public.[13] Nazi policymakers and program directors embarked on a mission to educate the masses through radio, but they eventually had to concede that radio's primary function was diversion.[14] The public simply wanted more popular and fewer classical offerings, and a statement in the official publication of the Reichs-Rundfunk-Gesellschaft rationalized in 1934 that "it would not be National Socialist [behavior] for German radio, from an exalted vantage point of 'education,' to presume to invade the free time of productive human beings."[15]

To the extent that music censorship did exist, it was not very well organized. Local commissioners functioned primarily as coordinators of the local concert season, approving bookings to avoid schedule conflicts but lacking any authority to control programming decisions.[16] Other agencies, such as the Amt Rosenberg (Alfred Rosenberg's ideological watchdog organization), were equally limited as censors and exerted influence over only a few party-controlled activities. The church might have been able to monitor its own music performances, but even in the official Nazi church, attempts to eliminate familiar Lutheran hymns that had Hebrew words in their texts met with open resistance from congregants.[17] Nor is there any compelling evidence that total control over musical production was ever a priority for Nazi cultural policy-makers in the twelve years of the Reich. Music censorship at most consisted of a few published and unpublished lists condemning certain Aryans as well as non-Aryans, including Alban Berg, Aaron Copland, and Serge Koussevitsky (but notably not including Felix Mendelssohn) along with a ruling that dealers and publishers receive permission before disseminating the works of émigrés. But the Reichsmusikprüfstelle, an office organized to handle the huge task of overseeing all music publication in Germany, at one point consisted of only four staff personnel, suggesting that censorship priorities obviously lay somewhere other than with music.[18] During the war, new restrictions were placed on music from enemy countries, but these measures, motivated by economic boycotts and copyright laws, were implemented in similar ways by other countries at war.[19]

Myth #3: The Nazis banned all jazz and atonal music.

This statement presumes, first of all, that mechanisms were in place to impose bans on certain types of music, which, as we will see in the case of jazz, is a great exaggeration. Secondly, the focus on jazz and atonal music derives from the infamous "Degenerate Music" (*Entartete Musik*) exhibit of 1938, which was modeled on the highly successful

"Degenerate Art" (*Entartete Kunst*) show that had opened a year earlier. This exhibit vilified jazz, "Jewish" operetta, music criticism, and individual conductors and composers, both Aryan and non-Aryan, who were singled out for having proliferated "degeneracy" through atonal composition and other musical means. But, as discussed below, the "Degenerate Music" exhibit was a high-profile event that attracted much attention but had little or no relevance for policy and practices before or after it took place. It is instead but one of countless examples of the incoherence of Nazi ideology and the even greater inconsistency between ideology and its implementation, that is, between theory and practice in the music of the Third Reich.

Finally, this myth, by referring generically to "the Nazis," raises the problematic question of who was a Nazi. Fraught with difficulties on its own, this question is further complicated by the legacy of postwar denazification programs. The aims of denazification were to seek out the worst criminals and, less realistically, to reeducate and reform the rest of the population. The process of denazification could be particularly frustrating for musicians, who were screened not only for their party membership but also for such traits as nationalist leanings and authoritarian personalities.[20] Although the program was eventually abandoned, it engendered a confused notion of what it meant to be a Nazi. Numerous Germans under investigation denied many of their actions of the preceding twelve years, exaggerated any minor hardships or conflicts as evidence of their "resistance," "persecution," or "apolitical behavior," and relied heavily on even casual (and sometimes fabricated) associations with Jews as evidence of their opposition. In the end, it was impossible to define what a Nazi was or to determine degrees of guilt or innocence. Even if it had been possible, the results would not have been particularly useful. The intense scrutiny of individuals that shaped much of the discussion about music in the Third Reich for many years after the end of World War II was revealing, but without an understanding of the operations and functions of musical life and its institutions, the simplistic classification of individuals floundered without any context or foundation.

The Germanization of Music

Of all of the artistic realms Goebbels claimed to have Germanized by the end of 1936, music was perhaps the most elusive. By its very nature, music usually conveys no clear messages or meanings, especially when it stands alone without any text, choreography, or other dramatic or visual cues. For this reason, it has been easier to assign arbitrary labels to music than to other forms of cultural output, but also more difficult to justify these labels. Thus, the progressive experiments of Arnold Schoenberg and his school could be designated as "Bolshevist" by the Nazis and "bourgeois" by the Soviets. Such elusiveness posed difficulties for using music as a propaganda tool: its ambiguity made it susceptible to arbitrary labels, but the same ambiguity could keep the labels from sticking. While Nazi ideologues such as Alfred Rosenberg and propaganda minister Joseph Goebbels were quite articulate in their views toward modernism in the visual arts, they had relatively little knowledge of music and showed far less interest in engaging in the aesthetic debates surrounding it.[21] In the twelve years of the Nazi regime, government and party interests never managed to establish any consistent aesthetic criteria for music, despite the loud outcries against musical "Judaism," "Bolshevism," and "Americanism." Furthermore, the Nazi system neglected to enforce effective measures to suppress those types of music it may have considered unacceptable.

The most coherent public presentation of any ideologically based musical criteria came in 1938 with the first Reich Music Days (Reichsmusiktage) in Düsseldorf and the accompanying exhibit on "Degenerate Music," though even these events failed to convey consistent guidelines and came into direct conflict with measures in practice. The stated purpose of the Reich Music Days was to foster communication between the creators of music and the public, providing a forum for composers, performers, bureaucrats, educators, and scholars to present their achievements to the "people's community."[22] The festivities lasted eight days and were spread all over the city, including concerts at local factories sponsored by the Kraft durch Freude (Strength Through Joy) organization.[23] High points included Richard Strauss conducting some of his own works, the Berlin Philharmonic's performance of Beethoven's Ninth Symphony, and an address by Goebbels. The event should have been able to illustrate the differences between "good" and "bad" music, but even Goebbels, a masterful orator in his own right, was strikingly vague in his keynote speech. The "ten commandments" he offered for German music in a half-hearted attempt to set the tone for the event provided only hazy notions such as: "the nature of music lies in melody" and not in theoretical constructs; "not all music is suited to everyone"; music is rooted in the *Volk*, requires empathy rather than reason, deeply affects the spirit of man, and is the most glorious art of the German heritage; and musicians of the past must be respected.[24] Goebbels was not alone in his inability to put his finger on what made music German. For decades, or even centuries prior to the Nazi era, music critics, musicians, and scholars had written countless books and articles on the subject, but could conclude only that German music was distinct for its depth, clarity, and "that certain something" that made it recognizably German.[25]

But what about un-German music or anti-German music—the music that was supposed to have been eradicated from Nazi society? The "Degenerate Music" exhibit, a focal point of the Reich Music Days, was intended to teach Germans how to recognize destructive musical influences and root them out from the new state. Instead, the exhibit offered only a confusing array of *ad hominem* attacks, many of them self-contradictory. Furthermore, a look at how music functioned in the Third Reich reveals that even the most relentlessly attacked subjects of the exhibit survived the regime unscathed.

The exhibit was modeled on the exhibit of "degenerate" art shown in Munich one year earlier, and its purpose was to present a picture of negative Jewish and foreign influences that had threatened German music until the Nazi revolution succeeded in eradicating them. But rather than clearly delineating the difference between good and bad, the exhibit merely threw together a confusing mixture of anything construed as alienating, intellectual, sarcastic, erotic, socialist, capitalist, or American. The cover of the exhibit catalogue is only the first illustration of this mélange, depicting a black saxophonist, with a Jewish star on his lapel, against a red background (a possible allusion to Bolshevism). The image of the black musician immediately incites an aversion to racial otherness, his saxophone invokes the old worries that had peaked in the 1920s about American culture becoming too influential, and the Jewish star apparently is meant to divulge the manipulative power lying behind this destructiveness. Elsewhere in the catalogue, further examples of fear-mongering draw on various conspiracy theories that involve Jews, Bolshevists, psychoanalysts, capitalists, and Expressionist artists. An unflattering portrait of Schoenberg accompanies an observation, notably by another Jew, that describes him as an explorer attempting to open up new horizons by turning sounds of anguish and hysteria into music.[26] A portrait of his student Anton von Webern, an Aryan, is captioned with the comment that the student exceeds the master "even in the length of his nose."[27] Another Aryan composer, Ernst Krenek, is targeted for "propagating race dishonor" with his hugely successful opera from the 1920s, *Jonny spielt auf!*, which featured a black jazz musician with criminal intentions as the central character.[28] The Jewish opera composer Franz Schreker, whose works had been quite successful throughout the 1920s, was compared to the sex researcher Magnus Hirschfeld and was accused of "setting all types of sexual-pathological confusion to music,"[29] and the works of Bertolt Brecht and Kurt Weill that satirized capitalism were represented literally as promoting greed and corruption.[30]

That the organizers relied heavily on the success of the "Degenerate Art" exhibit becomes clear in the frequent inclusion of similar images, simultaneously betraying their insecurities in confronting music on its own terms. The art exhibit had highlighted its attack on modern art graphically by arranging works in a crowded and chaotic fashion with walls strewn with graffiti-like commentary, and the music exhibit was set up in a similar manner.[31] The catalogue of the "Degenerate Music" exhibit also exploited the shock value of modern art and linked it to music wherever possible. It featured, for example, a sketch of a stage design for a Schoenberg opera by one of the defamed Bauhaus artists, Oskar Schlemmer. In addition, it reproduced caricatures of Jewish musicians that were drawn by Jewish artists,[32] and it captioned two abstract paintings with musical subjects by the "degenerates" Paul Klee and Carl Hofer with the inscription "degenerate art and degenerate music hand in hand."[33] The curator of the exhibit, Hans Severus Ziegler, was not a musician and clearly felt uncomfortable delving into musical issues, having stated outright in the catalogue text that the intention is not to "write prescriptions or circumscribe laws for the new formation of German musical life," but rather to educate the youth.[34] Owing to Ziegler's lack of musical competence, the text indulges in polemics against democracy, Bolshevism, and Jews, but with more attention to Jewish literary figures than to musicians. Any discussions of music are superficial, and the only significant overlap in text and illustrations lies in the references to Schoenberg (the text names him as the inventor of atonality who tried to undermine the essence of German musical expression, the triad).[35]

The "Degenerate Music" exhibit neither provided guidelines for music practice nor reflected current or future music policy. One may be shocked, for example, by the language and images of the repeated attacks against Schoenberg, but it is highly unlikely that such character assassination would have aroused much surprise in Germany in the 1930s, or even in the 1920s. Schoenberg had made a name for himself with the successes of *Pelleas und Melisande* (1910), *Pierrot lunaire* (1912), and *Gurrelieder* (1913), breaking down aesthetic norms by abandoning traditional harmony in his atonal works and later on replacing it with an equally discordant-sounding organization of tones (the twelve-tone or dodecaphonic system of composition). He inspired many to follow his example, but by the late 1920s the critical reception of his new works was less than enthusiastic. Many younger composers had set their minds on forging a stronger relationship with general audiences and shunned Schoenberg's esoteric experiments. Even the musically sophisticated critic Alfred Einstein cast doubt on Schoenberg's effectiveness. In 1928 Einstein described Schoenberg's recent works as "a secret closet to which only he has the key."[36] Having attended the 1930 premiere of *Von heute auf morgen*, Einstein criticized Schoenberg for his half-hearted attempt to compose a work for the masses by choosing a story with broad appeal but setting it to a twelve-tone score displaying "fanatical seriousness and an overwhelming lack of humor," resulting in a work of "pure self-gratification" that was "unsocial and inhumanly difficult."[37] Schoenberg had been named director of the prestigious composition master class at the Prussian Academy in 1925, and his public humiliation and resignation in 1933 attracted much attention as a first step in fulfilling the mission to remove all Jews from musical life. That Schoenberg was a Jew, however, and had recently declined in popularity provided a convenient coincidence that could be exploited in racist propaganda.

The denigration of Schoenberg and his compositional style did not, however, signal the death of atonality. Despite the "Degenerate Music" exhibit's focused criticism of the "destroyers" of "Germanic" tonality, several atonal and twelve-tone works were composed and heard in the Third Reich.[38] In fact, on the occasion of Schoenberg's sixtieth birthday in 1934, Herbert Gerigk, a music critic and employee of Nazi ideologue Alfred Rosenberg, targeted Schoenberg's Jewishness more than his experimentation. Unwilling to reject atonality outright, Gerigk claimed that in the right hands, i.e., those of a composer who is of pure blood and pure character, atonal composition could be an effective means of expression.[39] Twelve-tone works by younger composers were even commissioned by Nazi organizations and performed in prominent venues through the years of the Third Reich.[40]

As for the other individuals attacked in the "Degenerate Music" exhibit, it is important to note that almost all, including Schoenberg, were "safe" targets, as they had either emigrated or died by the time the exhibit was mounted and thus posed no threats of retribution to the organizers. Curiously, Ziegler's list of individual compositions by Jews and non-Jews that had "insulted German audiences" includes a passing reference to the work *L'histoire du soldat* but does not name its composer, Igor Stravinsky.[41] At the time of the exhibit, Stravinsky was actually enjoying great success in Germany[42] and was even named as a possible mentor and model for young composers of the Third Reich.[43] Stravinsky's style was indeed resonating in some of the most successful new compositions by Germans. His experiments with rhythm and meter, for example, clearly influenced Carl Orff's *Carmina Burana*, a work that enjoyed great success in Nazi Germany.[44]

The other prominent object of vilification in the exhibit was jazz, but the fate of jazz in Nazi Germany was also inconsistent with these attacks. Jazz, like Schoenberg's atonality, started out as an easy target. Throughout the 1920s, it came to symbolize foreign corruption in the minds of conservative music critics, leaders of the youth movement, and those practicing musicians who feared competition from the influx of foreign jazz musicians during the Depression.[45] Jazz, however, managed to live on in a variety of forms. First, "art jazz" (*Kunstjazz*), which incorporated jazz-inspired and ragtime-inspired syncopated rhythms and modes into operas, piano pieces, chamber music, and orchestral works, had become popular throughout Europe, infusing the *oeuvre* of Debussy, Stravinsky, Weill, and Hindemith and accounting for the huge success of Krenek's opera *Jonny spielt auf!*[46] Art jazz lived on to receive further acclaim in the Third Reich, most notably with the initial success of Boris Blacher's *Concertante Music for Orchestra*, which the Berlin Philharmonic performed in 1937.[47]

Even more ironic, after the "Degenerate Music" exhibit Germans acquired a more sophisticated appreciation for real jazz, which actually gained in popularity during the World War II. Soldiers clamored for it, and the German public threatened to tune into foreign broadcasts if German radio refused to offer it on the airwaves.[48] Nazi policy seemed to follow the principle that it was better to be lenient and give the public what it wanted than to impose restrictions and risk defiance. Despite some harsh punishments sporadically imposed by local authorities, central government measures against jazz performance were notably tentative.[49] On the radio, jazz was initially banned by Nazi broadcasting authorities, but in the course of the war it was noted that listeners were tuning in to foreign stations playing jazz and would inevitably hear foreign news broadcasts. Fear of this led the authorities to curtail any radio bans on jazz. Radio programs started to include works by jazz artists

Louis Armstrong, Duke Ellington, and Benny Goodman, but concealed their names, insisting that this was not "Negro and Jewish jazz" per se, but rather the "relaxed, strongly rhythmic music" that soldiers wanted to hear.[50] Popular demand also led to the formation of government-sponsored German jazz bands that would appeal to radio listeners. These would also perform demoralizing parodies of popular big band hits such as "FDR Jones," "Hold Tight," and "You're Driving Me Crazy" to Germany's enemies.[51] Jazz thrived beyond the radio waves as well. During the war, German soldiers stationed in occupied territories served as a conduit for forbidden recordings, purchasing them outside the German borders and smuggling them home.[52] Jazz also managed to thrive in nightclubs, many of which hired doormen to screen for suspected spies and installed elaborate warning mechanisms and foils in case of raids by Chamber of Music agents. Some of these nightclubs were even the frequent haunts of SS and SA officers who were jazz enthusiasts.[53]

The Germanization ("Dejewification") of the Music Community

While the campaign against "degenerate" music met with limited success, the Nazis government did manage to weed out and silence large numbers of "degenerate" musical personnel, especially Jews, targeting prominent figures and systematically depleting the numbers of "undesirables" active in Germany by means of emigration, deportation, or ultimately murder. While the elimination of "undesirable" music proved an ill-advised, even impossible program to pursue, the elimination of "undesirable" individuals continued.

To be sure, certain difficulties arose when trying to identify individuals as Aryans, Germans, and Nordics, on the one hand, or as Jews and other so-called "degenerates" on the other. In Nazi Germany, one could rejoice in the "Germanness" of Shakespeare, or Giuseppe Verdi, or even Jesus.[54] And it was just as feasible to humiliate publicly such "pure Aryans" as the Expressionist painter Emil Nolde, the composer Anton Webern, or the writer Heinrich Mann by branding them "degenerate." These inconsistencies, however, did little to impede the aggressive and largely successful systematic persecution of Jews, communists, and, to a lesser degree, others deemed deviant or inferior. The Nazi purge of artistic personnel affected the Sinti and Roma ("gypsies"), nonwhites, and political, social, and sexual "deviants," but Jews remained the central target.[55] The Germanization or, to use the official terminology, "dejewification" (*Entjudung*) of musical life in the Nazi state proceeded first in a series of high-profile acts against prominent individuals. Schoenberg was compelled to resign his post at the Prussian Academy, Bruno Walter was threatened and coerced into canceling his German engagements, and even the Aryan composer and president of the Reich Chamber of Music, Richard Strauss, temporarily became a pariah for refusing to break off his collaboration with the Jewish author Stefan Zweig. The purge then affected the less prominent, as musicians had to prove their Aryan lineage in order to gain working papers. Jews who earlier had managed to join the Chamber of Music and get their permits were systematically expelled beginning in 1936.[56]

Still, it was impossible to achieve a complete purge of all Jewish artists, since many exceptions were made for artistic reasons. The well-known phrase "I will determine who is a Jew" became something of a policy once leaders such as Göring and Goebbels became the protective patrons of their own musical institutions. Göring, as Prussian Prime Minister, inherited the Berlin State Opera and its orchestra, and managed to protect his institutions from any financial or bureaucratic control by the Ministry for Public Enlightenment and Propaganda. Goebbels, for his part, was Gauleiter of Berlin and played a similar role as patron of the city opera and the Berlin Philharmonic.[57] But rather than steer the aesthetic content of these venues, the two Nazi leaders concentrated on getting the best and the brightest stars for their ensembles and found themselves in a fierce rivalry with one another. They promoted the careers of several actors and directors known to be homosexuals or to have had close associations with communists and Jews, and they even tolerated productions that conveyed not-so-subtle criticisms of the Nazi regime, such as a scandalous production of Shakespeare's *Richard III* in 1937 that contained direct criticisms of brownshirts and SS men.[58] Goering even granted special permits to conductor Leo Blech and singer Alexander Kipnis, both "full-Jews," and to the singers Günther Treptow (whose grandmother was Jewish), Max Lorenz, and Frieda Leider (both married to Jews).[59]

The "dejewification" of culture industries in Nazi Germany put an end to the perceived unwelcome competition from Jews by leading to mass emigration of prominent Jewish musical figures[60] and eventually withdrawing working privileges from the rest. This undoubtedly increased job opportunities for Aryans, but also created a sizable class of unemployed Jewish musicians. With one stroke, Jews were legally barred from participating in cultural activities, leaving thousands in the arts with no means of support. Recognizing the serious economic implications of this sudden increase in unemployment, the Reich's propaganda ministry accepted a proposal from leaders of the Jewish community to establish theaters, orchestras, and other cultural programs run exclusively by Jews and presented exclusively to Jewish audiences.[61] The Jüdischer Kulturbund (Jewish Cultural League) started in the spring of 1933 in Berlin where it grew to include three theater ensembles, an opera ensemble, two symphony orchestras, a chamber theater, and numerous choral groups and chamber music groups, and also sponsored lectures, exhibits, film programs, cabaret, and dances. The league subsequently spread to at least one hundred cities, accounting for over 50,000 members by 1937.

The establishment of the Jewish Cultural League offered yet one more opportunity for Nazi officials to draw distinctions between "true German" and "Jewish" music. The government imposed three restrictions on the Jewish Cultural League's repertoire: it was prohibited from performing German works; it was encouraged to perform works by Jews; and it was allowed to perform foreign works as long as their content was not anti-German. At first the prohibition of German works was not strictly enforced, and the Jewish Cultural League, for the most part, exercised self-censorship. As a result, the league was subjected to official censorship only on a few occasions. League members avoided the obvious "Germans" such as Wagner, Weber, and Lortzing, although they were explicitly allowed to perform Handel's oratorios, most of which were based on Old Testament themes. Over time, restrictions on German music tightened as officials wanted to draw clearer distinctions between "German" and "Jewish." Thus, the Jewish Cultural League was not permitted to program Beethoven's works as of 1936, and Mozart became taboo after the annexation of Austria. Yet, although the Nazi government increased pressure on the league to concentrate exclusively on Jewish works, these restrictions were not as clear-cut as they seemed. In one case, an official in the Ministry for Public Enlightenment and Propaganda rejected the Jewish Cultural League's request to perform Mahler because he insisted that the composer of "The Wayfarer's Song" surely was Aryan.[62]

For many decades after World War II, music in Nazi Germany was commonly perceived as a strictly controlled regimen of march music, Wagner operas, and Beethoven symphonies, devoid of atonal music, jazz, or any other remnants of progressive "Weimar culture." Many of our assumptions still rest on a stubborn determination to assign labels of "Nazi" and "non-Nazi" to musical styles and to people. As a result, we have difficulty accepting evidence that does not fit neatly into these categories. Assumptions about the totalitarian nature of the Nazi system, Hitler's interference and control in all areas of culture, and the enforcement of rigid criteria for "good" and "bad" culture all stem from the argument put forth by Germans after the war that they had no choice but to conform. This conception of Nazi cultural policy derives from early historiographic trends, in which scholars tried to draw parallels between Nazi Germany and the Soviet Union.[63] Unfortunately, the persistence of the totalitarian concept in accounts of musical life in the Third Reich has only contributed to the caricature of Nazi musical life as controlled, inflexible, and artistically sterile.

Contrary to these popular assumptions, the vibrancy and creativity in German musical life did not cease in 1933, even though many of us would like to believe it did, such a cessation being easier to fathom than the notion that anything as lofty as music might have thrived in an environment of such unprecedented inhumanity. One of the great puzzles of the past half-century has been to understand how a nation that had produced such extraordinary artists as Goethe and Beethoven could be capable of committing such barbarous acts in the 1930s and 1940s. The postwar silence on this question was particularly deafening in the sphere of music, where a large number of prominent musical figures who enjoyed illustrious careers in the 1950s and 1960s managed to hide from the world the successes they had enjoyed in Hitler's Germany. It was not difficult for stars such as Herbert von Karajan, Elisabeth Schwarzkopf, and Carl Orff to deny their Nazi affiliations, because the world wanted to believe that musicians inhabited the elevated realm of art and would never lower themselves by associating with Nazi thugs.

The truth, however, is that music in Nazi Germany did thrive, even as Jewish musicians there languished. The Nazi regime was clever enough to recognize the importance of music to German culture and to allow musicians more freedom than many others working in the cultural realm. It was also clever enough to realize the importance of keeping the public happy and even compromised its own principles, such as its aversion to jazz, rather than risk dissatisfaction and revolt. Finally, Nazi policy-makers were also clever enough to capitalize on deep-seated resentment among German musicians against successful Jews in the music world, a resentment that stretched back at least to the days of Richard Wagner and lived on in the myth that Jews were occupying positions that belonged to "true Germans." Through a mixture of aggressive propaganda and loose-reined control, the Nazi regime created a situation in which German musicians could feel privileged and unfettered, and even comforted in the belief that they were making a tremendously important contribution to rebuilding Germany's morale and international cultural standing. The persecution of their Jewish colleagues could be rationalized as retribution for decades of alleged Jewish domination of the musical world. In the end, although no one could clearly distinguish between German music and Jewish music per se, the physical separation and ensuing eradication of Jewish musical personnel served to satisfy the requirements of Nazi ideologues and mitigate insecurities among the German music professions and the German nation as a whole.

Notes

1. *Deulig-Tonwoche* [no. 257, 2 December 1936], in *Cinematographie des Holocaust: Dokumentation und Nachweis von filmischen Zeugnissen. Ein Projekt des Fritz Bauer Instituts* [cited 26 May 2004]; available at http://www.cine-holocaust.de. This and all other translations are by the author unless otherwise indicated.

2. Alan Steinweis, *Art, Ideology, and Economics in Nazi Germany: The Reich Chambers of Music, Theater and the Visual Arts 1933-1945* (Chapel Hill: University of North Carolina Press, 1993), 103–120.

3. Numerous works have documented the achievements of musicians driven from Nazi Germany, including Horst Weber, ed., *Musik in der Emigration 1933-1945: Verfolgung, Vertreibung, Rückwirkung* (Stuttgart: Metzler, 1994); Reinhold Brinkmann and Christoph Wolff, eds., *Driven into Paradise: The Musical Migration from Nazi Germany to the United States* (Berkeley: University of California Press, 1999); Hanns-Werner Heister, Claudia Maurer Zenck, and Peter Petersen, eds., *Musik im Exil: Folgen des Nazismus für die internationale Musikkultur* (Frankfurt am Main: Fischer Verlag, 1993); Habakuk Traber and Elmar Weingarten, eds., *Verdrängte Musik: Berliner Komponisten im Exil* (Berlin: Berliner Festspiele und Argon Verlag, 1987); and Barbara von der Lühe, *Die Emigration deutschsprachiger Musikschaffender in das britische Mandatsgebiet Palästina* (Frankfurt am Main: Peter Lang, 1999).

4. In addition to a number of publications on the subject, a long-term recording project entitled *Entartete Musik* on the Decca label is dedicated to proliferating the works of composers who perished in the concentration camps.

5. See Michael Walter, *Hitler in der Oper* (Stuttgart: J.B. Metzler, 1995), 195–197, and Appendix H in this volume.

6. Hubert Kolland, "Wagner-Rezeption im deutschen Faschismus," in *Bericht über den internationalen musikwissenschaftlichen Kongreß Bayreuth 1981*, ed. Christoph-

Hellmut Mahling and Sigrid Weismann (Kassel: Bärenreiter, 1984), 498–502; Henry Bair, "National Socialism and Opera: The Berlin Opera Houses 1933–1939," *Opera* 35, no. 2 (1984): 130.

7. Fred K. Prieberg, *Musik im NS-Staat* (Frankfurt am Main: Fischer Verlag, 1982), 307; Michael Kater, *The Twisted Muse: Musicians and Their Music in the Third Reich* (New York: Oxford University Press, 1997), 35–39.

8. Richard Wilhelm Stock, *Richard Wagner und seine Meistersinger: Eine Erinnerungsgabe zu den Bayreuther Kriegsfestspielen 1943* (Nuremberg: Ulrich, 1938 [sic]); Michael Karbaum, *Studien zur Geschichte der Bayreuther Festspiele (1876-1976)* (Regensburg: Bosse, 1976), 91–93.

9. Joseph Goebbels, "Richard Wagner und das Kunstempfinden unserer Zeit," reprinted in *Die Meistersinger von Nürnberg: Texte-Materialien-Kommentare*, ed. Attila Csampai and Dietmar Holland (Munich: Rowohlt, 1981), 194–197.

10. Joseph Wulf, *Musik im Dritten Reich: Eine Dokumentation* (Berlin: Ullstein, 1983 [1966]), 257–261.

11. Albrecht Riethmüller, "Die Bestimmung der Orgel im Dritten Reich," in *Orgel und Ideologie. Bericht über das fünfte Colloquium der Walcker-Stiftung für orgelwissenschaftliche Forschung 5.-7. Mai 1983 in Göttweig*, ed. Hans Heinrich Eggebrecht (Murrhardt: Musikwissenschaftliche Verlags-Gesellschaft, 1984), 40–44.

12. Prieberg, *NS-Staat*, 256–259. See also Fritz Bunge, *Musik in der Waffen-SS* (Osnabrück: Munin, 1975).

13. Rita von den Grün, "Funktionen und Formen von Musiksendungen im Rundfunk," in *Musik und Musikpolitik im faschistischen Deutschland*, eds. Hanns-Werner Heister and Hans-Günter Klein (Frankfurt am Main: Fischer, 1984), 98–106.

14. Nanny Drechsler, *Die Funktion der Musik im Deutschen Rundfunk, 1933-1945* (Pfaffenweiler: Centaurus, 1988), 30, 35–36, 41–43, 86–95; Michael Kater, *Different Drummers: Jazz in the Culture of Nazi Germany* (New York: Oxford University Press, 1992), 47.

15. *Mitteilungen der Reichsrundfunkgesellschaft*, 1 February 1934, quoted in Drechsler, *Funktion der Musik*, 121.

16. Donald Wesley Ellis, "Music in the Third Reich: National Socialist Aesthetic Theory as Governmental Policy" (PhD diss., University of Kansas, 1970), 142–143.

17. Doris Bergen, *Twisted Cross: The German Christian Movement in the Third Reich* (Chapel Hill: University of North Carolina Press, 1996), 164–171.

18. Steinweis, *Art, Ideology, and Economics*, 138–141; Ellis, "Music in the Third Reich," 129–130.

19. Ellis, "Music in the Third Reich," 130–134.

20. David Monod, "Verklärte Nacht: Denazifying Musicians under Nazi Control," in *Music and Nazism: Art Under Tyranny, 1933-1945*, ed. Michael H. Kater and Albrecht Riethmüller (Laaber: Laaber Verlag, 2003), 298–299.

21. Jonathan Petropoulos, *Art as Politics in the Third Reich* (Chapel Hill: University of North Carolina Press, 1996), 21–45; Kater, *Twisted Muse*, 188–190.

22. Heinz Drewes of the Reichsmusikkammer, quoted in Werner Schwerter, "Heerschau und Selektion," in *Entartete Musik: eine kommentierte Rekonstruktion*, ed. Albrecht Dümling and Peter Girth (Düsseldorf: Landeshauptstadt Düsseldorf, 1988), 113.

23. Program reprinted in Dümling and Girth, *Entartete Musik*, 105–110.

24. Joseph Goebbels, "Zehn Grundsätze deutschen Musikschaffens," *Amtliche Mitteilungen der Reichsmusikkammer* 5, no. 11 (1938), facsimile in Dümling and Girth, *Entartete Musik*, 123; portions translated in Ellis, "Music in the Third Reich," 127. See Appendix G.

25. Bernd Sponheuer, "Reconstructing Ideal Types of the 'German' in Music," in *Music and German National Identity*, ed. Celia Applegate and Pamela Potter (Chicago: University of Chicago Press, 2002), 36–58; on the continued challenges to define German music faced by musicologists in the Third Reich, see Pamela M. Potter, *Most German of the Arts: Musicology and Society from the Weimar Republic to the End of Hitler's Reich* (New Haven: Yale University Press, 1998), 200–234.

26. Hans Severus Ziegler, *Entartete Musik: Eine Abrechnung*, 2nd ed. (Düsseldorf: Völkischer Verlag, 1939), 13.

27. "Anton Webern, ein 'Meisterschüler' Arnold Schönbergs, übertrumpfte seinen Dresseur noch um etliche Nasenlänge," Ziegler, *Entartete Musik*, 19.

28. "Ernst Krenek propagierte in 'Jonny spielt auf' die Rassenschande als die Freiheit der 'Neuen Welt'." Ziegler, *Entartete Musik*, 19. The work is defamed elsewhere in the catalogue (9) as "Bolshevist" and was probably also the inspiration for the cover illustration.

29. "Franz Schreker war der Magnus Hirschfeld unter den Opernkomponisten. Es gab keine sexual-pathologische Verirrung, die er nicht unter Musik gesetzt hätte." Ziegler, *Entartete Musik*, 15.

30. An illustration of Weill is accompanied by a facsimile passage of the seized autograph of *The Threepenny Opera*, with the commentary: "Der 'Schöpfer' der *Dreigroschenoper* Kurt Weill, persönlich—und seine Handschrift mit dem Selbstbekenntnis aus der 'Dreigroschenoper': '…nur wer im Wohlstand lebt, lebt angenehm.'" Ziegler, *Entartete Musik*, 17. A similar misrepresentation comes with a quote from *Mahagonny* describing the vices of gluttony, lust, boxing, and inebriation, followed by the commentary: "So lautet der Wahlspruch der von den Verbrechern zum Zwecke der Befriedigung aller niedrigen Instinkte gegründeten 'Stadt Mahagonny!'" Ziegler, *Entartete Musik*, 21.

31. Michael Meyer, "A Musical Façade for the Third Reich," in *"Degenerate Art": The Fate of the Avant-Garde in Nazi Germany*, ed. Stephanie Barron (New York: Los Angeles County Museum of Art/Harry Abrams, 1991), illustrations on 170, 173, and 180; description of the exhibit on 180–182.

32. Ziegler, *Entartete Musik*, 19.

33. Ibid., 25.

34. Ibid., 6.

35. Ibid., 13, 22–24.

36. Alfred Einstein, "Opera in Breslau: Schönberg's *Die glückliche Hand* [The Favored Hand], Handel's *Joshua*, and Ballet," *Berliner Tageblatt*, 26 March 1928, trans. in *Alfred Einstein on Music: Selected Music Criticisms*, Contributions to the Study of Music and Dance, vol. 21, ed. Catherine Dower (New York: Greenwood Press, 1991), 50.

37. Alfred Einstein, "Arnold Schönberg: *Von heute auf morgen* (World première in Frankfurt)," *Berliner Tageblatt*, 3 February 1930, trans. in Dower, *Einstein on Music*, 104–105.

38. Prieberg, *NS-Staat*, 126, 298–306.

39. "Wenn hier gegen Schönberg gesprochen wird, so richtet sich das nicht unbesehen gegen alles, das nicht restlos den Regeln der Harmonielehre entspricht. Auch der sogenannten Atonalität kann eine wertvolle Kunst herauswachsen, wenn nur der Mensch blutmäßig und charackterlich einwandfrei und schöpfersich ist, der dahinter steht." Herbert Gerigk, "Eine Lanze für Schönberg," *Die Musik* 27 (1934): 89.

40. Prieberg, *NS-Staat*, 303–306.

41. Ziegler, *Entartete Musik*, 18–20.

42. Joan Evans, "Stravinsky's Music in Hitler's Germany," *Journal of the American Musicological Society* 56, no. 3 (2003): 525–594.

43. Kater, *Twisted Muse*, 183.

44. Michael H. Kater, *Composers of the Nazi Era: Eight Portraits* (New York: Oxford University Press, 2000), 122–128.

45. Kater, *Different Drummers*, 26–28.

46. On *Kunstjazz* see J. Bradford Robinson, "Jazz Reception in Weimar Germany: In Search of a Shimmy Figure," in *Music and Performance during the Weimar Republic*, ed. Bryan Gilliam (Cambridge: Cambridge University Press, 1994), 107–143.

47. Kater, *Twisted Muse*, 231–232.

48. Kater, *Different Drummers*, chaps. 1 and 2.

49. Kater, *Different Drummers*, 52, 104.

50. Drechsler, *Die Funktion der Musik*, 24, 33, 42, 131.

51. Kater, *Different Drummers*, 122–135; see also chapter 5 of Horst Bergmeier and Rainer E. Lotz, *Hitler's Airwaves: The Inside Story of Nazi Radio Broadcasting and Propaganda Swing* (New Haven: Yale University Press, 1997). Appendix II (293–342) includes lyrics for more than eighty parodies of American and British songs.

52. Kater, *Different Drummers*, 49–51, 86–87, 138–146.

53. Kater, *Different Drummers*, 64, 101.

54. Boguslaw Drewniak, "The Foundations of Theater Policy in Nazi Germany," in *National Socialist Cultural Policy*, ed. Glenn R. Cuomo (New York: St. Martin's Press, 1995), 86; Birgitta Maria Schmid, "Musikwissenschaft im 'Dritten Reich'," in *Die dunkle Last: Musik und Nationalsozialismus*, Schriften zur Musikwissenschaft und Musiktheorie, vol. 3, ed. Brunnhilde Sonntag, Hans-Werner Boresch, and Detlef Gowony (Cologne: Bela Verlag, 1999), 98–99; Bergen, *Twisted Cross*, 155–157.

55. Steinweis, *Art, Ideology, and Economics*, 126–132.

56. Steinweis, *Art, Ideology, and Economics*, chap. 5; Kater, *Twisted Muse*, 75–85, 88–91.

57. Pamela M. Potter, "Musical Life in Berlin from Weimar to Hitler," in *Music and Nazism* [see n. 20], 90–101.

58. William Grange, "Ordained Hands on the Altar of Art: Gründgens, Hilpert, and Fehling in Berlin," in *Theatre in the Third Reich, the Prewar Years: Essays on Theatre in Nazi Germany*, ed. Glen W. Gadberry (Westport, CT: Greenwood Press, 1995), 75–89

59. Bair, "Berlin Opera Houses," 83–84.

60. Theodor Adorno, Rudolf Bing, Emanuel Feuermann, Otto Klemperer, Erich Korngold, Fritz Kreisler, Lotte Lenya, Paul Pisk, Arnold Schoenberg, William Steinberg, Fritz Stiedry, Ernst Toch, Bruno Walter, and Kurt Weill, among others, came to the United States.

61. Steinweis, *Art, Ideology, and Economics*, 120–126.

62. Bernd Sponheuer, "Musik auf einer 'kulturellen und physischen Insel': Musik als Überlebensmittel im jüdischen Kulturbund 1933–1941," in Weber, *Musik in der Emigration*, 108–135.
63. See Ian Kershaw, *The Nazi Dictatorship: Problems and Perspectives of Interpretation*, 3rd ed. (London: Edward Arnold, 1993), chap. 2.

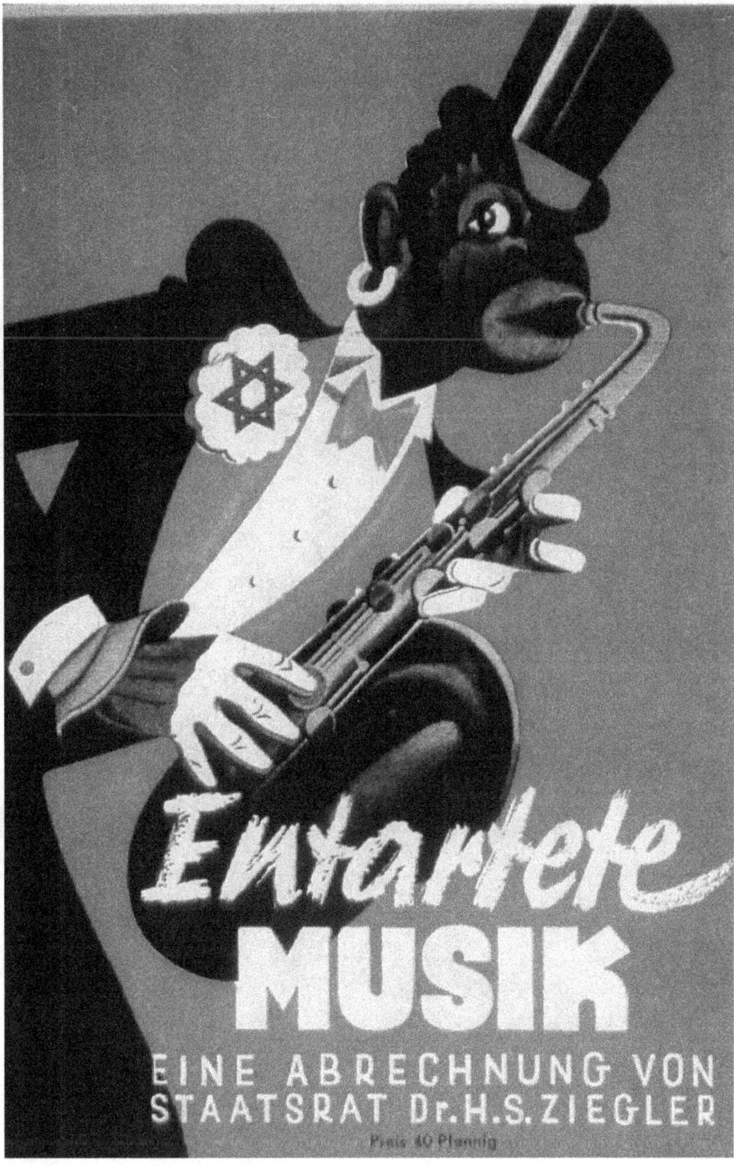

FIGURE 4.1. Cover for the brochure *Degenerate Music* (*Entartete Musik*), by H. S. Ziegler, issued for the Düsseldorf run of the exhibit *Degenerate Art* (*Entartete Kunst*), which occurred at the same time as the Reich Music Days
1938
Source: Bildarchiv Preussischer Kulturbesitz, via the United States Holocaust Memorial Museum

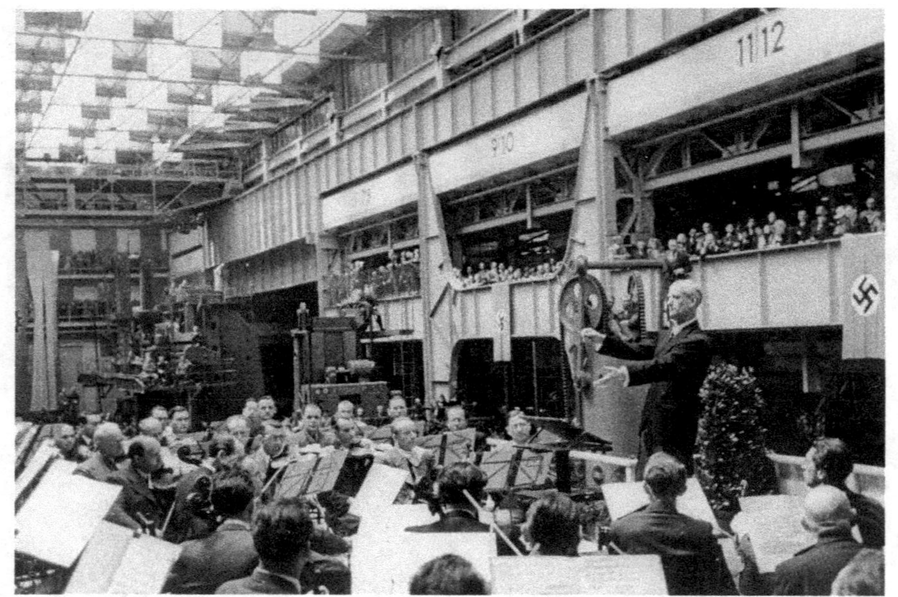

FIGURE 4.2. Wilhelm Furtwängler conducts the Vienna Philharmonic Orchestra in a concert in a Berlin factory, sponsored by the Reich Ministry for Public Enlightenment and Propaganda in connection with the National Socialist "Strength Through Joy" (Kraft durch Freude) recreational organization
17 May 1943
Source: Nederlands Instituut voor Oorlogsdocumentatie, via the United States Holocaust Memorial Museum

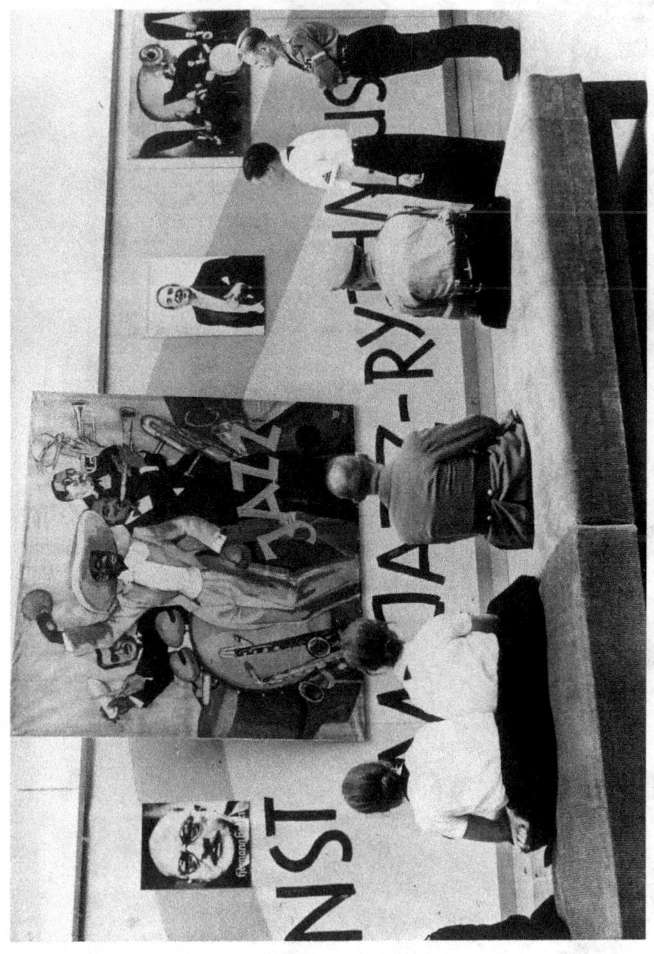

FIGURE 4.3. The vilification of jazz in the exhibition *Degenerate Music* (*Entartete Musik*) during the Reich Music Days in Düsseldorf   1938
Source: Ullstein Bild

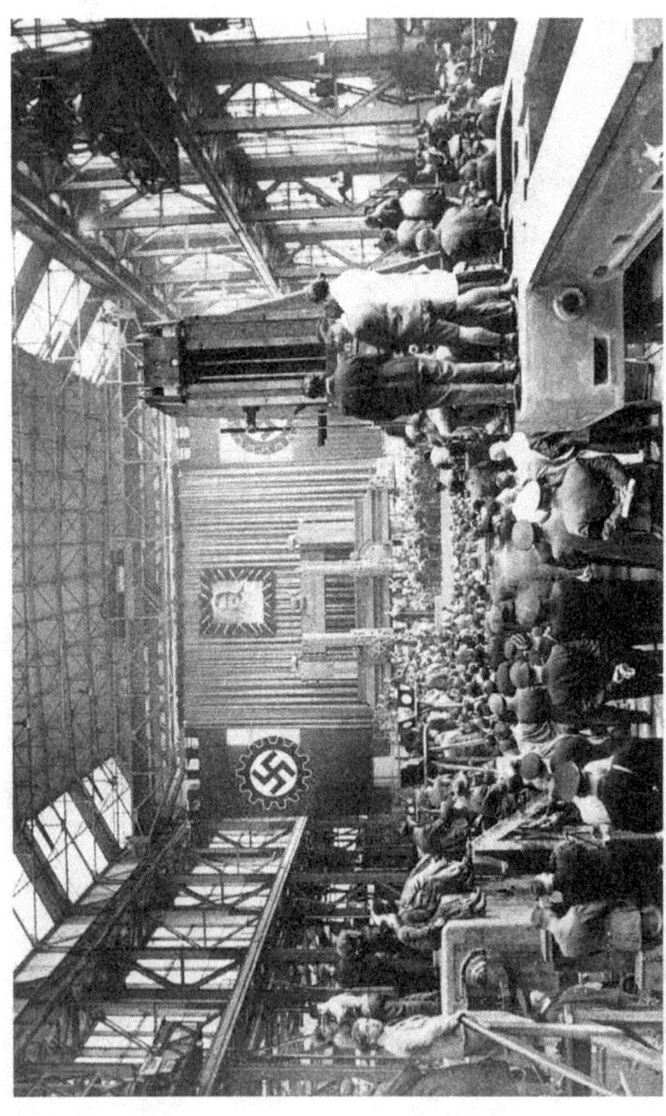

FIGURE 4.4. Reich Music Days 1938. Reich Symphony Orchestra performing at the Schiess-de Fries factory, Düsseldorf   23 May 1938

Source: Stadtarchiv Düsseldorf

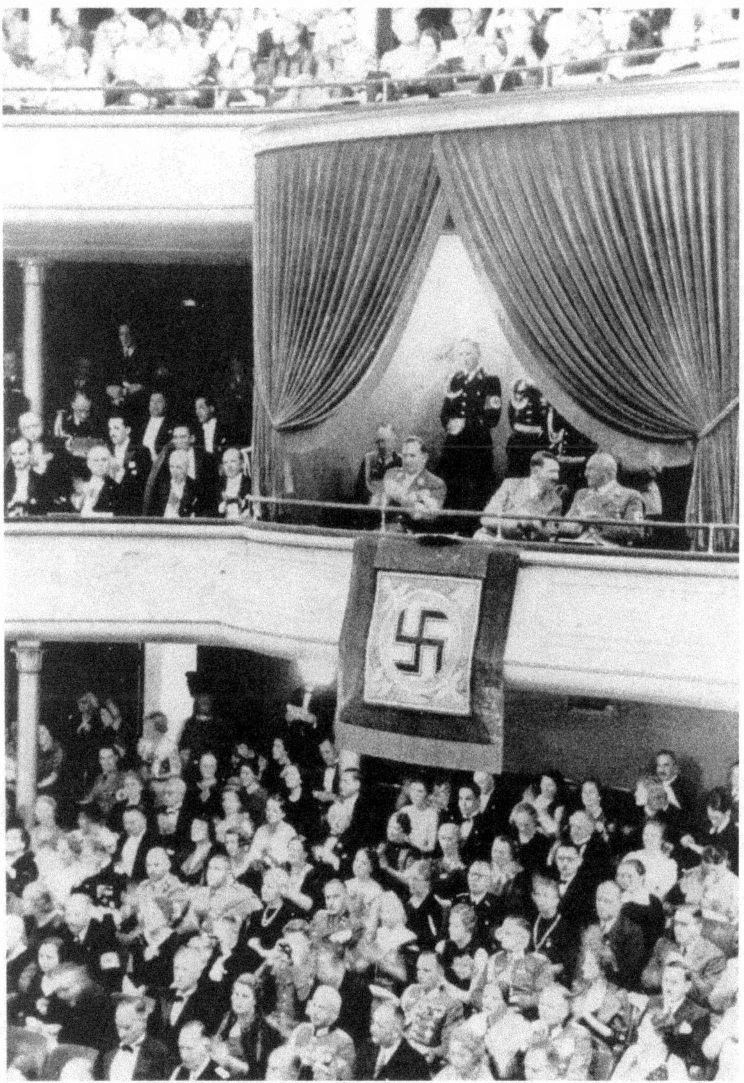

FIGURE 4.5. Adolf Hitler speaking with Julius Streicher in the Führer's box
(*Führerloge*) during a performance in Nuremberg of Richard Wagner's *Die Meistersinger von Nürnberg*
1938
Source: Museen der Stadt Nürnberg

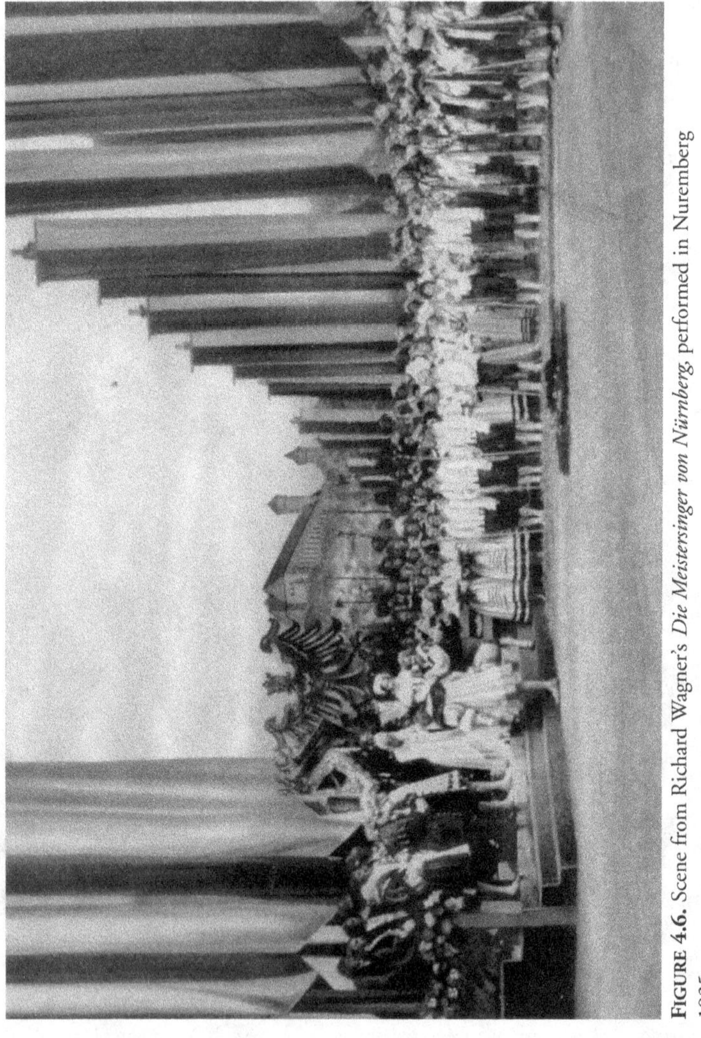

FIGURE 4.6. Scene from Richard Wagner's *Die Meistersinger von Nürnberg*, performed in Nuremberg 1935

Source: Museen der Stadt Nürnberg

Chapter Five

A Command Performance?
The Many Faces of Literature
under Nazism

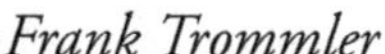

Frank Trommler

WHEN WE APPROACH NAZI LITERATURE, we usually know what we can expect: a blustering rhetoric of living and dying for the German *Volk*. Yet, at closer look, young love is always wholesome, family life is an earthly paradise, manual labor is pleasant and redemptive, and nature functions as a friend and support. When we approach the histories of this literature, we also know what we can expect: extensive discourses on the party and state apparatus of controlling the writers, on Goebbels's Ministry for Public Enlightenment and Propaganda, which supervised the Reichsschrifttumskammer (Reich Chamber of Literature), the Amt Schrifttumspflege (Office for the Cultivation of Literature), which Alfred Rosenberg used in order to keep Goebbels's propaganda empire in check, and on other institutions that were built after the concerted action of book burnings in 1933. We also find a rather uninspiring run-down of the lives and work of the usual suspects, from Friedrich Blunck, Hanns Jost, and Erwin Guido Kolbenheyer to the younger representa-tives Hans Baumann, Heinrich Anacker, and Gerhard Schumann. The problem is not that we do not know much about this literature (though this is in fact the case) but rather that we do not want to know much about it and prefer to remain content with the established wisdom on the poor literary quality of party-controlled publications.

It is hardly surprising that it fell to a few specialists, such as crit-ics Joseph Wulff, Dietrich Strothmann, Ernst Loewy, and Uwe-Karsten Ketelsen, to provide the scholarly tools for broader studies of the many forms of writing under National Socialism. Eager to illuminate the regime's systematic corruption of artistic production, they focused more on ideology and control than on the market, which had the unintended consequence of making the cultural apparatus look more consistent and efficient than it actually was.[1] Yet, they also established that the political dates of 1933 and 1945, while certainly important for the political assessment of this literature, were less relevant to the definition of its aesthetics and its conservative, often antimodernist outlook. Just as numerous authors had made their name with conservative or *völkisch* works before they were adopted by the Nazis, so too did many writers keep a broad readership in Germany and Austria long after the end of World War II.

Aware of these continuities, critics of the 1968 protest generation blasted the ideological components of this literature in terms of fascism and antifascism, illuminating important aspects of aesthetic and cultural production in the 1930s and 1940s, although they were less interested in the literary texts themselves.[2] The textual interest resurfaced in the 1990s, leading to a new kind of interpretive study that combines the experience of writing and reading in another German dictatorship, the German Democratic Republic, with a thorough understanding of state censorship under Hitler and Goebbels.[3] Such an understanding is now possible thanks to Jan-Pieter Barbian's painstaking reconstruction of the monstrous state and party apparatus of control and guidance between 1933 and 1945.[4] Similarly revealing is Volker Dahm's devastating documentation of the gradual exclusion of Jewish writers, publishers, and booksellers under National Socialism that extended, after the abrupt *Anschluss* of 1938, also to Austria.[5] Austria warrants mention as a distinct part of this appalling period of German history, not only because it produced some resistance to the command performance of German culture, but also because it provided especially strong support to the anti-Semitic and *völkisch* agenda of Nazi literary politics. The fate of theater also deserves separate mention because it became, under a host of competing authorities sustaining continuities with the 1920s, a significant catalyst in the campaign to promote classical literature and *völkisch* aesthetics.[6]

This essay focuses on the particularities of National Socialist literature, caught between representing an extension of German national culture on the one side, and a specific emanation of what was considered a National Socialist revolution on the other. I subscribe to the thesis that the success and failure of Nazi literature should not only be seen as a matter of creating a new canon of *völkisch* writing, but also as the result of an enormous effort to shape a particular form of reception, a Nazi reading experience strongly directed toward the communal and collective. At the same time, I will try to refrain from mirroring the intentions of Nazi literary politics, there being no need to prove here that the immense bureaucratic apparatus of control was as successful as Goebbels and Rosenberg pretended it to be. One of the best ways to contradict these assumptions is to shed light on the real market of books that Germans read in those years by using recent statistics on bestsellers (those books that reached printings of and above 300,000 copies) in Nazi Germany.

Promoting the Writer as *Dichter*

One aspect of Nazi literary politics cannot be disputed: the attention devoted to the individual writer, usually a male author whose portrait, with raised chin and determined look, serves both as his identifier and as a generic representation of the German *Dichter*. The promotion of the personal as representative of larger phenomena simultaneously enhances and diminishes the public significance of the individual writer in a development that can be traced back to earlier decades, when authors learned to make their self-perception as writers part of their aesthetic message. In novels, stories, poems, and plays, they were in constant negotiation with the public perception of writing and reading.[7]

There were many ways of projecting the writer's stature together with the work. Even if writers turned against politics, their *oeuvre* assumed a place in the political landscape.

Such projections had gained momentum in Expressionism when young authors like Johannes R. Becher, Ernst Toller, Georg Kaiser, Hanns Johst, Reinhard Johannes Sorge, and Walter Hasenclever trumpeted the overcoming of the chaotic present by the power of *Geist* and enthusiasm, and also proclaimed themselves the leaders of the new community, even if it was merely a reading or viewing community. In the words of Franz Blei in 1918: "While formerly there was a work and no visible person, today there is a person in the spotlight and, instead of a work, books that at best represent sketches, drafts, attempts."[8] Projections of this kind gave the literary life of the Weimar Republic its personal and often polemical flavor. They became especially poignant in the Depression years around 1930, when authors felt an overwhelming desire to politicize or depoliticize their work, trying to carve out a niche for their survival in an increasingly volatile literary market. While dozens of theaters were closing, publishing houses went bankrupt or severely reduced their output, fewer and fewer readers could afford books, and more and greater political demands pressed writers to take sides. Thus, authors felt the need to couch their literary works as projections of themselves as stoics, or party fighters, or nostalgics, or war veterans, or journalists, or therapists, or, the highest claim, *Dichter.*

There has been little analysis of this transformation of the author into a determining part of the literary message, yet its poignancy can be traced deep into the vicissitudes of exile, where the self-styled figure of the fighter against Hitler became the sustenance of literary survival. One might think of Thomas Mann, who had once styled himself as the leading conservative with the pretense of being apolitical during World War I. The same Thomas Mann changed his convictions in the Weimar Republic and became a democrat, endorsing the Social Democrats in the 1930 elections. After his emigration to the United States in 1938, he became a much-admired—and hated—king of the German exiles, holding the attention of a surprisingly large audience in this country as the representative of the "other" Germany. He appeared as the quintessential anti-Hitler, whom Roosevelt had invited to the White House, and who tried to explain the nasty German soul, both in a speech at the Library of Congress in 1945 and in his novel *Doctor Faustus.* Or one might think of Ernst Toller, who as a Jewish German in World War I had sacrificed much to embrace the Fatherland and who became the quintessential émigré fighter, a warm and passionate representative of the "other" Germany. Toller, in vivid contrast to Thomas Mann, lived and symbolized a German *Dichter* when he took his life in a New York hotel in 1939.

Shifting back to the writers in Nazi Germany, one cannot overlook other projections of the fighter—the cliché-ridden type of a militant youth inspired by *völkisch* idealism—as drawn by writers of the so-called "Junge Mannschaft" (young crew), such as Gerhard Schumann or Heinrich Anacker, who produced lyric proclamations of Germany's greatness mixed with adoration of the Führer. By contrast, there were also many writers who projected the aura of the prestige-conscious *Dichter,* a venerated figure among the German educated classes and a figure of exalted calling beyond the trivialities of politics and markets. An author like Hans Carossa, who was not a Nazi but was co-opted by Goebbels and made president of the Europäische Dichtervereinigung (European Writers' Association), might not have felt like a collaborator. But he was one, and after 1945 he showed a complete lack of remorse about the role he had played for the benefit of the system.

In other words, one should not forget that even if creative trajectories were strongly affected by the political upheavals and economic depression of the 1930s and the vicissitudes of a vast cultural bureaucracy, writers had some say over their literary work. As they conceived their plays, novels, and essays in full awareness of their standing within the public realm, their responsibilities reached far beyond the traditional observance of the market.

Why Literature?

Any attempt to situate literature among the arts in Nazi Germany will have to come to terms with two aspects—one surprising, and the other expected. The surprising aspect is that the regime undertook wide-ranging efforts to promote literature; the expected is that Hitler, in contrast to his attention to architecture and art, did not express particular interest in the contribution that literature could make to his vision of the new Reich. Concerning the promotional efforts, which cannot easily be separated from the controlling apparatus, one might be tempted to defer any broader recognition to the fact that the Nazis gave widest exposure to the book burnings a few months after they came to power. Did the book burning in May 1933 not demonstrate utter disregard for books? Do the statistics not speak a clear language? From a production high of 24,865 titles published in Germany in 1927, the curve dropped to 18,289 in 1933, to 15,585 in 1939, and to a mere 7,271 in 1944, an obvious decline in book production. The manipulation of book publication included the suppression of thousands of titles that could and should have expressed the spirit of social, political, and intellectual exploration.

And yet, the Nazi leadership embarked on a far-reaching campaign to promote reading, organizing annual "Wochen des Buches" (Book Weeks), financing comprehensive building programs for libraries, establishing an array of book prizes, and imploring the public to embrace the book as part of *völkisch* culture. Was this all determined by Goebbels's manipulation of propaganda? To pose the question more directly: what place was literature able to occupy, given that state and party agencies—especially Goebbels's Ministry for Public Enlightenment and Propaganda—found press, radio, and film more conducive as tools for the transmission of cultural policies? Why the enormous efforts to promote not only a particular brand of literature, but also the reading of books among all segments of the population, when Goebbels could be sure to reach and to shape mass opinion more directly through the use of modern technologies of communication?

A first answer obviously will have to focus less on the issue of manipulation of opinion than on the symbolic agenda of national renewal that referred to World War I and the efforts to define the national purpose with regard to German culture. That some of the most vicious attacks against representatives of the Weimar Republic were directed against writers and artists illuminates the importance of culture in the symbolic program of the nationalist and *völkisch* right. Taking as a case in point the burning of the books in university towns on 10 May 1933, one detects among the *völkisch* students an obsession with writers and books as political symbols—an obsession whose intensity also reflects an uncanny recognition of these symbols' power and is heightened by the labeling of these actions as spontaneous outbursts. In other words, while the social misery of the Depression had fueled social revolutionary rhetoric on the socialist left, university students expressed their revolutionary fervor by advocating a return to true German culture, to the right books and writers—who, however, remained unspecified. Not surprisingly, Goebbels, in his address at the book burning in Berlin, mentioned no specific authors or titles.[9] He took aim at "Jewish intellectualism" as subversive of the German *Geist* by expounding the blessings and duties of the Nazi movement, and by using the sinister symbolism of the event to consolidate the claim that the National Socialist revolution created a new community of the educated and the *Volk*, thereby renewing German culture from the bottom up.

Nazi leaders saw the action of student organizations as a kind of intellectual pogrom that they could use as a symbolic death warrant against the Weimar Republic. The Republic had allowed Jews, communists, and intellectuals to taint German culture. Renewal would mean a new devotion to literature defined as high art (*Dichtung*), which, as in the case of music, provided dignity and seriousness, helping the Nazis to gain acceptance among the educated classes. A crucial move, long hoped for by Germanists in the universities and conservative literary critics, was the redefinition of *Literatur* as *Dichtung*, which in the classical German tradition had become a term that accorded the depth of great poetry to any literary creation and commanded respect and veneration on the part of the audience. For literature in general, the bureaucratic term *Schrifttum* was reserved. Because the concept *Dichtung* had lost much of its cachet in the post–Expressionist period of the 1920s, its restitution as a central element of Nazi cultural politics[10] was a shrewd operation, one that helped denounce the anti-Nazi writings of emigrants as mere "literature," that is, the shallow, political, market-driven production of the Weimar Republic.

With the agenda to cherish and stimulate *Dichtung* as the core of the literary endeavor, Nazi functionaries claimed to be returning to literature the legitimacy it had lost in the Weimar era. Goebbels, more sophisticated and modern-minded as a propagandist than his rival Alfred Rosenberg, agreed with Rosenberg about the strategy of making veneration of *Dichter* and *Dichtung* mandatory for education and cultural practices. Officially abolishing critical reviews of art and literature was as much part of this strategy as the promotion of a particular kind of "*völkisch*" reading, in which readers experience themselves as part of a larger reading racial community (*die lesende Volksgemeinschaft*)." A short quotation from the 1942 *Bestimmungen über Erziehung und Unterricht in der Hauptschule* (Regulations on Education and Instruction in the Schools) illustrates the pretense of submitting to the powers of *Dichtung*: "Since the request has to be made that reading of the valuable German literature become again a love affair [*eine Herzensangelegenheit*] of the young, its attractiveness must not be spoiled by one-sided instructions. Literature itself should speak to the student, to his will-power and to his heart, and should expose him to moral decisions. In order to avoid the damaging plucking to pieces of a given piece of writing [*Zerpflücken und Zerreden*], one should refrain from an overly-long treatment of a whole text."[11]

Little needs to be said about the reverse of such *Dichtung* worship: the exclusion of a public sphere in which literature functions to instigate critical discourse about life and society. *Dichtung*, presented and consumed this way, creates an individual cocoon or a sense of community, but no public sphere. No wonder, then, that the regime made special efforts to subjugate theater as completely as possible under this doctrine. Ranking high in popularity, the broad network of German state, regional, and municipal theaters served as a gigantic generator of *Dichtung*-worship, fully endowed with famous or less famous priests who conjured the classical scenarios of Schiller, Kleist, Shakespeare, Goethe, Grabbe, Hebbel and others as encounters with greatness, fate, and a reverberating moral purpose.

Promoting *Dichtung* about and for the *Volk*

Elevating literature as *Dichtung* to a position that even conservative writers had not been able to maintain on their own, the Nazis were strongly invested in the symbolic agenda of culture and art. Yet this came at a price: although they had been brutally successful in persecuting the critical literature of their adversaries and settling upon a retrograde aesthetic (shortly after Goebbels came to power his flirtation with some Expressionist artists ended abruptly), the chances of engaging in a full-fledged effort to promote a genuine *völkisch* or National Socialist literature were less than optimal. The Nazis had not only stripped Germany of its best talents in the literary genre; they also had to negotiate between the claim of renewing the whole German culture from the bottom up and the promotion of a particular National Socialist culture.

In the regime's first years, many efforts and thousands of pages were devoted to connecting the two goals with the help of the concept of *Volk*, which, for lack of a precise definition, was marked as the crucial experience of being and feeling German.[12] Hitler's extensive use of the term in the realm of art was based on Wagner's writings, pointing to the need that the artist identify with the *Volk*, yet Hitler carried the definition clearly beyond Wagner's notion of *Volk* as a cultural community when he insisted on defining it as a racial community.[13]

No term was more indispensable to Nazi cultural politics than that of *Volk*. It provided the glue for that vague, unifying, and race-based projection of belonging. Yet, upon closer look, it also exposed a dual perspective on society: on the one hand it accommodated all classes and temperaments inside and outside of national borders, and was applied as a label of inclusion; on the other, based on exclusion, it signaled agency of an authentic and especially active segment of the population. As the function of National Socialist literature was delineated as providing the experience of *Volk* and *Volkstum*, the interpretations necessarily varied according to inclusive or exclusive definitions, that is, according to conservative visions of tradition, family, and community, or according to youthful self-empowerment and militancy.

The groupings of Nazi writers that we encounter in literary histories since the 1930s reflect these positions. They are defined by the thinking in occupations and skills that dominated the understanding of *Volk* in its everyday existence, with a strong bent toward the farmer, the worker, and the craftsman, and a certain disdain for the city-dwelling burgher whose working profile is lost in the bureaucracies of anonymous offices. Reinventing the concept of *Dichter* was popular because it played to the idea that the *völkisch* writer had a particular understanding of everyday existence in town and village, reflecting the attention to work and detail that guaranteed survival in a tough world.

This reenergizing of the writing profession through a new interest in nature and the simple life was a general phenomenon in the 1930s (one might think of Hemingway's fascination with the simplicity of country life in Spain during the Civil War) and has often been discussed, but rarely as a background to the wave of peasant novels and regional literature that swept Germany and Austria during and after the economic crisis of the Depression. In fact, little has been done to decipher this orientation toward customs and traditions (*Bräuche und Sitten*) and its hidden agenda of sociological exploration of what today is called "everyday life" or "folk culture." This orientation corresponded to an emerging branch of historiography that departed from historians' traditional aversion to the sociology of everyday life. As the historian Jürgen Kocka noted in a description of this kind of historiography, which scholars like Werner Conze developed in their approach to social history after 1945, *Volksgeschichte* was carried by a sense of sociological discovery, even if its ideology was retrograde and often racist. It received a particularly poignant formulation by Austrian scholars like Otto Brunner, who pursued a definition of *Volk* that was centered in the agrarian milieu, the "rural population" as the "humus soil of national folk culture" (*Volkstum*), thus giving postmonarchy rural Austria a strong standing in the German *Volkwerdung* (becoming a people).[14] In the 1930s and 1940s, Austrian writers indeed numbered among the most celebrated *Heimat- und Bauerndichter* (regional and peasant writers), for example, Karl Heinrich Waggerl, Gertrud Fussenegger, Friedrich Schreyvogl, Josef Friedrich Perkonig, and Bruno Brehm.[15]

Jean Améry, a Viennese writer who survived the Holocaust and stands above any association with *völkisch* literature, has given vivid testimony to the significance of this engagement with pre- or anti-industrial writings in the 1930s. He made a case for the model of most of the peasant novels, Knut Hamsun's *Growth of the Soil* (1917), which became a huge bestseller in Germany under the title *Segen der Erde* and was copied by Waggerl in his bestselling novel *Brot* (1930).[16] Featuring Hermann Stehr (*Der Heiligenhof*) and Ernst Wiechert (*Das einfache Leben*) as representative of the *Heimatroman* (regional novel) that he read with much dedication in his younger years, Améry argued that these and other, usually more Nazi-oriented chroniclers of village and farm life attained their prominence mainly through their therapeutic approach to this world. Authors like Friedrich Griese, Josepha Berens-Totenohl, or Richard Billinger left no doubt that industrialization destroyed traditional attitudes and values. Under the impact of the inflation of the 1920s and the economic crisis in the early 1930s, the view of the individual in his or her trials and tribulations within a palpable community responded to the anxieties of the disenchanted middle classes and corresponded to the therapeutic use of the concept of *Volksgemeinschaft* (people's community) that the Nazis usurped from the Social Democrats who, after World War I, had tried unsuccessfully to link it to the new democracy.

The practice of contrasting the literature of "blood-and-soil" (*Blut und Boden*, abbreviated *Blubo*) with the literature of "asphalt" (big-city literature) had been part of the conservative campaign against the progressive literature of the Weimar Republic. After 1933, its formulas became a crucial element in the *völkisch* and anti-Semitic rhetoric that increasingly dominated the discourse in newspapers, schools, and cultural institutions. Aside from invoking the image of Jewish *Zersetzung* (subversion) of German values and excluding "intellectualism," it projected the contrast between two modes of time usage: the redeeming experience of an eternal recurrence of time in rural nature juxtaposed against the big-city hassles that epitomize the senseless acceleration of time. The peasant novel was an especially appropriate vehicle for those interested in arresting time and projecting eternity as a valid experience. It gave credence to the Nazi manipulation of the sense of history (*Geschichtlichkeit*) as a way of claiming historical exceptionalism for the German *Volk*. Friedrich Griese, whose novels *Der ewige Acker* and *Das letzte Gesicht* were celebrated and widely read as exemplars of "blood-and-soil" literature, ties everything to the structure of the eternal recurrence of the seasons, of growth and decay, of life and death.[17]

In view of the tendency to eliminate the sense of historical conditioning toward that of eternal fate in individual and collective experiences, it is almost impossible to separate what was called historical literature from peasant or *Heimat* literature. Erwin Guido Kolbenheyer, the most celebrated author of historical novels and plays (*Paracelsus-Trilogy, Das gottgelobte Herz, Gregor und Heinrich*), was interested in placing events in his own biological-philosophical construct of history, which was not conditioned by the usual strictures of historiography.

The wave of biographical works, arguably the dominant literary genre in Europe from the 1920s to the 1940s, had its center in the ever-changing ways of presenting the individual in his or her *innere Erlebniswirklichkeit* (the internalization of experience), as Fritz Reck-Malleczewen called it in his biography of Charlotte Corday.[18] Karl Korn, later a prominent cultural critic with the *Frankfurter Allgemeine,* elucidated this literary device by pointing out that the reading masses wanted a truth that was refined from the mere facts by the illumination of the inner motives of the person, the unique individual experience.[19] As is shown by the fate of Reck-Malleczewen, who died as a conservative resistance fighter in Dachau shortly before the end of World War II, it is virtually impossible to distinguish non-Nazi from Nazi writers on the basis of writing style or even plots and themes. Ernst Wiechert, author of the exemplary peasant novel *Das einfache Leben*, is another case in point. Without changing his literary taste for the simple rural life, he learned to find fault with frivolous use of it on the part of the Nazis and denounced this publicly, though in poetic language. Goebbels interned him for several weeks in Buchenwald. Together with similarly conservative writers like Werner Bergengruen and Reinhold Schneider, Wiechert became a representative of what was called "inner emigration," not only to contrast it with the exile from Germany that many writers chose, but also in reference to the retreat into an inner realm of resistance.

Nazi Literature or National Culture?

Literary histories always point to a core group of writers that represented German literature in the Third Reich: Hans Friedrich Blunck, Hanns Johst, Friedrich Griese, Werner Beumelburg, Hans Carossa, Erwin Guido Kolbenheyer, Agnes Miegel, Hans Grimm, Wilhelm Schäfer, and a few others. Their prominent status clearly resulted from the brutal ousting of famous Weimar writers like Heinrich and Thomas Mann, Alfred Döblin, and Franz Werfel from the Prussian Academy of the Arts.[20] Blunck became the first president of the Reich Chamber of Literature in 1933. He had traced in his trilogy *Die Urvätersaga* of 1926–1928 the mythological origins of Nordic men with ostentatious symbolism and presented, in *Werdendes Volk* (1934), his version of the emergence of the German *Volk* through the lives of legendary heroes of North German history. In 1935 he was replaced by the more fanatical Hanns Johst, whose career as an effective playwright of historical plays, including the successful *Thomas Paine* (1927), came to a zenith with *Schlageter*, a dramatic hymn to a Nazi martyr that premiered in the presence of Hitler and the Nazi elite in 1933. As in the cases of Blunck and Johst, other writers, such as Wilhelm Schäfer, Agnes Miegel, Rudolf Binding, and Hans Grimm, became representatives of Nazi literature on the basis of their previous work, usually novels or plays with which they had attained standing as conservative or *völkisch* authors.

Grimm, for instance, in the novel *Volk ohne Raum* (1926) about the life journey of a young German to South Africa and back, had coined a term that the Nazis used to justify their expansion to the East.

While this hollow pantheon was built on borrowed prestige, another group of writers came to prominence through their successful projection of youthfulness. In poems, songs, and plays, these young authors provided textual glue for the performative arrangements by which Nazi organizations mobilized the masses. By concentrating on songs and dramatic scenes, they continued the practice of party songs and theatrics that had been used in the often violent confrontations of political movements before 1933. In some cases, the Nazis had stolen the communists' melodies and attached *völkisch* texts to them.[21] Most prominent was the group of writers known as the Junge Mannschaft, which included Heinrich Anacker, Baldur von Schirach (later Gauleiter of Vienna and leader of the Hitler Youth), Hans Baumann, Gerhard Schumann, and Herybert Menzel. Aiming to mobilize readers and performers in a collective celebration of the national revolution, they eschewed the private voice of poetry in favor of creating a communal identity. They conjured a mixture of aggressiveness and self-sacrifice that foreshadowed the increasing orientation toward war. In the first years of World War II this kind of rhetorical voluntarism served as a widely used propaganda tool.

The poems of these authors came closest to what was considered National Socialist literature, as did the politicized morality plays, the so-called *Thingspiele*, of which Eberhard Wolfgang Moeller's *Das Frankenburger Würfelspiel* and Richard Euringer's *Deutsche Passion* were recognized as the best examples. The *Thingspiel*, pretending to renew a Germanic tradition of communal performance, strove for "a drama that intensifies historical events to create a mythical, universal, unambiguous reality beyond reality."[22] With its masses of performers, choral elements, pantomime, dance, and music, it easily lent itself to the most outspoken claims for a cultic form of art, as Reich Theater Critic Rainer Schlösser put it in a programmatic speech in 1935.[23] Efforts to elevate the *Thingspiel* to a cultic representation of National Socialism brought the discussion about the function of National Socialist literature to a head. It laid bare the dichotomy between service to the nation as a whole and to National Socialism as a specific movement. Yet even more important, it made a decision inevitable as to whether National Socialism should be ritualized and celebrated, indeed performed, in a cultic form.

When *Thingspiele* were banned in 1937, most initiatives toward creating a peculiar National Socialist art had run their course. Hitler used the Parteitag Grossdeutschland (Party Congress of Greater Germany) of 1938—the congress after Austria's annexation—to oppose the cultic agenda in the realm of arts and culture. "First of all," he asserted, "National Socialism in its organization is a *Volksbewegung* [people's movement], but under no circumstances a *Kultbewegung* [cult movement]."[24] Hitler attacked every form of mysticism as a distraction from the racial program. He pointed to architecture, music, sculpture, and painting as representative expressions that spoke to the whole of the nation, and added theater, but also made clear, in his speech at the *Kulturtagung* (Conference on Culture) of the party congress, that he was against any cultic substitution for the direct experience of the National Socialist community in rallies and mass assemblies. Indeed, the propaganda apparatus that closely monitored the visual and textual appearance of the new state as a guardian of German culture made such substitution superfluous. Cultic celebrations would have lessened Hitler's direct grip on the imagination and devotion of the Germans.

Hitler mentioned poets or *Dichter* only fleetingly as guarantors of the use of clear language. The potential of *Dichtung* to crystallize the dynamics of National Socialism, as it had been envisaged in the early years of the regime, obviously no longer ranked high. No great literary works emerged to which Hitler could have pointed. At this time, and even more so during the war, with its priority of mobilizing the whole nation for battle, the definition of *Dichtung* as anchor of German culture reverted to the agenda that had dominated the mobilization of *Kultur* in World War I. What the tradition-bound bourgeoisie had maintained during the 1920s and 1930s—the reading of *Dichtung* as an identity-producing, emotional and, to some extent, social guidance—surfaced again as the fallback position or, more to the point, as the default leisure activity as official propaganda expanded and consumer goods disappeared. This kind of literature, even in the works of its most celebrated representatives Goethe, Schiller, Hölderlin, and Kleist, was rarely able to render what Hitler demanded from art: grandeur and timelessness. It was more therapeutic than a call to arms, more a celebration of the depth of *Volk* and communal feeling than an awe-inspiring presentation of space and greatness. This function fell to architecture and Wagner's music.

Ways and Limits of Promoting Nazi Literature

The genre of war literature that began to blossom in the late 1920s seemed to crystallize the militant temper of the early years of the Nazi regime, a temper that defined the writings of the Junge Mannschaft. It did not take long, however, to realize that the topic had run its course. Only a few authors like P.C. Ettighoffer, whose war novel *Gespenster am Toten Mann*, already published in 1931, remained a bestseller, were able to hold the attention of the public. To be sure, youthfulness as *Haltung*, as a social and emotional attitude, mostly meant sacrificial heroism and enthusiasm, expansion and military adventure.[25] It was magnified in countless initiatives to promote war literature, such as the works of Ernst Jünger, Werner Beumelburg, Edwin Erich Dwinger, and others.

And yet, the general message of these works was not exactly the youthful enthusiasm that Goebbels's propaganda machine tried to spread. This enthusiasm was massaged with the myth of the battle of Langemarck, according to which hundreds of students had sacrificed their lives while singing the *Deutschlandlied*.[26] But the invocation of such patriotic sacrifice was overshadowed by the gray and gruesome routines to which the survivors of World War I gave somber testimony. The descriptions of trench warfare did not exactly instill the steely romanticism (*stählerne Romantik*) that Goebbels had postulated in 1933 for the new National Socialist art and literature, but rather documented the loss of youthfulness in the battles of Verdun, the Somme, and Ypres. In a study of the preferred reading materials of soldiers in the winter of 1941–42, Goebbels's own ministry observed that soldiers ranked highest light entertainment, such as detective novels, romances, or adventure stories, but showed no interest in works of a political nature or in war literature.[27]

Combining the promotion of militant youthfulness with the bestowal of prestige on the new pantheon of German *Dichter*, the cultural bureaucracy relied to a considerable extent on the work of right-wing *Germanisten*, or included them in the new promotional machine. While literary scholars like Josef Nadler, Franz Koch, and Heinz Kindermann collaborated within the universities, Hellmut Langenbucher monitored belletristic literature as the first and increasingly prominent head of the central readers' department in Alfred Rosenberg's Amt Schrifttumspflege (Office for the Cultivation of Literature).[28] The thinking in leadership and hierarchies that penetrated everything in Nazi Germany easily outflanked considerations of aesthetic innovation and achievement. Typical strategies of simulating movement in the literary realm, or at the literary "front," as it was later called, consisted of awarding high-sounding prizes to established writers, assembling numerous *Dichter* on the pages of mass brochures, and organizing literary gatherings in Weimar in order to provide the population with faces—mostly of men, but also of some motherly women. Usually, they were presented as successors to Goethe, Schiller, or Eichendorff. This strategy culminated in yearly *Weimarer Dichtertreffen* (Weimar writers' meetings), which Goebbels instituted in 1938 as instruments for integrating important writers into his propaganda machine; in return they received increased recognition as the embodiment of German culture. In this way, Goebbels secured the collaboration of the conservative writer Hans Carossa, who in 1941 became the president of the Europäische Dichtervereinigung (European Writers' Association), which was supposed to unite German and foreign writers. Apart from sitting together in Weimar, these authors did not find they had much in common while the war was raging. And yet, Goebbels found foreign writers who complied with his strategy of prestige-peddling, most conspicuously Knut Hamsun, who received his highest recognition in Germany and continuously invested and scattered his worldwide prestige as an advocate for Nazi Germany.

In their prestige and youthfulness, the writers' perceived image represented an indispensable part of their work. Images of the youthful writer, as well as of the Goethe-successor, inserted themselves into the reading. Given the enormous promotion of *völkisch* and conservative literature, reading this literature could indeed be experienced as an activity in consonance with a larger community. Hans Frank, a Nazi legal expert and Governor General in German-occupied Poland, summarized the efforts to create a distinct National Socialist form of literary reception: "As beneficial as public help [in enhancing the book] is, the decisive step can only be made by the individual who takes the book home, experiences it and makes its experience available to those with whom it has, in some ways, a communal bond; and by trying to make sure that word does not remain word, but again finds the path where all important books come from: to an exemplary, deeply rooted, *volkhaft* life."[29] Reading was not to remain a solitary activity, but rather to become the basis for a collective experience of a *lesende Volksgemeinschaft* (reading racial community). Youth organizations and, of course, the Hitler Youth were the preferred targets of this policy. Caring for books in school and youth camps became part of everyday duties. "Reading" was often a euphemism for listening to and practicing speech-making for the purposes of political indoctrination.

In the second, war-oriented phase of the Third Reich, this promotion of reading had much less of an impact. The Nazis, although concentrating more on the reception than the production of *völkisch* literature, did not find a way to transform reading from an uncontrollable private act to a social or collective affair. They constantly warned against "reading rage" (*Lesewut*) as an antisocial activity. It is my thesis (although I cannot expand on it here beyond fleeting remarks) that a successful approach to the literature of the "inner emigration" has to start with an analysis of reading, reading behavior, and the strategies used by literary opponents to direct readers into a different kind of reception. Inner emigrants like Ernst Wiechert, Werner Bergengruen, or Reinhold Schneider were indeed interested in guiding the readers to a different *Haltung* toward their books and stories. While deeply entangled in the thematic and emotional ambiguities of the 1930s and 1940s, they rarely produced new plots, stories, or aesthetic innovations. What they intended and were often able to do, however, was to activate readers to read the works for double meaning and critical associations. As Ernst Jünger remarked, censorship hightens literary sensitivity. Jünger's novel *Auf den Marmorklippen* of 1939 is the most frequently quoted example of this kind of double meaning. It presents a parable of Hitler's ascent and violent rule, but can also be understood as a parable of other dictatorial regimes, such as that of the communists in the Soviet Union.

Inner emigrants used a variety of strategies to subvert the official pressure on reading as a communal activity, hence the isolating nature of much of their writing. When criticizing them as individualists in a self-styled cocoon, one should not forget the threats to which they responded. They were often under considerable danger of persecution. Theirs was a threatening reality not only full of political fervor, but also marked by an onslaught on the reader's independence and integrity.

Subverting or at least diverting the pressures to comply with the official reading agenda took many forms, of course. The most important, which occurred without much fanfare, was the everyday decision not to read *völkisch* literature. Goebbels was aware that the mood of the German public, as in the realm of film, favored entertainment, often called *gute Unterhaltung*. While the consumption of other goods shrank every year after 1939, the consumption of books could play a compensating role in the Nazi economy only if this *gute Unterhaltung* were allowed on the market.

It is hardly a coincidence that an article about the question "Was wird gelesen?"(What is being read?), with a list of current bestsellers, appeared in Goebbels's flagship weekly *Das Reich* in 1940.[30] Based on polls taken in three Berlin bookstores and one lending library (*Leihbücherei*), it focused on an urban readership. The guiding question was whether the war-related increase of interest in books diminished the quality of reading material. The answer was no. The store "Das gute Buch," geared toward the middle and upper middle classes, remained popular. None of the Nazi writers mentioned above had authored the listed top books. Who were the writers? They were international bestselling authors from the United States, Hungary, Italy, Switzerland and Norway, among them Margaret Mitchell with *Vom Winde verweht*, Erskine Caldwell with *Einst wird kommen der Tag*, Zsolt Harsanyi with *Ungarische Rhapsodie* and *Mit den Augen einer Frau*, Alba Céspedes with *Das andere Ufer*, Daniele Varè with *Laughing Diplomat*, John Knittel with *Via Mala*, and Olav Gulvaag with *Es begann in einer Mittsommernacht*. They were also national bestselling authors, among them Kurt Kluge with *Der Herr Kortüm*, William von Simpson with his family novels about East Prussia, *Die Barrings* and *Der Enkel*, Ernst Moritz Mungenast with *Der Zauberer Muzot*, and Ina Seidel with *Lennacker* and others. Like others, Karl Aloys Schenzinger, with the top bestsellers *Anilin* and *Metall*, pursued a national, at times nationalist, agenda, but he had become famous as the quintessential *Tatsachenautor* (or *Wissenschaftsautor*), the nonfiction writer of the day whose books were still on the bestseller lists after 1945. Kuni Tremel-Eggert, in her bestselling novel *Barb: Der Roman einer deutschen Frau*, had achieved great renown with her story of a woman whom the Nazis understood as exemplary. But only four titles from the poll of Berlin bookstores resonated clearly with the politics of the day: books by Goebbels (*Kampf um Berlin*); Reichspressechef (Reich Press Chief) Otto Dietrich (*Auf den Strassen des Sieges*); Erich Gritzbach with a book on Göring; and the autobiographical war novel by the famous submarine commander Günter Prien (*Mein Weg nach Scapa Flow*).

Christian Bock, the author of this article on readership, did not claim to deliver a scholarly survey. Yet, his evidence of considerable overlap between the titles in the stores and even those most in demand at a lending library makes him a serious source of information about reading habits under Hitler and Goebbels. His results have been fully confirmed by a recent survey of the bestselling novels on the German market between 1933 and 1945. On a retrospective bestseller list of

Nazi Germany (with bestseller understood as fiction or nonfiction books printed in at least 300,000 copies or more) the group of Mitchell, Caldwell, Gulbranssen, Seidel, and Simpson is well represented. The leader is Schenzinger with almost a million copies of *Anilin*, followed by Tremel-Eggert with *Barb: Der Roman einer deutschen Frau* and the humorous, nonpolitical novel by Ehm Welk, *Die Heiden von Kummerow*, which remained a bestseller in East Germany after the war. The top-selling novels of the humorist Heinrich Spoerl, *Die Feuerzangenbowle*, *Der Gasmann*, *Wenn wir alle Engel wären*, and *Der Maulkorb*, were easily made into movies, but posed some challenges for censors; they also remained popular after World War II.

Tobias Schneider, the author of the study "Bestseller im Dritten Reich," summarizes his findings about the forty bestselling titles by dividing them into two large groups. Citing ten genuinely National Socialist novels and thirty nonpolitical novels, he clearly documents the much smaller percentage of Nazi titles (one quarter).[31] He stresses that mere publication numbers in Nazi Germany do not allow conclusions concerning books' actual popularity, since National Socialist literature was heavily promoted by propaganda organizations, most visibly in the case of the books by Tremel-Eggert and Hans Zöberlein. Calling them "artificial bestsellers," he traces a boom in this literature in the early years of the regime (1933–1935), then stagnation, and then, after an initial boom in the early war years, a clear decline. Earlier studies had pointed to the enormous popularity in the 1930s and 1940s of *Wissenschaftsromane*, the nonfiction books that were later called *Sachbücher*.[32] Under the auspices of the regime's Four-Year Plan, which was to prepare Germany for war, the topics of technology, innovations, and science were promoted. Hans Dominik, Germany's most successful author of science fiction, was able to expand his broad readership from before 1933, especially among the younger generation.[33] He also remained successful after 1945.

In view of the small number of genuine Nazi novels among the bestsellers, Schneider concludes: "The average reader in the Third Reich preferred to read not Nazi novels but science-based, humorous, and foreign novels."[34] This corresponds to the parameters of film production, in which Goebbels's goal to keep Germans well entertained so that they would fulfill their duties in the service of the state reigned supreme. After thirty years of research that was heavily tilted toward reconstructing the censorship and control apparatus of Nazi-era literature, such an assessment helps set the record straight on the production, promotion, and reading of literature. It does not contradict the existing scholarship, but invites us to rethink the cultural traditions, market forces, and mere everyday behavior that shape literary practices in a dictatorship. For example, there are still no broader studies on the ways in which literature, in all its genres between high and popular, fit into the regime's view of German society as a consuming society. Literature, theater, arts, and culture had a particular role to play when consumer goods became scarce. Were they seen merely as compensation for the lack of these goods? A Nazi ideologist like Alfred Rosenberg certainly did not want to have to address questions like this.

A Look beyond 1933–1945

This brings me to a concluding point that I think should also be explored with fewer inhibitions. It puts the overbearing apparatus of bureaucratic registration, sponsorship and control in a somewhat different light. If one considers this apparatus, particularly its core institution of Goebbels's Ministry for Public Enlightenment and Propaganda and the Reich Chamber of Culture, in light of the scarcity of public support structures in the Weimar Republic, one can only express astonishment at the importance that the Nazi state attributed to this realm. That the various institutions between Joseph Goebbels, Alfred Rosenberg, Philip Bouhler (chief of the party's Censorship Committee for the Protection of National Socialist Literature, and of the Study Group for German History Books and Educational Material), and other highly placed ideologues often worked at cross purposes, creating interspaces and niches in which dissidents gained a voice, confirms the significance of *Kultur* as a barometer of the success of the Nazi revolution. While Walter Benjamin's notion of the aesthetization of politics was complemented by that of the politicization of aesthetics, the astonishing embrace of high culture under this regime generates questions concerning its long-term impact on the conceptual and practical standing of arts and culture in Germany and Austria. What does this period mean for the transformations of aesthetic production and reception with regard to a mass audience that uses a restricted market but cannot generate capital for more long-term sponsorship of the arts?

Public initiatives to organize writers, artists, and film and theater people in response to the devastating economic depression of the 1930s were not restricted to Germany. They occurred in several countries, including the United States, although in different forms. Scrutiny of this context should help differentiate the specifics of Nazi censorship and suppression, just as it should offer a broader understanding of the social and intellectual forces that accompanied the catastrophic crisis and breakdown of the liberal system around 1930. Such a perspective delineates different versions of empowering state authority, conservative values, and collective rescue fantasies, and also different versions of withdrawal into cocoons of privacy, melancholy, and existentialism. Obviously, the liberal, market-driven cultural life of the 1920s was transformed. At the core of this transformation lies the organizational institutionalization of several cultural spheres. This did not happen in Nazi Germany alone, but in Germany it was linked to censorship and a heinous anti-Semitic agenda.

In his impressive study *Art, Ideology, and Economics in Nazi Germany*, Alan Steinweis has documented the transformation process in which professional organizations seeking relief from the ruinous consequences of the market forces played into the hands of the new rulers, in essence asking that the government raise the incomes of "cultural producers." Enter Goebbels, with his "improvised but purposeful" agenda, as Steinweis calls it, of assembling artists, musicians, writers, and theater and film people in a unified organization, promising to enhance their status and living standards without seriously affecting their artistic autonomy. In this way, the Reichskulturkammer initially appeared beneficial. Yet, expulsion from the Reichskulturkammer meant loss of livelihood. The professional and social misery that the work of this seemingly beneficial institution brought upon Jews cannot be overlooked.

The state-sponsored structuring of cultural, educational, and recreational activities, which prior to 1933 had been pursued to a considerable extent under the tutelage of social democratic or middle-class organizations, encompassed theatrical and musical performances as well as the production of books and the building of libraries. The centralization of this effort under the Nazi regime had its own modernizing effects, since Germany's culture and education had long been a regional affair. Volker Dahm has argued that the regional outlook and organization of culture remained extremely strong, presenting clear limits to centralization under the Nazis.[35]

There can be little doubt, however, that the dynamics of institutionalization that had led to terrible abuse under the racist laws of the Nazi state also remained a dominant force in the sponsorship of arts and culture in the two German states in the second half of the twentieth century. In this respect, East Germany followed closely in the totalitarian footsteps of the Third Reich. A history of cultural politics and arts sponsorship in these societies as well as in Austria would be incomplete without a chapter on the Nazi conversion of culture into an element of the welfare state. To give an example, one cannot write about the project for old-age pensions for writers, which grew out of the social reforms of the Brandt government in the early 1970s, without mentioning the principled efforts toward such pensions in the late 1930s. They had been a pet project of Joseph Goebbels, but had to be abandoned due to more pressing wartime issues.

An assessment of culture as an element of the welfare state may not be the expected way of concluding an essay about literature under National Socialism. It is, indeed, part of an argument that can be made only after a more extensive study of arts and culture in Germany and Austria between 1933 and 1945, with a view to the fate of culture under Stalinism as well. And yet, although it provides only a glimpse into the creation and use of literature in the mid twentieth century, this view does offer a clue to a more comprehensive understanding of the elevation of arts and culture in the hour of their most appalling submission to political regimes. Obviously, the issue is not only one of National Socialism, but also of communism. A command performance in a dictatorship? Of course. Yet there are many ways of participating in or digressing from that performance. They are no less the result of institutional and economic conditions than of aesthetic and ideological decisions.

Notes

1. Dietrich Strothmann, *Nationalsozialistische Literaturpolitik: Ein Beitrag zur Publizistik im Dritten Reich* (Bonn: Bouvier, 1960); Joseph Wulf, ed., *Literatur und Dichtung im Dritten Reich: Eine Dokumentation* (Gütersloh: Sigbert Mohn, 1963); Ernst Loewy, *Literatur unterm Hakenkreuz: Das Dritte Reich und seine Dichtung. Eine Dokumentation* (Frankfurt am Main: Europäische Verlagsanstalt, 1966); Uwe-Karsten Ketelsen, *Völkisch-nationale und nationalsozialistische Literatur in Deutschland 1890-1945* (Stuttgart: Metzler, 1976), and *Literatur und Drittes Reich* (Schernfeld: SH-Verlag, 1992).

2. Horst Denkler and Karl Prümm, eds., *Die deutsche Literatur im Dritten Reich: Themen—Traditionen—Wirkungen* (Stuttgart: Reclam, 1976).

3. Christiane Caemmerer and Walter Delabar, eds., *Dichtung im Dritten Reich? Zur Literatur in Deutschland 1933-1945* (Opladen: Westdeutscher Verlag, 1996); Günther Rüther, ed., *Literatur in der Diktatur: Schreiben im Nationalsozialismus*

und DDR-Sozialismus (Paderborn: Schöningh, 1997); Heidrun Ehrke-Rotermund and Erwin Rotermund, *Zwischenreiche und Gegenwelten: Texte und Vorstudien zur 'Verdeckten Schreibweise' im "Dritten Reich"* (Munich: Fink, 1999).

4. Jan-Pieter Barbian, *Literaturpolitik im 'Dritten Reich': Institutionen, Kompetenzen, Betätigungsfelder* (Frankfurt am Main: Buchhändler-Vereinigung, 1993).

5. Volker Dahm, *Das jüdische Buch im Dritten Reich* (Munich: Beck, 1993, first published in Frankfurt am Main: Buchhändler-Vereinigung, 1979 and 1981). See also Otto Seifert, "Die Eingliederung Österreichs–das Manöver für die Kulturbarbarei in Europa," in Otto Seifert, *Die große Säuberung des Schrifttums: Der Börsenverein der Deutschen Buchhändler zu Leipzig 1933 bis 1945* (Schkeuditz: GNN, 2000), 159–193.

6. John London, ed., *Theatre under the Nazis* (Manchester and New York: Manchester University Press, 2000). This volume contains the informative chapter by Rebecca Rovit, "Jewish Theatre: Repertory and Censorship in the Jüdischer Kulturbund, Berlin," 187–221. See also Thomas Eicher, et al. eds., *Theater im "Dritten Reich": Theaterpolitik, Spielplanstruktur, NS-Dramatik* (Seelze-Velber: Kallmeyer, 2000).

7. Frank Trommler, "Targeting the Reader, Entering History: A New Epitaph for the Inner Emigration," in *Flight of Fantasy: New Perspectives on Inner Emigration in German Literature, 1933-1945*, ed. Neil H. Donahue and Doris Kirchner (New York: Berghahn, 2003), 125f.

8. Franz Blei, "Fragmente zur Literatur," *Summa* 3 (1918): 134.

9. Goebbels's speech at the burning of "un-German" writings on 10 May 1933, in *Die Bücherverbrennung: Zum 10. Mai 1933*, ed. Gerhard Sauder (Munich and Vienna: Hanser, 1983), 254–257.

10. As an example see Erwin Guido Kolbenheyer, *Wie wurde der deutsche Roman Dichtung?* (Munich: Langen/Müller, 1937).

11. Norbert Hopster and Ulrich Nassen, *Literatur und Erziehung im Nationalsozialismus* (Paderborn: Schöningh, 1983), 45.

12. Wulf Koepke, "Volk und Dichtung," in *Leid der Worte: Panorama des literarischen Nationalsozialismus*, ed. Jörg Thunecke (Bonn: Bouvier, 1987), 153–176.

13. Arne Fryksén, "Hitlers Reden zur Kultur: Kunstpolitische Taktik oder Ideologie?" in *Probleme deutscher Zeitgeschichte*, Lund Studies in International History 2, ed. Göran Rystadt, et al. (Stockholm: Läromedelsförlagen, 1970), 258.

14. Jürgen Kocka, "Ideological Regression and Methodological Innovation: Historiography and the Social Sciences in the 1930s and 1940s," *History and Memory* 2, no. 2 (1990): 130–138.

15. Klaus Amann, "Die Brückenbauer: Zur 'Österreich'-Ideologie der völkisch-nationalen Autoren in den dreißiger Jahren," in *Österreichische Literatur der dreißiger Jahre: Ideologische Verhältnisse, Institutionelle Voraussetzungen, Fallstudien*, ed. Klaus Amann and Albert Berger (Vienna: Böhlau, 1985), 60–78.

16. Jean Améry, *Bücher aus der Jugend unseres Jahrhunderts* (Stuttgart: Klett-Cotta, 1981), 28f. On the peasant novel, see Peter Zimmermann, *Der Bauernroman: Antifeudalismus—Konservatismus—Faschismus* (Stuttgart: Metzler, 1975); Gerhard Schweizer, *Bauernroman und Faschismus: Zur Ideologiekritik einer literarischen Gattung* (Tübingen: Tübinger Vereinigung für Volkskunde, 1976); Andrea Kunne, *Heimat im Roman: Last oder Lust? Transformationen eines Genres in der österreichischen Nachkriegsliteratur* (Amsterdam: Rodopi, 1991).

17. See Friedrich Griese's preamble to his novel *Das letzte Gesicht* (Munich: Langen-Müller, 1934), 5, which ends with the words "Ein Geschlecht vergeht, das andere kommt, die Erde aber bleibt ewiglich" (A generation passes, another one comes, but the earth remains forever).

18. Quoted in Karl Korn, "Literarische Ernte 1937," *Die Tat* 29 (1937): 623.

19. Ibid., 624.

20. Inge Jens, *Dichter zwischen rechts und links: Die Geschichte der Sektion für Dichtkunst an der Preussischen Akademie der Künste, dargestellt nach den Dokumenten* (Munich: Piper, 1971).

21. Fritz J. Raddatz, "Lied und Gedicht der proletarisch-revolutionären Literatur," in *Die deutsche Literatur in der Weimarer Republik,* ed. Wolfgang Rothe (Stuttgart: Reclam, 1974), 405.

22. Günther Rühle, *Zeit und Theater. Diktatur und Exil, 1933-1945,* vol. 3 (Berlin: Propyläen, 1974), 782. See also Karl-Heinz Schoeps, *Literature and Film in the Third Reich,* trans. Kathleen M. Dell'Orto (Rochester: Camden, 2004), 153.

23. Rainer Schlösser, *Das Volk und seine Bühne: Bemerkungen zum Aufbau des deutschen Theaters* (Berlin: Albert Langen, 1935).

24. Adolf Hitler, *Reden des Führers am Parteitag Grossdeutschland 1938* (Munich: Eher Verlag, 1939), 39.

25. See Ralf Schnell's fruitful discussion about *Haltung,* based on a 1937 article by Gerhard Schumann, in *Dichtung in finsteren Zeiten: Deutsche Literatur und Faschismus* (Reinbek: Rowohlt, 1998), 103–119.

26. Ketelsen, *Literatur und Drittes Reich,* 172–198.

27. Hans-Eugen Bühler, *Der Frontbuchhandel 1939-1945: Organisationen, Kompetenzen, Verlage, Bücher. Eine Dokumentation* (Frankfurt am Main: Buchhändler-Vereinigung, 2002), 35.

28. Schoeps, *Literature and Film,* 40, n. 22.

29. Hans Frank, "Betrachtungen über das Buch," *Schule der Freiheit* 9, nos. 13/14 (1942): 273.

30. Christian Bock, "Was wird gelesen? Eine Rundfrage in Berliner Buchhandlungen," *Das Reich,* 15 December 1940. Translation in Appendix I.

31. Tobias Schneider, "Bestseller im Dritten Reich: Ermittlung und Analyse der meistverkauften Romane in Deutschland 1933–1944," in *Vierteljahrshefte für Zeitgeschichte* 52, no. 1 (2004): 77–97.

32. Rudolf Radler, ed., *Die deutschsprachige Sachliteratur* (Munich and Zurich: Kindler, 1979), 19–23. See also various contributions in Walter Delabar et al., eds., *Banalität mit Stil: Zur Widersprüchlichkeit der Literaturproduktion im Nationalsozialismus* (Bern: Lang, 1999).

33. William B. Fischer, *The Empire Strikes Out: Kurd Lasswitz, Hans Dominik, and the Development of German Science Fiction* (Bowling Green, OH: Bowling Green State University Press, 1984), 179–262.

34. Schneider, "Bestseller im Dritten Reich," 96, n. 31.

35. Volker Dahm, "Nationale Einheit und partikulare Vielfalt: Zur Frage der kulturpolitischen Gleichschaltung im Dritten Reich," *Vierteljahrshefte für Zeitgeschichte* 43, no. 2 (1995): 221–265.

Chapter Six

THE ART WORLD IN NAZI GERMANY: CHOICES, RATIONALIZATION, AND JUSTICE

Jonathan Petropoulos

IT HAS BEEN FOUR YEARS SINCE I FINISHED *The Faustian Bargain*. The organizers of the Miller Symposium have given me the opportunity to revisit issues in the book and incorporate new information that I have found during my subsequent work on Nazi art plundering. This is work, I might add, that I have often done as a legal consultant, as there continue to be a number of cases involving stolen cultural property that was never restituted. The Holocaust was not only the most systematic program of murder in history; it was also the greatest theft, and the repercussions continue to reverberate in American courts.[1] However, there are many different kinds of justice. One variant might be labeled historical justice. It focuses on those persons responsible for important events in the past. Certain individuals evaded justice during their lifetimes, but they can nonetheless be held to account by subsequent generations. While historians of the Third Reich have debated whether it is appropriate to accuse and judge, there is widespread agreement that our task is to understand our subjects and to comprehend motivations and contextual factors.[2] To facilitate this undertaking, this essay is structured in trinities so as to explore three thematic categories with respect to three key figures. I will first introduce the three figures, each of whom represents a different profession within the art world, and then consider the themes of choice, rationalization, and justice.

Introductions

Arno Breker (1900–1991) was the most highly lauded and commercially successful artist of the over 13,000 who were officially sanctioned artists during the Third Reich.[3] Breker was a close friend of Albert Speer, Hitler's chief architect and later Minister for Armaments during the war, who gave him numerous commissions, including for the two iconic figures that adorned the main entry to the new Reich Chancellery in Berlin.[4] The talented sculptor was a beneficiary of Goebbels's propaganda machine, and his work was publicized in magazines, newspapers, and newsreels. For example, on his fortieth birthday in July 1940, Breker was the subject of a lavishly illustrated photo spread in the Nazi party periodical *Der Illustrierte Beobachter*. The title of the article, which captured its baldly ideological slant, was "Der ewige deutsche Kunst" (Eternal German Art).[5]

Indeed, Breker's art was upheld as representative of the regime and expressive of key ideological tenets: the racial superiority of Aryans, the martial prowess of Germans, and the connection to the classical world and all that was supposedly sublime. Breker's success as the leading artist in the Third Reich made him a wealthy man. Hitler gave him a palace that had been constructed by Frederick the Great, as well as special tax breaks and *Dotationen*, cash gifts in the hundreds of thousands of marks.[6] Breker had a large factory that produced his sculptures. After the war, former employees accused him of treating them like slaves and subjecting workers to inhumane conditions.[7] But during the Third Reich, Arno Breker was virtually unassailable. A powerful figure in the cultural bureaucracy who sat on prize committees, he had direct access to Hitler, Goebbels, Speer, Göring, Himmler, and others. Breker's position is perhaps best summed up by a former colleague who noted, "one glance from Breker was enough to render critics deathly silent."[8]

Karl Haberstock (1878–1956) was the leading art dealer in the Third Reich.[9] Successful in the art trade prior to 1933, he had emerged in the 1920s as the doyen of right-wing circles whose members often objected to buying from Jewish dealers. Haberstock was a friend of Hans Thoma, a notable Bavarian painter (later favored by many Nazis for his renderings of idyllic landscapes) who executed his portrait in 1912. This friendship exemplified the niche in the market filled by the dealer. As one contemporary museum official noted about Haberstock in the 1920s, "[his] clientele, drawn mostly from reactionary German circles, also had a natural taste for 19th century German art, as opposed to 'degenerate' French products of the same period or their own progressive German contemporaries."[10] His flourishing business enabled him to move to a veritable palace on the fashionable Kurfürstenstrasse in Berlin, but Haberstock's business increased most precipitously when

Hitler became a customer in 1935. The dictator purchased the painting *Venus und Amor* by the Italian High Renaissance artist Paris Bordone, which he placed in the Berghof, his mountain retreat. Soon, other Nazi leaders, including Göring, Goebbels, Speer, and Minister of the Interior Wilhelm Frick, became customers.[11]

Haberstock exerted so much influence on Nazi leaders with regard to art that he was a virtual official in the regime's cultural bureaucracy. For example, he played a leading role in "liquidating" the so-called "Degenerate Art," and also helped draft the May 1938 law making the de-accessioning from state collections a legal act. He also sat on a commission for selling works abroad and served as the liaison to his friend, Swiss dealer Theodor Fischer, who organized the major sale of 125 works, the "Paintings and Sculpture of Modern Masters from German Museums," in Lucerne in June 1939.[12]

Lest one imagine that his involvement in the regime's *Kunstpolitik* (politics of art) was motivated by public service (or even solely by ideological predilection, although Haberstock was a party member), it should be noted that the dealer profited handsomely from his own involvement in the purging of modern art from state collections. To cite one example, Haberstock personally exerted pressure on the Staatsgalerie in Stuttgart to sell the painting *Pensioners' House* by Max Liebermann, a Jewish artist who was widely reviled in the Third Reich. The museum was induced to accept Anton Graff's *Portrait of Professor Hommel* in exchange. This unobjectionable painting was worth approximately 4,000 Swiss francs, while the Liebermann fetched 20,000–25,000 Swiss francs abroad. Haberstock reaped the resulting profits.[13] This was but one of many transactions that grew out of his involvement in the Liquidation Commission (Verwertungs-Kommission). In 1939, Hitler sent Haberstock to Vienna to help sort out the art plundered from the city's affluent and cultured Jewish population. But despite the bountiful harvest "reaped" from the Rothschild, Bondy, Wittgenstein, and Gomperz families, among others, Haberstock faced stiff competition from other Nazi authorities and was unable to profit from the "reorganization" of these collections.[14] He therefore resumed his work as a dealer.

Haberstock also garnered huge wartime profits in the occupied lands, particularly occupied France. He kept a suite at the Paris Ritz, and his wine bills, which are in the U.S. National Archives, are a story unto themselves.[15] The dealer often bought from Jews who were under duress. Indeed, among his papers in the Municipal Art Collections in Augsburg are auction catalogues from the sale of confiscated Jewish collections.

Haberstock, ever the precise record-keeper (a common attribute among dealers, where knowledge leads to profits), took care to annotate the catalogues and record the buyer of each work. The catalogue for the sale of Jacob Goldschmidt's collection on 25 September 1941 at Hans Lange's auction house in Berlin, for example, includes Haberstock's handwritten notations that Propaganda Minister Goebbels purchased an Adolph von Menzel painting for RM 31,000.[16] During the war, Haberstock engaged in so many deals with sellers under duress that some historians have compared him to actual Nazi looting agencies. As Malcolm Goldstein wrote, "In effect, Haberstock was in competition with the Einsatzstab Reichsleiter Rosenberg, or ERR, [the primary Nazi plundering agency in France] for as much Jewish-owned art as he could get his hands on."[17]

Many of the works Haberstock acquired went to Hitler and the Führermuseum, including two remarkable paintings by Rembrandt: *Portrait of Titus* and *Landscape with Castle* (also known as the Nicholas Rembrandts). Haberstock found these works, which had once hung in the Hermitage, in the possession of the important Parisian art firm of Wildenstein & Cie.[18] The firm had been Aryanized or, more specifically, handed over to a non-Jewish trustee named Roger Dequoy, who liquidated the stock. Haberstock also purchased a number of paintings from the Aryanized gallery that did not go to Hitler. For example, he acquired works by Gustave Courbet and Claude Lorraine and sold them for a sizeable profit to Swiss nationals, who in turn sold them to clients that included the art museum in Bern. The latter refused to restitute the property, despite claims made by the Wildensteins, and still exhibits the works today.[19]

These transactions are meant to illustrate the complicated, wide-ranging, and lucrative nature of Haberstock's dealings. It is most important to recognize, however, that his primary customer was Dr. Hans Posse, the famed director of the Dresden Gemäldegalerie (Dresden Painting Gallery), who in 1939 was appointed to oversee the Führermuseum.[20] This project, Hitler's effort to create the greatest museum in the world, was not only founded on the premise that it would contain plundered art, but also remained top secret until Posse's death in December 1942.[21] Haberstock kept this secret as he profited handsomely from the sale of dozens of works to the Führermuseum.

Ernst Buchner (1892–1962), the director of the Bayerische Staatsgemäldesammlungen (Bavarian State Painting Collections), or BSGS, held one of the three most important museum posts in Germany, comparable to the directorships in Berlin and Dresden. The BSGS were housed at that time in 15 museums, palaces, and castles throughout Bavaria, including castles like Neuschwanstein near Füssen and painting galleries such as the Neue and Alte Pinakotheken in Munich. The latter, which also housed the Wittelsbach royal collection, was the crown jewel of Bavarian museums. Appointed Generaldirektor in late 1932, Buchner joined the Nazi party in May 1933, several months after the "seizure of power," a step he later claimed to have taken in order to preserve his position.[22] Indeed, for a native of Munich whose father was a well-regarded local painter, the position at the BSGS was the fulfillment of a dream. Buchner fashioned himself as a German nationalist and was hardly a supporter of the Weimar Republic, although he was initially tentative about the Nazis. He avoided extending his hand in the "Hitler-greeting" and naively believed that he could carry out his duties in an unpolitical manner. Initially, his instructions from Berlin included the purging of all Jewish and politically subversive staffers, but there were none of the former (excepting one curator who was already on his way out), and Buchner was able temporarily to sustain delusions about his position.

Circumstances began to change in 1937 when he and other museum officials were ordered by Hitler and Goebbels to permit their collections of modern, "degenerate" art to be cleansed. Buchner was sincerely opposed to this program. He refused to meet with President of the Reich Chamber for the Visual Arts Adolf Ziegler and his purging commission, and he demanded that the affected museums be compensated for the losses.[23] But Buchner had started down the slippery slope, and with Munich deemed "the city of German art" by Hitler (it is no coincidence that the "Degenerate Art" exhibition opened there and that the "Great German Art Exhibition" had its annual run nearby on the Prinzregentenstrasse), it was difficult to remain aloof from the Nazi *Kunstpolitik*.[24]

Buchner's involvement in the regime's art policies proceeded apace, and by 1938 he was purchasing objects from Jews taking flight. He was well aware that he was acquiring works for the museums under his supervision at well below market prices. At times, he made payments directly to the Gestapo, whose agents had seized the works in question. Buchner also worked with the Gestapo as he helped the secret police store seized works in buildings such as the Bavarian National Museum.[25] After the outbreak of war, he bought art in occupied territories for the museums, paying for these objects in inflated Reichsmarks. The advantage held by German buyers subsequently led Allied authorities to label such purchases "technical looting."[26] Ernst Buchner also helped compile a kind of wish list for the Nazi authorities of German-owned works that had gone abroad during the preceding centuries, and he led a commando that plundered the Van Eyck brothers' *Mystic Lamb Altar* from Vichy France. After World War I, the Germans had been forced to relinquish several panels to the Belgians as compensation for the destruction of the library in Leuven, among other acts. Later in the war, Buchner safeguarded plundered art at Neuschwanstein and other castles. This was art that the Einsatzstab Reichsleiter Rosenberg (ERR), an agency within the Nazi party, had seized throughout Europe. The Neuschwanstein repository held over 21,000 art objects stolen from French Jews, as well as records relating to the plundering operation.[27] Buchner could have had no illusions about the origin of this cultural property.

Choices

Although trained at the famed art academy in Düsseldorf, Arno Breker's career took off during the 1920s when he lived in France. A protégé of naturalist sculptor Aristide Maillol, and friendly with modernists like Jean Cocteau, with whom he socialized in Paris during the late 1920s and early 1930s, Breker was viewed by many as Maillol's successor in a tradition of naturalist sculptors that originated with Auguste Rodin. Breker not only had associates and customers in France; he also spoke French fluently. These considerations are relevant because they concern the issue of choices. In short, it would have been easy for Breker to remain in France during the 1930s. Many German artists, of course, chose emigration.[28] It would be interesting to compare visual artists to musicians, people in the film industry, and academics to see which field had the highest percentage of flight.[29] Because visual artists were not tied to language in the same way that many others were, they faced relatively few obstacles to continuing their work abroad. Stephanie Barron writes, in the introduction to her exhibition catalogue, *Exiles and Emigrés*, that "[t]hroughout the 1930s a great number of artists continued to flee the country: Beckmann to Amsterdam, Rudolf Belling to New York and then Turkey, Lyonel Feininger to New York, Raoul Hausmann to Ibiza, Kandinsky to Paris, Kokoschka to Prague and then London, Schwitters to Norway and then London."[30] This list is far from exhaustive, for George Grosz, John Heartfield, Josef Albers, Laszlo Moholy-Nagy, and many others come to mind. For Breker, emigration, or simply remaining outside Germany, was a real option. Indeed, for many who wished to continue to exhibit and sell art, it was perhaps the only viable one.

Yes, Otto Dix chose "inner emigration," but he was already established and financially comfortable.[31] For a young, ambitious artist, the choice was between collaboration and emigration.

As a major dealer of Old Masters, Karl Haberstock had international business contacts. During the 1920s, he had established a small branch in London. Subsequently, he concluded deals with nearly all the major European dealers of the time, for example, the Wildensteins in Paris, the Cramers in the Netherlands and, as mentioned earlier, with Theodor Fischer in Switzerland. Karl Haberstock also had excellent linguistic skills; he spoke French and English fluently. In short, he and his wife Magdalena had the means and the contacts to reestablish themselves outside of Germany. Of course, many art dealers, most of whom were Jewish, emigrated and did well abroad. Paul Graupe, Curt Valentin, Karl Nierendorf, and Karl Buchholz in New York, and Galka Scheyer in Los Angeles offer but a few examples.[32] Haberstock had options other than flight. He could have remained in Germany and avoided exploitative practices. Even if it was not always easy to draw boundaries, he could have made it a policy not to purchase Aryanized Jewish property, not to buy in the occupied lands, and not to sell to Nazi leaders. He was sufficiently wealthy to have lived comfortably with a diminished income.

Ernst Buchner was in a more difficult situation. He was an expert in old German art (the Cranachs, Dürer, and Grünewald, among others), which was not valued around the world in the same way as in Germany, especially Nazi Germany. It would therefore have been difficult for him to find a museum post abroad. In North America, the Busch-Reisinger Museum at Harvard was the only institution devoted exclusively to Germanic art.[33] Still, many museum directors did leave Germany. Alois Schardt, who had been the director of the Berlin Nationalgalerie and the Städtische Museum in Halle, moved to Los Angeles, where he taught and gave lectures. Alexander Dorner, once a museum director in Hannover, took over the Rhode Island School of Design. Georg Swarzenski, forced out of the Städel Museum in Frankfurt, went to Harvard. In terms of remaining in Germany, Buchner faced challenges similar to Breker's. The museums Buchner oversaw featured public exhibits subject to Nazi *Gleichschaltung* (coordination), and they were therefore buffeted by ideologues like Joseph Goebbels and Alfred Rosenberg. Although Buchner could not remain entirely aloof from propaganda, he did not have to participate in the Nazi plunder of art in the way he did. Even though he remained in Germany, he retained a range of options that would have limited his involvement in criminal activities. He could have chosen to focus on scholarship, evaluations, and other kinds of consulting that would not have necessitated his direct involvement in Nazi *Kunstpolitik.*

Rationalizations

Arno Breker wrote extensively about his life after the war, and he described his work in the 1930s and 1940s as part of an international movement.[34] The aesthetic that he and Speer helped define for art and architecture in Nazi Germany, he claimed, could be found in countries around the world. To support his case, Breker pointed to projects in Washington, D.C., such as the roughly contemporaneous Jefferson Memorial. He also noted with a certain pride that Stalin had extended feelers to see if the sculptor would consider accepting commissions to work in the Soviet Union. Because Breker had held a fellowship at the German Academy in Rome in 1932–1933, he also pointed to the style of the Italian fascists as an influence.[35] In addition to rationalizing his bombastic, monumental style by referring to similar work outside Germany, Breker believed that his influence in the German cultural bureaucracy helped mitigate the influence of Nazi radicals. For example, he later maintained that he had tried to intervene against the "degenerate art" purges and that he had helped artist friends such as Aristide Maillol and his Jewish model Dina Vierny in France during the war.[36] But clearly these assertions came within a framework of denial; he even claimed that his works were not ideological.

Karl Haberstock maintained that he was just a businessman, buying and selling objects. By selling modern art abroad, he argued, he was preserving it for humanity. As a member of the Ministry for Public Enlightenment and Propaganda's Liquidation Commission, he went on record opposing the destruction of seized works, although that happened on at least one occasion in March 1939.[37] Like the other two figures considered here, Haberstock pointed to the help he had provided to Jews. He cited the Mendelsohn family in Germany and the famed art historian Max Friedländer in the Netherlands as examples.[38] His was a selective memory, for he did not mention that he had bought the entire contents of Friedrich and Louise Gutmann's home in Heemstede, Holland, just before the German-Jewish émigré and his wife were deported to Germany in 1942. The founder of the Dresdner Bank, Friedrich Gutmann was beaten to death by Göring's agents. Göring had wanted to purchase his famed silver collection, much of which he would not sell. Louise was shipped to Theresienstadt and then Auschwitz, where she perished.[39] Haberstock and his partner, Munich dealer Julius Böhler, liquidated the contents of the Gutmanns' Heemstede residence. Haberstock also visited a storage facility in Paris on the Boulevard Raspail, where he "carried away some eight paintings" belonging to the Gutmanns, which he in turn sold.[40] Among them was Edgar Degas's *Landscape with Smokestacks*, a pastel over monotype from 1890 that currently hangs in the Art Institute of Chicago.[41] Haberstock later explained the vast wealth he had accumulated by pointing to the fact that Germany had been winning the war; during that time, he rationalized, material benefits would naturally result.

Ernst Buchner also portrayed himself as a bulwark against Nazi Party radicals. When he attended meetings of museum directors during the 1930s, he was horrified by some of their ideas, such as those in Walter Hansen's address on Rembrandt as a Jewish artist, a lecture presented in Berlin in November 1937. Buchner had stood up to Hitler with regards to the proceeds from the sale of modern art, stressing that the revenue must come back to museums and be utilized for the acquisition of desirable works. This protest, it should be noted, was successful, and, like most other museum directors, he received funds from the proceeds of the liquidation action. Buchner also maintained a positive self-image through his work to safeguard works of art during wartime. Like other museum directors and curators, he pioneered techniques for protecting cultural property against aerial bombardment and combat more generally. The Generaldirektor consulted with conservation specialists and other museum officials, and passed on recommendations to Martin Bormann and other Nazi officials concerning the best tactics for safeguarding art. In the latter years of the war, he would personally escort shipments from the Bavarian State Painting Collections to rural repositories. His efforts to protect art extended to the Van Eyck brothers' altarpiece, which was placed in the Altaussee salt mine. Buchner almost certainly believed his involvement in the removal of the precious artwork was grounded in a concern for its preservation.

Ernst Buchner's ideas and rationalizations were not entirely constant, but changed according to the policies of the regime and the course of foreign political affairs. From 1939 to 1942, the peak of Hitler's success, Buchner underwent a transformation such that it would be accurate to label him a Nazi, and not merely an opportunistic German nationalist. He helped draft lists of artworks taken by the French and English from German lands over the preceding centuries. This program for "*die Rückführung von Kulturgütern deutscher Provenienz*" (the repatriation of cultural objects of German provenance), which was overseen by Joseph Goebbels, was a blatantly ideological project.[42] During the early years of the war, at a time when German armies enjoyed relative success on the battlefield, he advocated a kind of literal-minded cultural imperialism: as the most powerful country in Europe, it was natural that Germany would control Europe's cultural patrimony. Furthermore, he believed that his mission with an SS commando to secure the Van Eyck altar was simply helping to address a historical injustice, the Treaty of Versailles. However, after 1943, such rationalizations would be replaced by notions of humanitarian work and what he perceived as apolitical technocratic service.

Justice

Arno Breker went before a denazification court in Donauwörth, Bavaria, in 1948. He faced serious charges, as the prosecution sought to place him in category II (a major offender) of a five-tiered scale (with category I being most culpable and V being exonerated). Breker was charged with being a propagandist, a friend of Hitler's, an employer of slave labor, and a profiteer. The denazification trial proved elaborate; it entailed collecting hundreds of affidavits from Albert Speer and other notables. While Breker's case elicited some negative publicity in the press (he was mocked in some headlines as "Hitler's Michelangelo"), he was ultimately let off with the designation "*Mitläufer,*" or fellow-traveler (category IV) and fined DM 100.[43]

This permitted Breker to return to sculpting. He established a niche in radical right-wing circles, but also found broader acceptance and was commissioned to do portraits of Salvador Dali and others. On his own, Breker executed works of Chancellor Konrad Adenauer, among other establishment figures, by which he strove to give the impression that he had been fully rehabilitated.[44] While this was not entirely the case, he received considerable support from German corporate executives, fulfilling commissions for the Gerling Konzern in Cologne, among others. One critic called him the "*Hofkünstler des deutschen Wirtschaftswunders*" (court artist of the German economic miracle).[45] Indeed, building upon the findings of the denazification board, which interpreted his activities during the Third Reich in a most generous manner, he fabricated a web of life-lies comparable to that woven by filmmaker Leni Riefenstahl, who also denied responsibility for fashioning a Nazi aesthetic or bolstering the regime.[46] Arno Breker lived comfortably until his death in 1991. Today there is a museum near Düsseldorf dedicated to his memory, and there are numerous websites that pay tribute to him as a "world class artist."[47]

Karl Haberstock went before a *Spruchkammer* (tribunal) at Ansbach, near Nuremberg in Bavaria. Like Breker, he faced serious charges stemming from his connections to Nazi leaders and for selling plundered art. The American Office of Strategic Services (OSS) agents from the Art Looting Investigation Unit had initially recommended that he be tried as a war criminal, but Haberstock saved his own neck by testifying at the International Military Tribunal at Nuremberg and helping American authorities with restitution efforts.[48] In Ansbach, Haberstock was initially placed in category III, but on appeal the judge reduced the sentence to category IV or *Mitläufer*, and lowered the fine from DM 200,000 to DM 127,000.[49] According to Military Government Law No. 52, which regulated the art trade in the American occupation zone by requiring dealers to obtain a license, this made him eligible to return to art dealing, which Haberstock did.[50] He abandoned his bombed-out gallery in Berlin and operated out of his home overlooking the English Garden in Munich. Interestingly, Hermann Göring's chief art dealer, Walter Andreas Hofer, lived upstairs from Haberstock after the war and also continued in the art trade. Those in the know after the war referred tongue-in-cheek to their common apartment building on the Königinstrasse as the "*braune Haus*," a reference to the former Nazi Party headquarters.

Others were not so amused by the rehabilitation of art dealing careers. Two members of the OSS Art Looting Investigation Unit, Theodore Rousseau, the illustrious curator at the Metropolitan Museum of Art, and S. Lane Faison, Jr., a professor of art history at Williams College, corresponded after seeing an article in *The New Yorker* that mentioned Haberstock. Rousseau wrote Faison: "this may amuse you. They make me all the more angry when I think of the wretched [Bruno] Lohse [an art dealer in the employ of Göring who went before a court in Paris]. According to the latest news, even [Gustav] Rochlitz [another Nazi dealer] is out and doing business!"[51] The former OSS art looting experts were frustrated primarily by the limitations of justice. While they recognized that the Nazi dealers were able to revive their careers, they seemed less aware that these dealers possessed assets taken from Holocaust victims that were never restituted. Rochlitz and Lohse, for example, had surrendered to the Americans a cache of paintings hidden near Neuschwanstein at the war's end. Some of the works belonged to the Gutmann family. This was not, however, the entirety of their holdings, and investigators continue to work to this day to hunt down works of problematic provenance that have been in their possession.[52]

The art that Haberstock owned was placed in a foundation, and then put on permanent loan to his home town of Augsburg, where it was housed in the Schäzler Palais. It is still there today and includes works by Rembrandt, Canaletto, and Cranach, among others. Haberstock was honored for this act of generosity and made an honorary citizen, which included the keys to the city as well as a street named after him, the Karl Haberstock-Strasse. Karl Haberstock died in 1956. His wife and behind-the-scenes partner, Magdalena, continued to be honored in his place until her passing in 1983. Several catalogues documenting the holdings of the Haberstock Foundation were produced between 1960 and 1991. Despite the inclusion of essays on Karl Haberstock's career, there was scarcely a word about his activities during the Third Reich.[53] Indeed, until 1999, one had to walk past a bust of him upon entering the museum. Many citizens of Augsburg were suffering from a serious case of historical amnesia.[54]

Ernst Buchner was also apprehended by the OSS Art Looting Investigation Unit, which recommended that he be tried as a war criminal and never again be permitted to return to his post in museum administration. The Americans never followed through with this suggestion, and Buchner faced a Spruchkammer in Munich. This resulted, not surprisingly, in Buchner being placed in category IV as a fellow-traveler (Lutz Niethammer selected an apt title for his book on denazification in Bavaria, "*Die Mitläufer-fabrik*" or "fellow-traveler factory," since 98 percent of those who went through denazification were placed in categories IV or V).[55] This enabled Buchner to return to his position as general director of the Bavarian State Painting Collections. Because the position was filled at the time of his legal rehabilitation, he worked on his scholarship as he collected his salary. Buchner returned to his post in 1952 and oversaw the final stages of the rebuilding of the Alte Pinakothek, the beautiful building designed by Leo von Klenze. He was celebrated as a savior of art, a national hero who had saved German artistic treasures.[56] Upon the reopening of the Alte Pinakothek, he escorted luminaries such as the first President of the Federal Republic, Theodor Heuss, and Bavarian Governor Wilhelm Högner, on a tour of the museum. Some questions about his role in securing the Van Eyck altar surfaced toward the end of his tenure as Generaldirektor, but he retired gracefully, with a full pension and additional support as a scholar affiliated with the Bavarian State Painting Collections.[57] Buchner died in 1962 and his papers, as specified by German privacy laws (*Datenschutz*), remained closed for the next thirty years. This naturally helped to preserve certain myths about Buchner.

Conclusions

In keeping with the theme of a trilogy, I offer three general points in closing. The first concerns the value of a biographical or prosa-pographical approach. By focusing on individuals, it permits a better understanding of the distinctive constraints, thought processes, and experiences of individuals. It allows, I believe, greater insight into the motivation and thinking of our subjects, one of the chief challenges to historians. Yes, we must put these individuals in a broader context and understand structures, processes, and larger trends. But it is important not to lose sight of the individual.

Second, the study of the art world during the Third Reich cannot be separated from ethical considerations. While I am not so naïve as to hold artists and intellectuals to higher ethical standards, these peo-ple have often thought about such matters. Their inclination toward self-awareness provides a basis for reflection on issues of morality and personal responsibility. I have always maintained that the history of propaganda and art plundering cannot be disentangled from the his-tory of the Holocaust. Theft was an important juncture on "the twisted road to Auschwitz."[58] It was part of the radicalization process. It pro-vided perpetrators with a material reward, and perhaps an incentive, for participating in the persecution. Self-enrichment was a motive among perpetrators more often than has been recognized.[59] Depriving people of their property contributed to the dehumanization process. Once they were impoverished, and then in many cases deported to ghettos in the East, it was easier to think of them as different and inferior. More-over, we must not forget that members of the art world were important cogs in the propaganda machine; years of indoctrination were neces-sary before most perpetrators became willing to implement a genocidal program. Furthermore, Jewish assets were converted by the Nazis into resources that helped fuel the war machine.[60]

Third, it is important to realize that these figures are neither entirely culpable nor innocent. Like so many others in the Third Reich, they fall somewhere in a gray zone.[61] There is ambiguity in their character and their actions, which is what makes them so fascinating and so much like us. Arno Breker, Karl Haberstock, and Ernst Buchner struggled with ethical issues. They were, at times, troubled by the policies of the Nazi regime. On certain occasions, they exhibited compassion and even courage. But they also, ultimately, came up short. Theirs was an ethical failure, and the reverberations of such failures extend far and wide. One can invoke philosopher John Roth's question, "How is the Holocaust a warning?"; one can point to journalist Gitta Sereny's formulation about "the fatal interdependence of all human actions"; or one can refer to Nobel laureate Elie Wiesel's formulation, "traditional ideas and acquired values, philosophical systems and social theories-all must be revised in the shadow of Birkenau."[62] Furthermore, the careers of the three figures examined here raise questions regarding what philosopher Berel Lang calls, "the Third Reich and the breakdown of professional ethics."[63] Lang emphasizes the challenges of exploring this issue, noting "codes of professional conduct, like any other moral codes, are more likely to fail or to change under the pressure of external coercion than without it."[64] One must therefore recognize that the professional codes of the time were mutable and in some ways ambiguous, and accordingly approach these figures not in a prosecutorial manner but as a historian, employing one's powers of empathy.

This is nonetheless an admonitory tale. Despite the intellectual and artistic prowess of these individuals, they were unable to resist cooptation into the Nazis' criminal programs. As literary critic George Steiner noted in his now classic book, *In Bluebeard's Castle*, "Art, intellectual pursuits, the development of the natural sciences, many branches of scholarship flourished in close spatial [and] temporal proximity to massacre and the death camps.... Why did humanistic traditions and models of conduct prove so fragile a barrier against political bestiality?"[65] Indeed, in a formulation echoing that offered at the outset of this essay, namely that the Nazis were not only the greatest mass murderers but also the greatest thieves, one must recognize that the Nazis were not only among the most malevolent leaders in history, but also among those most focused on culture and cultural policy. During the Third Reich, there was an inextricable nexus of culture and barbarism, to the point that many concentration camps, including the unparalleled killing factory at Auschwitz, featured orchestras.[66]

The phrase "Nazi culture" is not an oxymoron. Hitler, Göring, Himmler, and their cohort at the top level of the regime, as well as Breker, Haberstock, and Buchner, among those in the second rank, devoted tremendous time and energy to cultural matters, not only the visual arts but also opera, film, theater, and even interior design, among still other spheres.[67] Very often, those in both the first and second rank took an instrumental approach to culture, seeing it as an expression of ideological tenets, as a vehicle for creating a group ethos, and as a means of self-definition.[68] Culture was so important during the Third Reich that it served as a kind of glue, holding together divergent ideas and personalities, linking the leaders with the masses, and ultimately becoming a defining feature of the regime. Contemporary critic Walter Benjamin offered a profound and prescient insight in 1936 when he mused on the politicization of aesthetics and the aestheticization of politics.[69]

Notes

1. Michael Bazyler, *Holocaust Justice: The Battle for Restitution in America's Courts* (New York: New York University Press, 2003), xi.
2. Concerning the issue of historians making moral judgments, see Richard Evans, *The Coming of the Third Reich* (London: Penguin, 2003), xx.
3. Joseph Wulf, *Die bildenden Künste im Dritten Reich: eine Dokumentation* (Frankfurt am Main: Ullstein, 1963), 109. Wulf cites figures from the Reich Chamber of Visual Arts that list 10,500 painters and 3,200 sculptors.
4. Albert Speer, *Inside the Third Reich* (New York: Macmillan, 1970), 203–204, 234–236, 244, 403, 417.
5. "Ewige Deutsche Kunst: Arno Breker zum 40. Geburtstag," *Illustrierte Beobachter* 29, 18 July 1940. For another ideological reading of Breker's work see Werner Rittich, "Zum 40. Geburtstag von Professor Arno Breker," in *Kunst im Deutschen Reich* 4 (Ausgabe B) (1940), 1.
6. See Magdalena Bushart, "Kunstproduzent im Dienst der Macht," in *Skulptur und Macht*, ed. Magdalena Bushart (Berlin: Fröhlich und Kaufmann, 1983).
7. Archive of the Institut für Zeitgeschichte, Munich, ZS-2410, account of Marta Mierndorff, "Der Untergang der Steinbildhauerwerkstätten Arno Breker GMBH in Wriezen/Oder."
8. Amtsgericht Munich, Breker file, Konrad Hämmerling to Spruchkammer Donauwörth, 20 January 1947.
9. This is a judgment shared by many other scholars of the art world during the Third Reich. See, for example, Günther Haase, *Kunstraub und Kunstschutz: eine Dokumentation* (Hildesheim: Georg Olms Verlag, 1991), 47.
10. National Archives and Records Administration (NARA), Record Group (RG) 226, Entry 92, Box 505, Theodore Rousseau, "Detailed Interrogation Report No. 13: Karl Haberstock" (Washington, D.C.: Strategic Services Unit, Art Looting

Investigation Unit, 15 September 1945), 1. For more on Haberstock's career, see National Gallery of Art, MSS3 (Faison papers), Box 4, Haberstock statement (in translation), 4 June 1945.

11. See Haberstock's ledgers, or *"Geschäftsbücher"* from 1937 to 1941 in Städtische Kunstsammlungen Augsburg, Haberstock Nachlass, Bd. XXVIII.

12. The German phrasing was "Gemälde und Plastiken moderner Meister aus deutschen Museen." See Germanisches Nationalmuseum, Nachlass Haberstock I, vol. II, Hofmann to Goebbels, 28 November 1938; and NARA, RG 239, Entry 73, Box 79. More generally, see Stephanie Barron, "The Galerie Fischer Auction," in *"Degenerate Art": The Fate of the Avant-Garde in Nazi Germany*, ed. Stephanie Barron (New York: Los Angeles County Museum of Art/Harry Abrams, 1991), 135–170. See also Andreas Hüneke, "Dubiöse Händler operieren im Dunst der Macht," in *Alfred Flechtheim: Sammler, Kunsthändler, Verleger*, ed. Hans Albert Peters and Stephan von Wiese (Düsseldorf: Westfälisches Landesmuseum, 1987), 103; Esther Tisa Francini, Anja Heuss, and Georg Kreis, *Fluchtgut–Raubgut: Der Transfer von Kulturgütern in und über die Schweiz 1933-1945 und die Frage der Restitution* (Zurich: Chronos, 2001), 200–207; and Stefan Frey, "Die Auktion in der Galerie Fischer in Luzern am 30. Juni 1939–ein Ausverkauf der Moderne aus Deutschland," in *Überbrückt: Ästhetische Moderne und Nationalsozialismus*, ed. Eugen Blume and Dieter Scholz (Cologne: Walther König, 1998), 275–291.

13. Francini et al., *Fluchtgut–Raubgut*, 217.

14. See Bundesarchiv Berlin (BAB), R43II 1269a, for documents pertaining to Haberstock's tenure in Vienna. For a list of looted art collections in Vienna, see Tina Walzer and Stephan Templ, *Unser Wien: "Arisierung" auf österreich* (Berlin: Aufbau Verlag, 2001), 178–179.

15. For Haberstock's wine bills and other records, see NARA, RG 260, Entry Ardelia Hall, Boxes 446–448.

16. For the annotated auction catalogues, see Städtische Kunstsammlungen Augsburg, Haberstock Nachlass. Note that scholars are currently engaged in careful and systematic studies of the so-called "Judenauktionen"; this is difficult and laborious because there is no one place that holds all the auction catalogues. For a discussion of relevant sources, see Francini et al., *Fluchtgut–Raubgut*, 44. More generally, see Anja Heuss, "Die Reichskulturkammer und die Steuerung des Kunsthandels im Dritten Reich," in *Sediment: Mitteilung zur Geschichte des Kunsthandels 3*, ed. Zentralarchiv des Deutschen und Internationalen Kunsthandels (Bonn: Zentralarchiv des Deutschen und Internationalen Kunsthandels, 1998), 49–61.

17. Malcolm Goldstein, *Landscape with Figures: A History of Art Dealing in the United States* (New York: Oxford University Press, 2000), 181.

18. S. Lane Faison, "Supplement to Consolidated Interrogation Report No. 4" (Washington, D.C.: Strategic Services Unit, OSS, Art Looting Investigation Unit, 15 December 1945), attachment 57, "Partial List of Purchases for Linz Made in France Bought through Haberstock." The paintings were sold in 1942 for RM 3 million ($1.2 million) and now hang in the Louvre.

19. The Kunstmuseum Bern claimed that it had purchased the works in good faith, and a Swiss court ruled in the museum's favor in 1951. According to Swiss law (as opposed to U.S. law), one can have legal title to an object, even when it is stolen, if it was purchased in good faith. See Francini, et al., *Fluchtgut–Raubgut*, 416–418.

20. See Birgit Schwarz, "Hitlers Sonderbeauftragter Hans Posse," *Dresdener Hefte* 77, no. 1 (2004): 77–85.

21. Francini et al., *Fluchtgut–Raubgut*, 224. Note that there is some controversy over the precise number of paintings collected for the Führermuseum. Francini, Heuss, and Kreiss use a figure consistent with S. Lane Faison's 1945 Office of Strategic Services report and estimate "approximately 6,000," while Birgit Schwarz, in her new study, reduces the number to 3,935. See Birgit Schwarz, *Hitlers Museum: Die Fotoalben Gemäldegalerie Linz* (Vienna: Böhlau, 2004), 21. See also S. Lane Faison, "Consolidated Interrogation Report No. 4. Linz: Hitler's Museum and Library" (Washington, D.C.: Strategic Services Unit, OSS, Art Looting Investigation Unit, 15 December 1945).

22. Bayrisches Hauptstaatsarchiv (BHSA), MK 44778, Ernst Buchner, "In eigener Sache," 15 June 1945.

23. BHSA, MK 40849, Buchner's report on the "*Entartete Kunst*" program, 16 July 1937.

24. See Münchener Stadtmuseum, ed., *München–"Hauptstadt der Bewegung"* (Munich: Münchener Statdtmuseum, 1993).

25. BHSA, MK 44778, Statement of Otto Marx, 13 September 1945. See also Theodore Rousseau, "Detailed Interrogation Report No. 2: Ernst Buchner" (Washington, D.C.: Strategic Services Unit, OSS, Art Looting Investigation Unit, 31 July 1945), 5.

26. Gerard Aalders, "By Diplomatic Pouch: Art Smuggling by the Nazis," *Spoils of War International Newsletter* 3 (December 1996), available at http://spoils.libfl.ru/spoils/eng/spoil3_2.html#13.

27. Contemporaneous German documents about the ERR plunder in Neuschwanstein are reproduced and translated into French in Jean Cassou, ed., *Le Pillage par les allemands des oeuvres d'art et des bibliothèques appartenant á des juifs en France* (Paris: Centre Documentation Juive Contemporaine, 1947).

28. See, for example, Keith Holz, *Modern German Art for Thirties Paris, Prague, and London: Resistance and Acquiescence in a Democratic Public Sphere* (Ann Arbor: University of Michigan Press, 2005); and Keith Holz and Wolfgang Schopf, *Im Auge des Exils: Josef Breitenbach und die Freie Deutsche Kultur in Paris 1933-1941* (Berlin: Aufbau Verlag, 2001).

29. Current studies are inconclusive about which among the cultural professions were most inclined toward emigration. See, for example, Jarrel Jackman and Carla Borden, eds., *The Muses Flee Hitler: Cultural Transfer and Adaptation, 1930-1945* (Washington, D.C.: Smithsonian Institution Press, 1983); and Anthony Heilbut, *Exiled in Paradise: German Refugee Artists and Intellectuals in America from the 1930s to the Present* (Boston: Beacon Press, 1983).

30. Stephanie Barron, "European Artists in Exile: A Reading Between the Lines," in *Exiles and Emigrés: The Flight of European Artists from Hitler*, ed. Stephanie Barron and Sabine Eckmann (New York: Los Angeles County Museum of Art/Harry Abrams, 1997), 14.

31. Eva Karcher, *Otto Dix, 1891-1969: Leben und Werk* (Cologne: Benedikt Taschen, 1988). See, more generally, Neil Donahue and Doris Kirchner, eds., *Flight of Fantasy: New Perspectives on Inner Emigration in German Literature 1933-1945* (New York: Berghahn Books, 2003).

32. One can identify many émigré dealers in the useful reference work by Nancy Yeide, Konstantin Akinsha, and Amy Walsh, *The AAM Guide to Provenance Research* (Washington, D.C.: American Association of Museums, 2001).

33. See Kuno Francke, "The Germanic Museum at Harvard," *Art and Archeology* 28, no. 6 (1929): 233–239; and Peter Nisbet and Emilie Norris, *The Busch-Reisinger-Museum: History and Holdings* (Cambridge, MA: Harvard Art Museums, 1991).

34. See, for example, Arno Breker, *Paris, Hitler et Moi* (Paris: Plon, 1970); Arno Breker, *Im Strahlungsfeld der Ereignisse: Leben und Wirken eines Künstlers* (Preussisch Oldendorf: K. W. Schütz, 1972); and Arno Breker, *Schriften*, ed. Volker Probst (Bonn: Marco, 1983).

35. See Dietmar Schenk and Gero Seelig, "Die Deutsche Akademie in Rom: Felix Nussbaum und Arno Breker in der Villa Massimo, 1932–33," in *Die Kunst hat nie ein Mensch allein besessen*, ed. Akademie der Künste (Berlin: Henschel Verlag, 1996), 433–436.

36. Amtsgericht Munich, Arno Breker file, Dina Vierny statement, 27 February 1947.

37. Documents about the Verwertungskommission can be found in the Germanisches Nationalmuseum, Nachlass (NL) Haberstock, as well as BAB, R 5001/21020. This latter includes records of a 2 November 1938 meeting where Franz Hofmann from the Ministry for Public Enlightenment and Propaganda raises the idea of burning art in a propagandistic act, and of Haberstock's recommendation at the 20 February 1939 meeting that the objects be auctioned off.

38. NARA, RG 226, Entry 92, Box 505, Theodore Rousseau, "Detailed Interrogation Report No. 13: Karl Haberstock" (Washington, D.C.: Strategic Services Unit, Art Looting Investigation Unit, 15 September 1945), 7.

39. The purchase agreements concluded between the Gutmanns and Haberstock and Julius Böhler are in Haberstock's papers in the Städtische Kunstsammlungen Augsburg. Some of Julius Böhler's papers are in the Archiv der Industrie- und Handelskammer in Munich. See also Gerard Aalders, *Nazi Looting: The Plunder of Dutch Jewry during the Second World War* (Oxford: Berg, 2004).

40. Hector Feliciano, *The Lost Museum: The Nazi Conspiracy to Steal the World's Greatest Works of Art* (New York: Basic Books, 1997), 184.

41. Howard Trienens, *Landscape with Smokestacks: The Case of the Allegedly Plundered Degas* (Evanston, IL: Northwestern University Press, 2000).

42. See Anja Heuss, *Kunst- und Kulturgutraub: Eine vergleichende Studie zur Besatzungspolitik der Nationalsozialisten in Frankreich und der Sowjetunion* (Heidelberg: Universitäts-Verlag C.Winter, 2000), 277–283.

43. "Der 'Michelangelo Hitlers'," *Die Abendzeitung*, 2 October 1948.

44. See Volker Probst, *Der Bildhauer Arno Breker* (Bonn: Galerie Marco, 1978).

45. See Kurt Reutti's formulation in Geheime Staatsarchiv Preussischer Kulturbesitz, I HA Rep. 92 Reutti Nachlass, NL 1, Kurt Reutti, "Erinnerungen," 197. See also Magdalena Bushart, "Überraschende Begegnungen mit alten Bekannten: Arno Brekers NS-Plastik in neuer Umgebung," in *NS-Kunst: 50 Jahre danach. Neue Beiträge*, ed. Berthold Hinz (Marburg: Jonas, 1989), 35–54.

46. See Riefenstahl's interview in Ray Muller's film, *The Wonderful, Horrible Life of Leni Riefenstahl* (New York: Kino International, 1995). See also Susan Sontag, "Fascinating Fascism," in *The Nazification of Art: Art, Design, Music, Architecture and Film in the Third Reich*, ed. Brandon Taylor and Wilfried van der Will (Winchester, UK: Winchester Press, 1990), 204–218.

47. See the website for the Arno Breker Society International at http://www.meaus. com/articles/guardian.html. Breker is not the only rehabilitated artist who previously enjoyed success during the Third Reich. See Gregory Maertz, *The Invisible Museum: The Secret Postwar History of Nazi Art* (New Haven, CT: Yale University Press, forthcoming).

48. Rousseau, "Detailed Interrogation Report No. 13: Karl Haberstock," 7.

49. Landesarchiv Berlin, Spruchkammer file of Karl Haberstock, Akte No. 2045: Berufungskammer Senat Nürnberg, Zweigstelle Ansbach, 16 December 1949.

50. See NARA, RG 260, Ardelia Hall, Box 86, Office of the Military Government of the United States, press release of 22 March 1949, that cites MG Law No. 52 of 1945.

51. National Gallery of Art, S. MSS3 (Faison papers), Box 2, Theodore Rousseau to S. Lane Faison, 16 November 1948. They make reference to Janet Flanner's article, "Annals of Crime: The Beautiful Spoils," *The New Yorker*, 22 February 1947, 31–44.

52. For the discovery of the cache at Gipsmühle near Neuschwanstein, see Thomas Carr Howe, *Salt Mines and Castles: The Discovery and Restitution of Looted European Art* (Indianapolis and New York: Bobbs-Merrill, 1946), 241–242. The author recently discovered a valuable work of art illegally removed from Italy that was housed for over fifty years in Rochlitz's farmhouse in this same area. Efforts are currently underway to restitute this piece to the rightful owner.

53. Städtische Kunstsammlung Augsburg, ed., *Gemälde der Stiftung Karl und Magdalene Haberstock* (Augsburg: Städtische Kunstsammlungen, 1960), and Städtische Kunstsammlungen Augsburg, ed., *Mythos und Bürgerliche Welt: Gemälde und Zeichnungen der Haberstock-Stiftung* (Augsburg: Städtische Kunstsammlungen, 1991).

54. Brita Sachs, "Nicht rümen, sondern aufklären: Jonathan Petropoulos sprach in Augsburg über Karl Haberstock, Hitler's Kunsthändler," *Frankfurter Allgemeine Zeitung* 38, 14 February 2001, 52.

55. Lutz Niethammer, *Die Mitläuferfabrik. Die Entnazifizierung am Beispiel Bayerns* (Berlin: J. H. W. Dietz, 1982). See also Christian Zentner and Fridemann Bedürftig, eds., *The Encyclopedia of the Third Reich*, vol. I (New York: Macmillan, 1991), 190.

56. See, for example, "Hüter der Kunst: Dr. Buchner, *Die Welt*, 23 June 1953."

57. Karl Schumann, "Münchens Pinakotheksdirektor im Kreuzfeuer," *Mannheimer Morgen Post*, 29 December 1956; Susanne Carwin, "Unter der Sonne des Artikels 131," *Frankfurter Hefte* 11 (November 1956): 789–797.

58. Karl Schleunes, *The Twisted Road to Auschwitz: Nazi Policy Toward German Jews, 1933-1939* (Urbana: University of Illinois Press, 1990), 259–262.

59. Jonathan Petropoulos, "The Nazi Kleptocracy: Reflections on Avarice and the Holocaust" in *Lessons and Legacies VII: The Holocaust in International Perspective*, ed. Dagmar Herzog (Evanston, IL: Northwestern University Press, forthcoming).

60. Michael MacQueen, "The Conversion of Looted Jewish Assets to Run the German War Machine," in *Holocaust and Genocide Studies* 18, no. 1 (2004): 27–45.

61. See Jonathan Petropoulos and John Roth, eds., *Gray Zones: Ambiguity and Compromise in the Holocaust and its Aftermath* (New York: Berghahn Books, 2005).

62. John Roth, *Holocaust Politics* (Louisville, KY: Westminster John Knox Press, 2001), 138–176. Gitta Sereny, *Into That Darkness: An Examination of Conscience* (New

York: Signet, 1983), 15. Elie Wiesel, speech of 23 October 2000, quoted in Roth, *Holocaust Politics*, 138.

63. Berel Lang, *The Future of the Holocaust* (Ithaca, NY: Cornell University Press, 1999), 92–104.

64. Ibid., 94.

65. George Steiner, *In Bluebeard's Castle: Some Notes Towards the Redefinition of Culture* (New Haven: Yale University Press, 1971), 31. More recently, Frederic Spotts has explored some of these issues in what he calls, "the grand paradox," in Frederic Spotts, *Hitler and the Power of Aesthetics* (Woodstock and New York: Overlook Press, 2003), 29. See also Robert Jan van Pelt, "Bearers of Culture, Harbingers of Destruction: The Myth of the Germans in the East," in *Art, Culture, and Media Under the Third Reich*, ed. Richard Etlin (Chicago: University of Chicago Press, 2002), 98–135.

66. Guido Fackler, "'We all feel this music is infernal…'; Music on Command at Auschwitz," in *The Last Expression: Art and Auschwitz*, ed. David Mickenberg, Corinne Granof, and Peter Hayes (Evanston, IL: Northwestern University Press, 2003), 114–125.

67. See, for example, Sabine Weissler, *Design in Deutschland: 1933-1945* (Giessen: Anabas-Verlag, 1990).

68. For an elaboration of these points, see Jonathan Petropoulos, *Art as Politics in the Third Reich* (Chapel Hill: University of North Carolina Press, 1996).

69. Walter Benjamin, "The Work of Art in the Age of Mechanical Reproduction," in *Illuminations: Essays and Reflections*, ed. Hannah Arendt (New York: Schocken Books, 1969), 241. See also the reflections on Benjamin and National Socialist cultural policy in Otto Karl Werckmeister, "Hitler the Artist," *Critical Inquiry* 23 (winter 1997): 270–297.

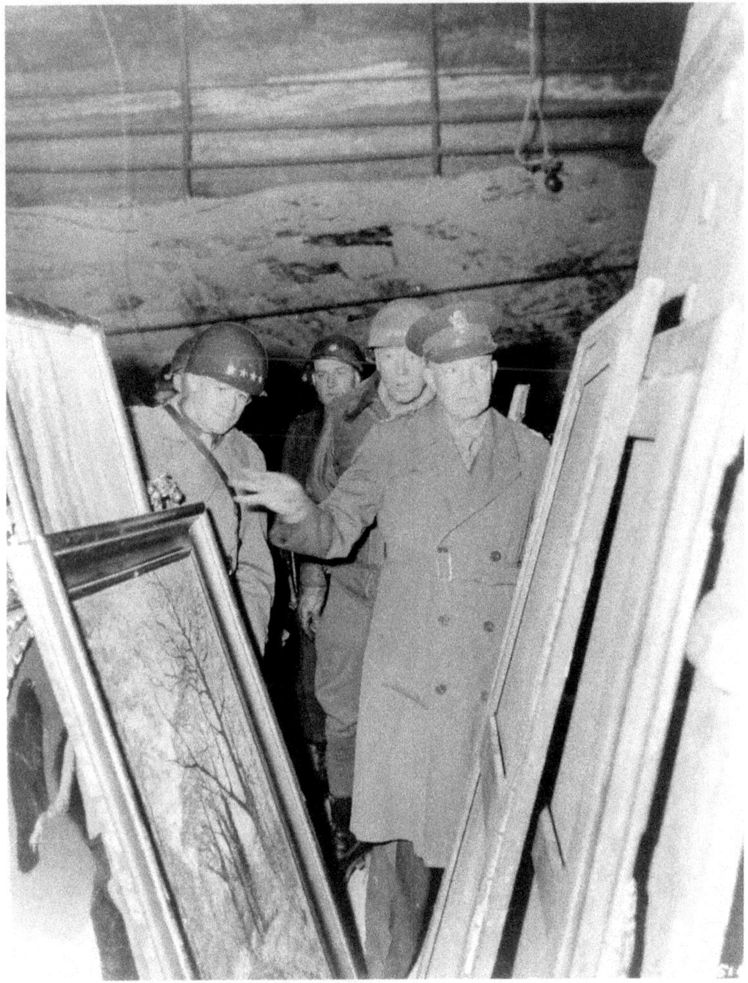

FIGURE 6.1. General Dwight D. Eisenhower, accompanied by General Omar Bradley and General George S. Patton, inspecting stolen art treasures in the Merkers salt mine, where they were stored by the German government
12 April 1945
Source: The National Archives and Records Administration, via the United States Holocaust Memorial Museum

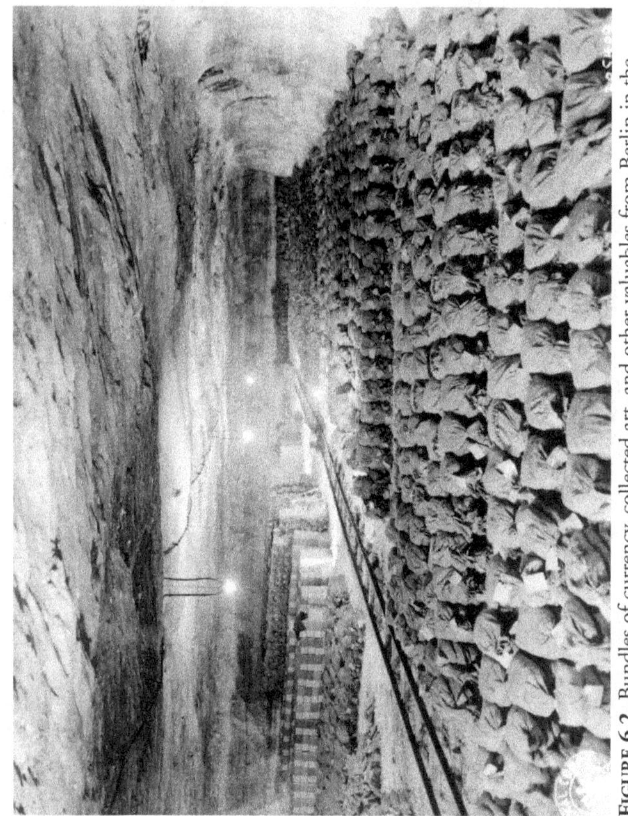

FIGURE 6.2. Bundles of currency, collected art, and other valuables from Berlin in the Merkers salt mine where they were stored by the German government 15 April 1945
Source: The National Archives and Records Administration, via the United States Holocaust Memorial Museum

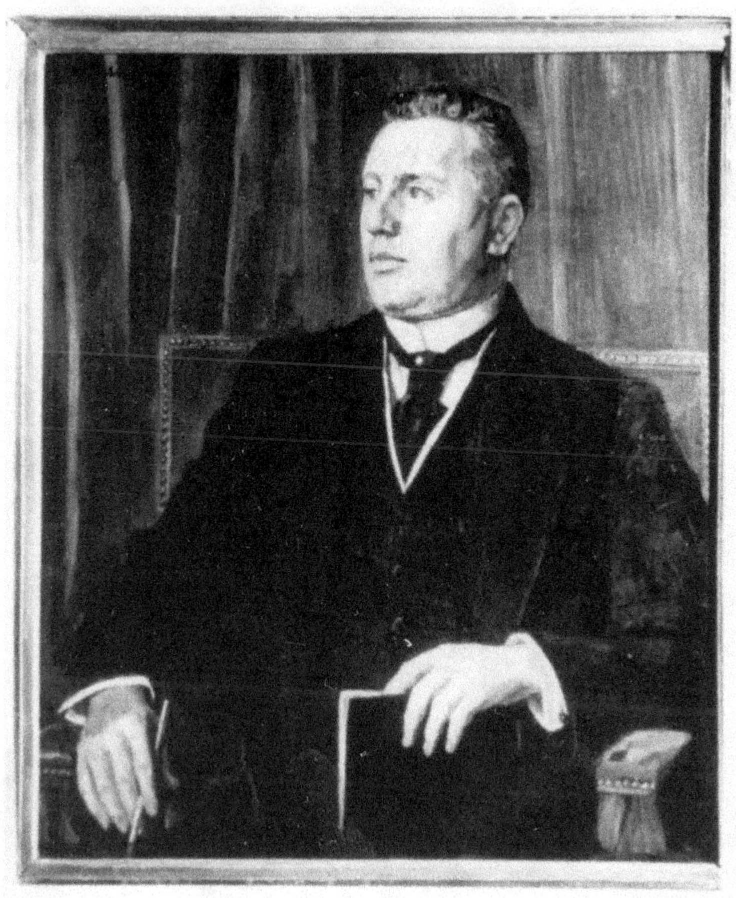

FIGURE 6.3. Painting of Karl Haberstock by Wilhelm Trübner
1914
Source: Städtische Kunstsammlung Augsburg

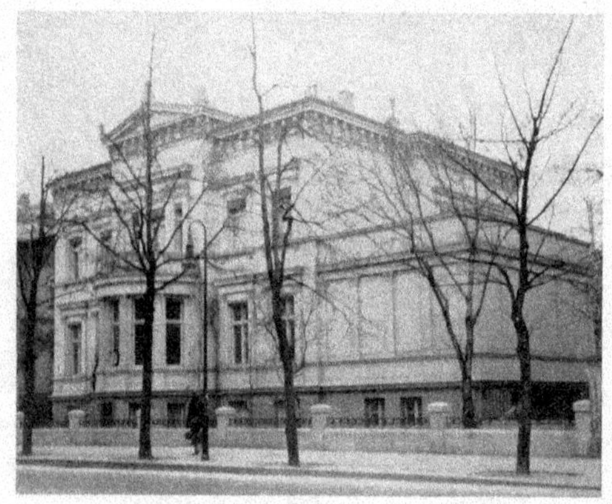

FIGURE 6.4. Photograph of the Karl Haberstock Gallery in Berlin 1940
Source: Die Kunst im Deutschen Reich (Berlin: Zentralverlag der NSDAP, June 1940)

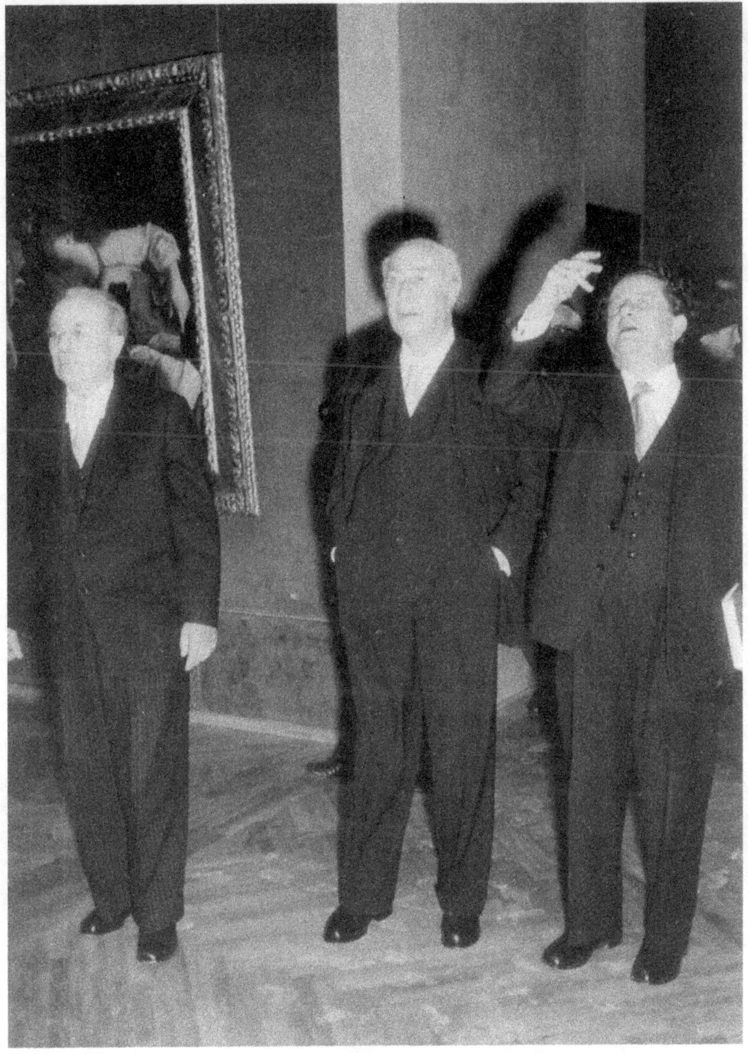

FIGURE 6.5. Premier Wilhelm Hoegner, Federal President Theodor Heuss, and General Director Ernst Buchner at the reopening of the Alte Pinakothek in Munich 7 June 1957
Source: Bayerische Staatsgemäldesammlungen, Munich

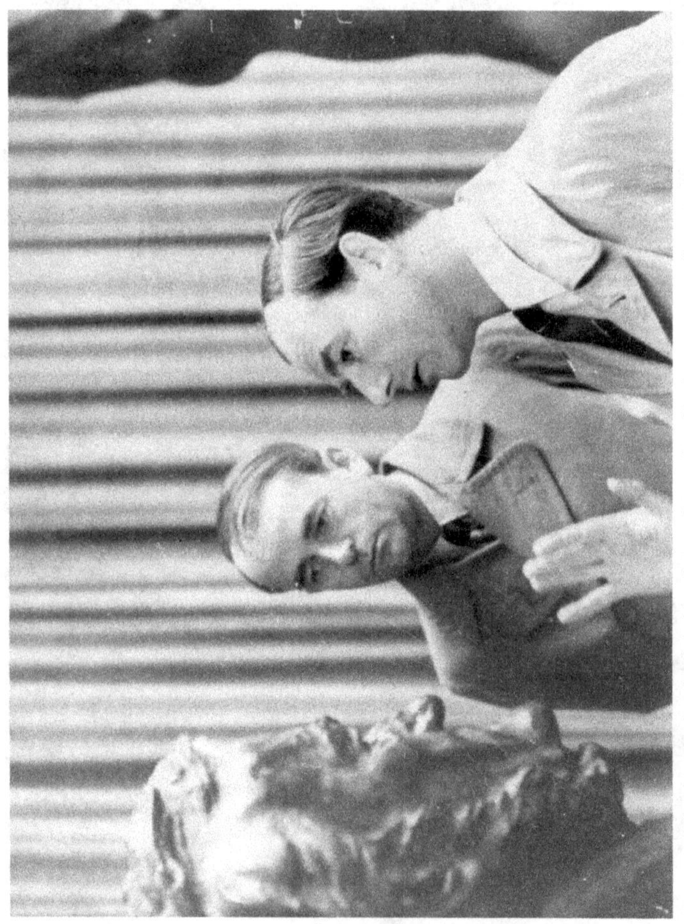

FIGURE 6.6. Arno Breker (right) describing a bust of Richard Wagner to Albert Speer   ca. 1941
Source: Bundesarchiv, Berlin

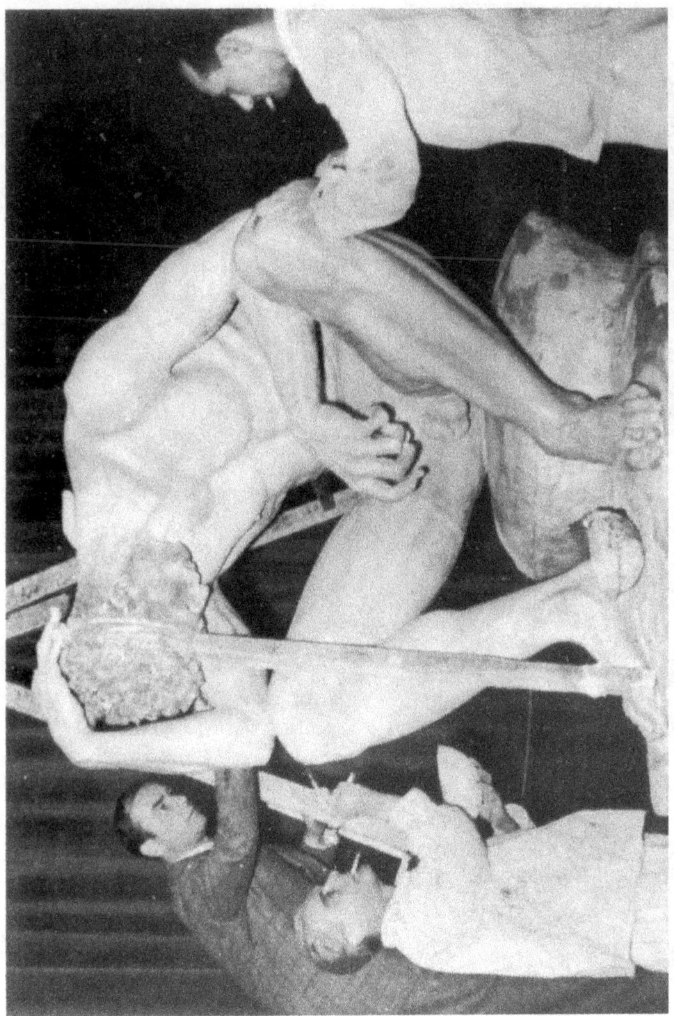

FIGURE **6.7.** Arno Breker (top left) preparing a sculpture for an exhibition in Paris   1942
Source: Bayerisches Hauptstaatsarchiv, Munich

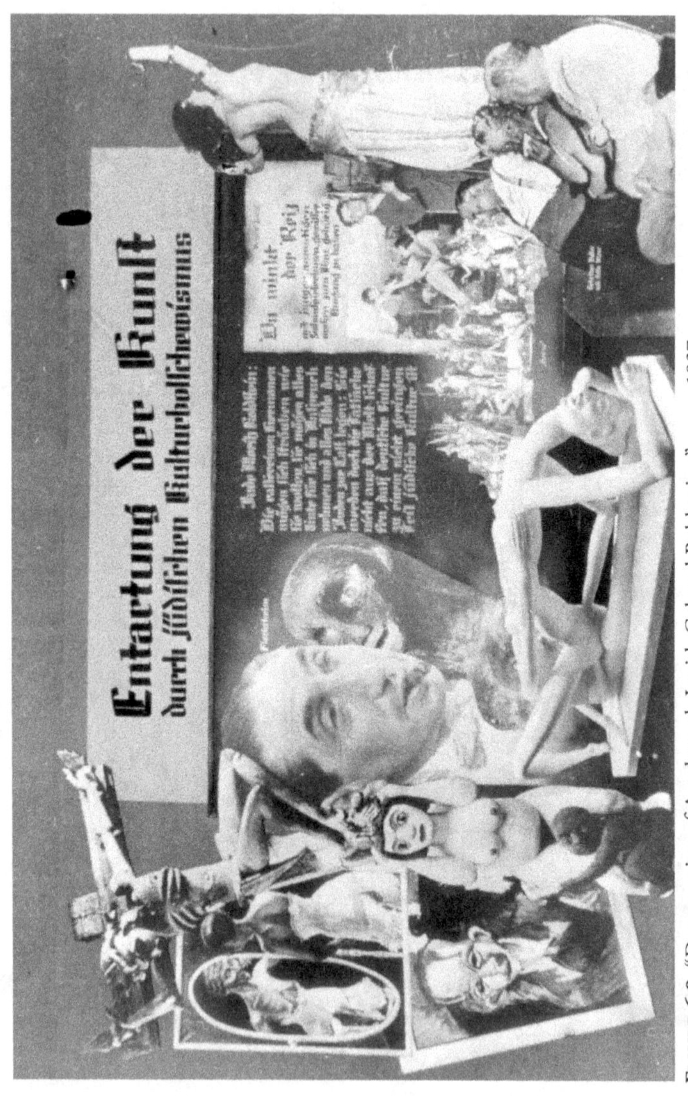

Figure 6.8. "Degeneration of Art through Jewish Cultural Bolshevism"   1937
Source: Bildarchiv-Österreichisches Institut für Zeitgeschichte, Vienna

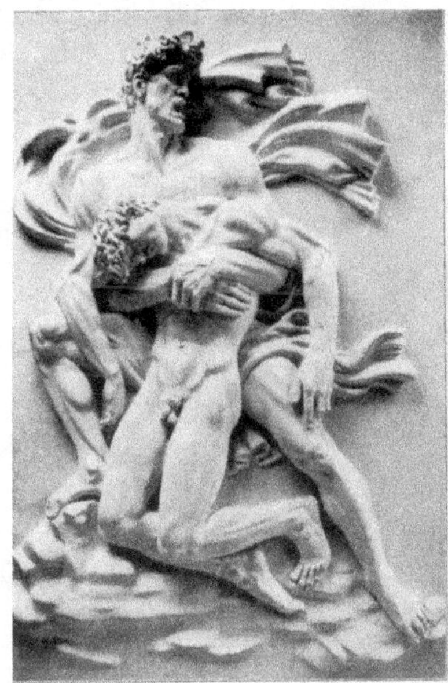
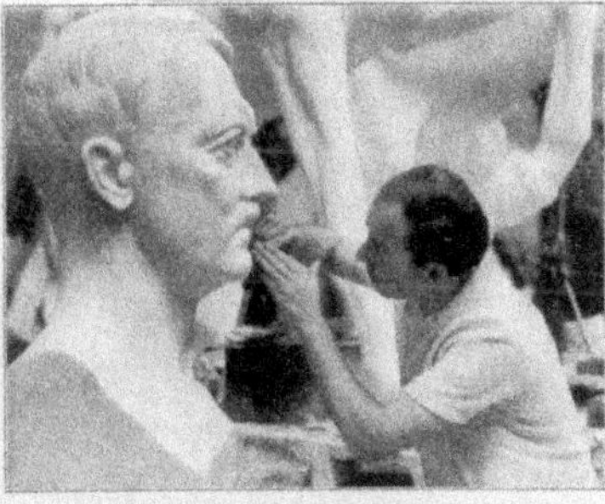

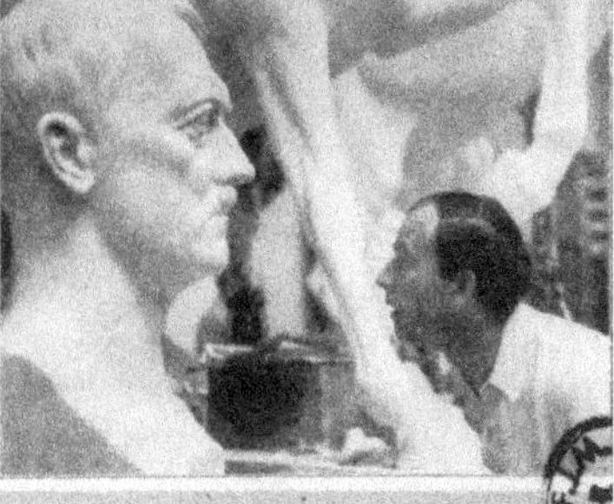

FIGURE 6.9. "'Eternal German Art,' Arno Breker on his 40th Birthday"
1940
Source: Bayerisches Hauptstaatsarchiv, Munich

LETTER FROM WILHELM FURTWÄNGLER TO JOSEPH GOEBBELS

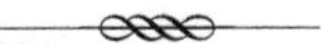

12 April 1933

Dear Reich Minister,

In view of my work over many years with the German public and my inner bond with German music I take liberty of drawing your attention to events within the world of music which in my opinion need not necessarily follow from the restoration of our national dignity which we all welcome with joy and gratitude. My feelings in this are purely those of an artist. The function of art and artists is to bring together, not to separate. In the final analysis, I recognize only one line of division—that between good and bad art. But while the line of division between Jews and non-Jews is being drawn with a relentless, even a doctrinaire, sharpness, even where the political attitude of the person concerned gives no grounds for complaint, the other line of division, extremely important, if not decisive, in the long run—that between good and bad—is being far too much neglected.

Musical life today, weakened anyway by the world crisis, radio, etc., cannot take any more experiments. One cannot fix the quota for music as with other things necessary for life like potatoes and bread. If nothing is offered in concerts, nobody goes to them. So that for music the question of quality is not simply an idealistic one, but a question of life and death. If the fight against Jews is mainly directed against those artists who, lacking roots themselves and being destructive, try to achieve an effect through kitsch, dry virtuosity and similar things, then this is quite all right. The fight against them and the spirit they embody cannot be pursued emphatically and consistently enough. But if this fight is directed against *real* artists as well, this will not be in the interests of cultural life, particularly because artists anywhere are much too rare for any country to be able to dispense with their work without loss to culture.

It should therefore be stated clearly that men like Walter, Klemperer, Reinhardt, etc. must be allowed in future to express their art in Germany.

Once again, then, let our fight be directed against the rootless, subversive, leveling, *destructive* spirit, but not against the real artist who is always creative and therefore constructive, however one may judge his art.

In this sense I appeal to you in the name of German art to prevent things from happening which it may not be possible to put right again.

Very respectfully yours,
[signed] WILHELM FURTWÄNGLER

Source: J. Noakes and G. Pridham, eds., *Nazism, 1919-1945*, vol. 2: *State, Economy and Society, 1933-1939* (Exeter: University of Exeter, 1984), 407.

LAW FOR THE ESTABLISHMENT OF A PROVISIONAL CHAMBER OF FILM

14 July 1933

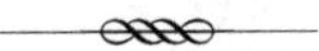

The government of the Reich has decreed the following law, herewith announced:

§ 1. With the goal of standardizing the film industry, a provisional Chamber of Film based in Berlin is hereby established as a corporation under public law.

§ 2. It is the responsibility of the provisional Chamber of Film to promote the German film industry within the framework of the national economy, to represent the interests of the individual groups within this unit as well as in the wider realm of Reich, states, and counties (or county units), as well as bring about a just equilibrium in the working lives of those in the profession.

§ 3. Membership in the Chamber of Film is required for all employers who professionally, or as non-profit organizations, produce, sell, or show to the public films, or who, as film-makers, collaborate in the production of films. Membership can be denied or a member excluded from the Chamber of Film only when evidence exists that the applicant does not possess the required reliability to practice filmmaking.

Whoever maintains a studio (or atelier) for the making of films or for the processing of films (copying amenities), or possesses copyrights or patents in the area of filmmaking is considered a film producer.

Production managers, directors, composers, writers, conductors, musicians, cameramen, architects, film and sound technicians, leading actors, supporting cast members, extras, supernumeraries, and the like are all considered to be filmmakers.

§ 4. The provisional Chamber of Film has a board, which consists of three members. The chair and deputy chair are viewed as the legal representatives of the Chamber of Film.

The board is constituted by the Reich Minister for Public Enlightenment and Propaganda. The Reich Minister for Public Enlightenment and Propaganda and the Reich Minister of Trade and Commerce each appoints a representative to the board.

The board conducts the daily business of the Chamber of Film.

§ 5. In an advisory capacity to the board is an administrative council, to which the various groups within the film industry appoint one or more members.

§ 6. The bylaws of the Chamber of Film require the approval of the Reich Minister for Public Enlightenment and Propaganda; the same applies for the rules of the associations connected to the Chamber of Film.

§ 7. The Reich Minister for Public Enlightenment and Propaganda is authorized to issue statutory orders and general administrative decrees (possibly of a supplementary nature) for the purpose of carrying out this law.

Berlin
14 July 1933

Reich Chancellor
Adolf Hitler

Reich Minister for Public Enlightenment and Propaganda
Dr. Goebbels

Source: *Reichsgesetzblatt*, 1, No. 82 (Berlin: Reichsverlagsamt, 1933–1938): 483–484. Translated by David Scrase, University of Vermont.

THE REICH CHAMBER OF CULTURE LAW

22 September 1933

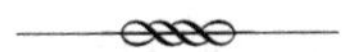

The Reich Government has passed the following law, which is announced herewith:

§ 1. The Reich Minister for Public Enlightenment and Propaganda is commissioned and empowered to combine the members of the professional groups in his area of responsibility in corporations under public law.

§ 2. In accordance with § 1 the following entities will be established:

1. a Reich Chamber of Literature
2. a Reich Chamber of the Press
3. a Reich Chamber of Broadcasting
4. a Reich Chamber of Theater
5. a Reich Chamber of Music
6. a Reich Chamber of the Visual Arts

§ 3. In establishing the chambers listed in § 2 the regulations are to be applied that were decreed in the law for the establishment of a provisional Chamber of Film of 14 July 1933 (RGBI. I. p. 483) together with the regulations to carry out this law.

§ 4. The establishment of the chambers is to follow the guidelines for structuring the professions that were passed by the Reich government.

§ 5. The corporations listed in § 2 are, together with the provisional Chamber of Film, which is to be designated the Reich Chamber of Film, to be incorporated in the Reich Chamber of Culture. The Reich

Chamber of Culture is under the supervision of the Reich Minister for Public Enlightenment and Propaganda. Its headquarters are to be in Berlin.

§ 6. The Reich Minister for Public Enlightenment and Propaganda and the Reich Minister for Trade and Commerce are authorized to work together to bring trade regulations into alignment with the regulations of this law.

§ 7. The Reich Minister for Public Enlightenment and Propaganda is authorized to enact legal decrees and general administrative guidelines, possibly of a supplementary nature, in order to implement this law. The legal decrees and general administrative guidelines, which touch upon the financial or commercial interests of the Reich, require the approval of the Reich Minister of Finance or the Reich Minister of Trade and Commerce.

Berlin
22 September 1933

Reich Chancellor
Adolf Hitler

Reich Minister for Public Enlightenment and Propaganda
Dr. Goebbels

Source: Reichsgesetzblatt, 1, No. 105 (Berlin: Reichsverlagsamt, 1933–1938): 661–662.
Translated by David Scrase, University of Vermont.

First Decree for the Implementation of the Law for the Reich Chamber of Culture

1 November 1933

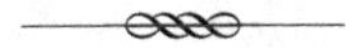

Based on § § 6 and 7 of the Law for the Reich Chamber of Culture of 22 September 1933 (RGB1.1, p. 661) the following decree is hereby drawn up:

I. Establishment of the Chamber

§ 1. With the coming into effect of this decree the following listed organizations will become corporations under public law with the subsequent appended titles:

1. the Reich Alliance of German Musicians, Inc.:
    Reich Chamber of Music
2. the Reich Alliance of the Visual Arts:
    Reich Chamber of Visual Arts
3. the Reich Chamber of Theater
    Reich Chamber of Theater
4. the Reich Association of German Writers, Inc.,
    Reich Chamber of Literature
5. the Reich Association of the German Press
    Reich Chamber of the Press
6. the National Socialist Chamber of Broadcasting, Inc.,
    Reich Chamber of Broadcasting

§ 2. The chambers listed in § 1 together with the Reich Chamber of Film make up a corporation under public law that bears the name Reich Chamber of Culture.

§ 3. It is the responsibility of the Reich Chamber of Culture to promote German culture responsibly for the people and the Reich through collaboration among the members of all the areas of creative activity under the leadership of the Reich Minister for Public Enlightenment and Propaganda, to regulate the economic and social concerns of the cultural professions, and to work to balance the aims and strivings of the member groups.

The Reich Minister for Public Enlightenment and Propaganda can determine special tasks, which may be/are assigned to the Reich Chamber of Culture and its individual subgroups. § 7, section 2 of the new law remains unaffected.

II. Membership of the Chamber

§ 4. Whoever engages in the creation, reproduction, the intellectual or technical processing, the promotion, conservation, the direct sale or mediated sale of cultural assets, must be a member of the individual chamber relevant to the cultural activity.

Promotion includes the production and sale of technical circulation.

§ 5. For the purposes of this decree, cultural assets are:

1.   all artistic creations or performance achievements whenever they are transmitted to the public,
2.   all other artistic creations or performances, when transmitted to the public through print, film, or radio.

§ 6. For those engaged in cultural endeavors as set forth in § 4, it is irrelevant whether the activity is

a)   practiced professionally or for charity,
b)   conducted by individuals, through societies, clubs, or private foundations, through public corporations or public organizations,
c)   practiced by Reich citizens or foreigners,
d)   carried out by employers or persons in an employer capacity unless the activity involved is purely mercantile, office-connected, technical or mechanical.

§ 7. For the purposes of this decree, any type of reproduction is to be considered equivalent to print according to § 2. section 2 of the Law for Editors.

§ 8. The production of draft products is not considered to be the processing of cultural assets in the sense of this decree.

§ 9. The president of each individual chamber can determine that certain cases of insignificant or occasional exercise of an activity listed in § 4 do not justify membership in that chamber.

§ 10. Acceptance into a particular chamber can be denied or a member excluded whenever there are facts that demonstrate that the person in question does not possess the necessary reliability and aptitude to practice the activity.

III. Chamber Constitution

§ 11. The Reich Minister for Public Enlightenment and Propaganda is the president of the Reich Chamber of Culture. He appoints one or more deputies or business managers. The presidents of the individual chambers constitute a board of the Reich Chamber of Culture. The representatives of the president of the Reich Chamber of Culture along with the business manager of the Reich Chamber of Culture are ex officio members of the Reich Chamber of Culture with access to its deliberations.

The legal representative of the Reich Chamber of Culture is the president, or his deputy.

§ 12. A Reich Cultural Senate may be established within the Reich Chamber of Culture. The president may appoint as members of the senate outstanding personalities who have rendered valuable service to the people and to culture.

§ 13. The president of the Reich Chamber of Culture appoints a president to each individual chamber. A presidential council of minimally two members is at the president's disposal. The members of this presidential senate are also appointed by the president of the Reich Chamber of Culture. The president appoints one or more members of the presidential council as representatives or business managers.

The legal representation of the individual chambers is the president, or, if prevented from serving in that capacity, his deputy.

§ 14. The presidents of the individual chambers have at their disposal an advisory board, which consists of members of the individual groups comprising each chamber.

The advisory board is convened by the president. It is to have a voice in important questions. It may petition a president. The members of the advisory board are appointed and dismissed by the president.

§ 15. The individual chambers are subdivided into the subject associations or units for the areas of activity they represent. By belonging to one of the subject associations represented in the chamber the members are *ipso facto* members of the individual chamber and the Reich Chamber of Culture.

Direct membership in an individual chamber is possible only when there is no appropriate subject association. In such cases the president of the individual chamber makes the decision to accept the application or not. The president may demand that the persons who have to belong to the chamber join together and form a subject association or branch unit.

Direct membership in the Reich Chamber of Culture is not possible.

§ 16. The president of the individual chamber makes the decision regarding the subject association's application to join the chamber. He must admit it to membership if

a)   the prerequisite in § 4 for the members of the association is met
b)   the statutes correspond to the regulation in § 20
c)   the association is, in the judgment of the president, able to fulfill the duties expected of it.

§ 17. If admittance is refused, the subject association may appeal to the president of the Reich Chamber of Culture. The president of the Reich Chamber of Culture must furthermore decide to accept the application or not whenever there is a split decision regarding admittance among the membership of the individual chamber.

§ 18. Whoever practices an activity as outlined in § 4 and does not fall into the situation as outlined in § 9 has the right to apply for membership in the relevant subject association and can, if not accepted, appeal to the president of the relevant chamber. Admittance can be refused only if § 10 applies.

§ 19. The president of the Reich Chamber of Culture formulates the bylaws of the Reich Chamber of Culture. The president of each individual chamber formulates the bylaws of each individual chamber, which require the approval of the president of the Reich Chamber of Culture.

§ 20. Subject associations must bring their bylaws into alignment with the Law for the Reich Chamber of Culture, with its implementation decrees, and with the bylaws of the chamber. Each set of bylaws needs the approval of the president of each individual chamber. The president of the individual chamber can demand the appointment and dismissal of the chairs and business managers of the subject associations or of their regional associations.

§ 21. The president of the Reich Chamber of Culture rules upon cases of disagreement among the presidents of any of the individual chambers. He can take on the responsibility for decisions in matters of interest common to several chambers even when there is no disagreement between them.

§ 22. The president of the Reich Chamber of Culture can reverse or dismiss decisions of the individual chambers and take over the matter under consideration and make his own decision.

§ 23. The president of the Reich Chamber of Culture prepares the budget for the Reich Chamber of Culture.

The presidents of the individual chambers prepare the budgets for each individual chamber, which have to be approved by the president of the Reich Chamber of Culture.

§ 24. All adjunct and full members of the chambers are subject to membership dues. The determinations regarding the imposition of dues are to be laid before the Reich Minister for Public Enlightenment and Propaganda, who will consult with the Reich Minister of Finance according to § 7 section 2 of the law.

Whoever is a member of more than one chamber is committed to a fee that is no higher than the highest fee among those requested by the chambers he is a member of.

The costs of the Reich Chamber of Culture are to be split among the individual chambers.

IV. Responsibilities of the Chamber

§ 25. The Reich Chamber of Culture and the individual chambers may determine the conditions for the enterprise, for the establishment and completion of undertakings in the area of their jurisdiction, and may make decisions concerning important questions within this area, especially concerning the manner and formulation of contracts with the organizations they encompass. These decrees may not violate aspects of international law.

Decisions according to section I in the areas of the book trade, music, art, and radio commerce require the approval of the Reich Minister for Public Enlightenment and Propaganda and the Reich Minister of Trade and Commerce.

§ 26. Measures taken in accordance with § 25 preclude any compensation for expropriation.

§ 27. Communication between the Reich Chamber of Culture and the individual chambers and the Reich government may take place only through the Reich Minister for Public Enlightenment and Propaganda.

§ 28. The presidents of the individual chambers may levy fines against anyone

1. who, contrary to § 4 of this decree is not a member of the chamber but who practices one of the activities in its purview
2. who, as a member of the chamber or by virtue of his responsibilities in a subject association, contravenes the decrees of the chamber
3. who, as a member of the chamber, or by virtue of his responsibilities in a subject association, makes false statements.

§ 29. Upon request the police authorities are required to enforce § 4 of this decree as well as the decrees of the individual chambers according to § 25. Courts and administrative offices are required to provide legal and management help to the Reich Chamber of Culture and its individual chambers.

§ 30. Membership dues for the chambers are collected in the same fashion as state taxes. Fines of the chambers are collected according to regulations governing the levying of administrative fines.

V. Final Determinations

§ 31. The regulations of the Law for the Establishment of a Provisional Chamber of Film of 14 July 1933 (RGB1.1, p. 483) and the Decree Concerning the Establishment of a Provisional Chamber of Film of 22 July 1922 (RGB1.1, p. 531) remain unaffected as long as they do not contravene the determinations of this decree.

§ 32. The regulations of §§ 1 sections 1, 32, 33a, 33b, 35b, 43, 49, 55–63, and of the titles VI and VIa of the trading regulations are not applicable whenever they contravene the determinations of the Law for the Reich Chamber of Culture, the determinations of this decree, or the decrees passed in relation to § 25.

§ 33. This decree will come into force on a date to be determined by the Reich Minister for Public Enlightenment and Propaganda.

Berlin, 1 November 1933
Reich Minister for Public Enlightenment and Propaganda
Dr. Goebbels

Reich Minister for Trade and Commerce
Dr. Schmitt

Source: Reichsgesetzblatt, 1, No. 123 (Berlin: Reichsverlagsamt, 1933–1938): 797–800.
Translated by David Scrase, University of Vermont.

ACTIVITIES OF THE CULTURAL ASSOCIATION OF GERMAN JEWS [JEWISH CULTURAL LEAGUE]

Frankfurter Israelitisches Gemeindeblatt, April 1934

The Cultural Association of German Jews needs you!

The need for the work of the Cultural Association has already been proved in Berlin. Cologne and Munich followed suit with plans and work. Frankfurt on Main, with its significant Jewish tradition and its special Jewish tasks, must also give a lead in these efforts. We have received authority from the State Commissioner for the independent organization of artistic and creative work. Like the centers of the Cultural Association in the main cities, so Frankfurt will be the starting-point for the work done in the District Rhein-Main. The smaller and smallest Jewish communities in cities and the countryside will join in actively and passively.

The creative artists appeal to you! Our program includes music, theater, lectures and art.

Finding work for members of artistic and crafts professions.

Training at all levels for Jewish musicians, painters and sculptors. There is a task here for the Youth Associations that is appropriate to our times.

The aim of our work is the cooperation of all those who take part, actively or passively, in Jewish cultural life, both artists and audience, and this can be achieved only if all Jewish organizations play their part. Every individual is jointly responsible and will decide with us on the success of our work.

Our appeal is addressed to all! We all need contact with elation, consolation, joy!

Therefore: Register as a member of the Cultural Association of German Jews, Frankfurt on Main.

Source: Yitzhak Arad, Israel Gutman, and Abraham Margaliot, eds., *Documents on the Holocaust: Selected Sources on the Destruction of the Jews of Germany and Austria, Poland, and the Soviet Union,* trans. Lea Ben Dor, 8th ed. (Lincoln and London: University of Nebraska Press, and Yad Vashem, Jerusalem, 1999), 68.

The German Authorities and the Cultural Association of German Jews [Jewish Cultural League]

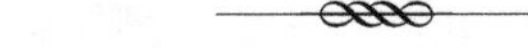

19 June 1934

Hans Hinkel
Staatskommissar
NSDAP [Nazi Party] *Gau* Hessen-Nassau
District Office, Frankfurt am Main

In reply to your inquiry of June 6, 1934, I wish to state that, for a variety of reasons, it is to be permitted for the Jews to join together in an Organization, the Cultural Association of German Jews (*Kulturbund deutscher Juden*), which will be supervised by the State Police and other Party organizations. The main reasons for this [permission], apart from intentions connected with foreign policy, is the easier supervision and the concentration of the intellectual-artistic Jews in an organization where Jews will "make art" only for Jews. Permission has been given generally for the State of Prussia, because the Secret State Police, which is mainly responsible for the supervision, gave its express approval. The existence of this Jewish organization will depend on its observance of various conditions. One of these conditions is that the gatherings of the Association will not be advertised publicly. Immediately on receipt of your communication I was in touch with Dr. Singer, the head of the local central office of the Association, with the urgent request that he inform the associated organizations and responsible colleagues that in future publicly exhibited posters or announcements in shops would no longer be tolerated and would endanger the whole work of the Association.

Heil Hitler!

Source: Yitzhak Arad, Israel Gutman, and Abraham Margaliot, eds., *Documents on the Holocaust: Selected Sources on the Destruction of the Jews of Germany and Austria, Poland, and the Soviet Union*, trans. Lea Ben Dor, 8th ed. (Lincoln and London: University of Nebraska Press, and Yad Vashem, Jerusalem, 1999), 67.

TEN PRINCIPLES FOR THE CREATION OF GERMAN MUSIC

Joseph Goebbels

In his significant cultural-political speech on the occasion of the Reich Music Days in Düsseldorf, Reichsminister Dr. Goebbels stated, among other things, the following:

This festival of music is, for the first time, a review of musical culture in our time. It gives an account of what we have accomplished and sets forth the goals both for the immediate future and for the foreseeable future. May the fame of Germany as the nation of music be once again revealed and substantiated here on this occasion. And, above all, may the principles that have since time immemorial been the source and the driving force behind our German music again be set forth and recognized. They are:

1. The essence of music does not lie in a program or in theory, in experimentation or in structure. It lies in melody. Melody as such elevates the heart and revives the spirits; for this reason it is not trite or reprehensible because it is sung by the people on account of the ease with which it can be memorized.

2. Not all music is accessible to everyone. For this reason, the kind of popular music that appeals to a wide audience is to be preferred. This is especially so in an epoch in which the nation's leaders are obliged to provide relaxation, entertainment, and refreshment for its people, who are confronted with today's deep anxieties.

3. Like every other art form, music has its origins in the mysterious and deep powers that are rooted in the people. It can, accordingly, be shaped and formed in a way appropriate to the people's needs

and to their powerful drive to make music only by those descendents who are steeped in their nation's heritage. Judaism and German music are opposites that, by their very nature, stand in stark contradiction to one another. The struggle against Judaism in German music, which Richard Wagner, alone and without any help or support, once took up, is for this reason still our great task today. This battle is no longer the battle of a knowledgeable genius, standing alone, but one that is being fought by a unified people.

4. Music is the most sensual of the arts and for this reason appeals more to the heart and the emotions than to the intellect. But where does the heart of a nation beat more strongly than in the masses, where the heart of a nation is truly at home? It is therefore the unavoidable duty of our musical leaders to let the people share in the treasures of German music.

5. For the musical person, to be unmusical is more or less like being blind or deaf. Thank God that he graciously created music for us to hear, experience, and passionately love.

6. Music is the art form that moves the human spirit most; it has the power to soothe pain and to turn mere happiness into ecstasy.

7. If melody is at the source of music, then it follows that a music for the people may not be limited to pastorales or chorales. Music must always return to lively melody as the root of its being.

8. Nowhere are the treasures of the past so richly and inexhaustibly spread out as in the area of music. To hold them up and give them to the people is our most important and rewarding task.

9. The language of musical tones is sometimes more effective than the language of words. For this reason, the great masters of the past represent the true majesty of our people and are deserving of reverence and respect.

10. And as children of our people they are the true monarchs of our people by God's grace and are destined to receive the fame and honor of our nation and to multiply.

Berlin. 28 May 1938

Reichsminister for Public
Enlightenment and Propaganda
Dr. Goebbels

Source: Amtliche Mitteilungen der Reichsmusikkammer 5, No. 11, Berlin (1938). Translated by David Scrase, University of Vermont.

FROM HITLER'S "SPEECH ON CULTURE" (*KULTURREDE*)

Nuremberg Party Congress, 5-12 September 1938

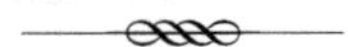

Music as absolute art behaves toward us according to unknown laws. At this stage we do not yet know precisely what the reasons are for melodious sound on the one hand or for dissonance on the other. It is, however, certain that music is most able to capture the emotions and feelings that move our spirit, and that it is least qualified to satisfy our intellect. For this reason it often happens that the intellect and an ear for music are not found in the same body. In order to give utterance to its thoughts the intellect makes use of language. A world of feelings and moods that cannot be easily captured in language can be revealed through music. Music can accordingly exist without recourse to language; it can of course contribute to a heightening of the impression of certain language formulations through the emotional elements it brings with it. The more music leads to pure illustration, the more important it is that the plot be brought forth and made visual. The natural ability of the great artist will contribute an additional all-pervading mood and therefore also an effect above and beyond the mere plot that can be attained only through music. This kind of art, whose goal is to portray a basic, and therefore general, character as emotion, rose to a peak in the works of the great Bayreuth master. But apart from him a number of divinely gifted musicians have succeeded in procuring for certain dramatic works a striking fundamental value in their music. The great symphonic composers strive for more general moods, but likewise need certain guidelines that they clothe in language as an introduction for the listener.

It is, however, totally impossible to express a worldview or intellectual matters musically. With the aid of music or, better, studies of earlier times, a picture of a historical age can be produced; it is, however, impossible to try to interpret or even expand on intellectual insights or political processes musically. For this reason there is neither a musical history of the party nor a musical philosophy; likewise there is no musical illustration or interpretation of philosophical ideas, for these purposes are exclusively the domain of language. Indeed, it is the task of our poets and thinkers to have such command of language that they not only reproduce clearly and graphically those ideas and insights that float before them, thereby acting as a mediator to their fellow humans, but also elevate them to a work of art by virtue of their command of the tonal elements that lie in language. We Germans can count ourselves lucky that we have at our disposal a language that is both beautiful and rich, although to be sure, difficult. To learn how to master it is a wonderful task and an ability to use it is likewise an art. To express in language the thoughts of our worldview must be possible and is indeed possible. To portray these thoughts musically is neither possible nor necessary. It is therefore nonsense to think that in the musical introduction to, say, a congress, you must attempt to show the history of the party or, even, that you are able to do so. In such cases, the accompanying text has to prevail and clarify to the audience the thoughts of the composer. This is, however, as has already been emphasized, not at all necessary. What is necessary is to provide the general rules for the development and guidance of our nation's life in the area of music. It is not necessary to excite the astonishment of the stunned audience through the technically brilliant confusion of sounds but to captivate its heart through the awakening perception and total beauty of the sounds. It is not the intellectual understanding that is the force behind our musicians but an overflowing musical genius. If the basic proverb is ever to apply, "he whose heart is full runneth over at the mouth," that is to say, whenever one is so excited about something that one cannot stop talking about it, it is here. In other words, whoever is so imbued with or overcome by the feeling of the greatness of beauty or by the pain or the suffering of an age and its people, can with God's help open up what is within through sound. The technical ability is, as always, the obvious prerequisite for the revelation of an inner predisposition.

I consider it of paramount importance that precisely our musicians take this realization to heart. The last century brought forth numerous musical geniuses from our people. I have attempted to explain in earlier speeches the reasons for the fading of such figures. But it would be bad if National Socialism were, on the one hand, to defeat the spirit of an age that caused our musical creativity to wane, while, on the other hand, leading music onto the wrong track because of a false objective. It would be even worse were it to lead music somewhere just as bad as the general confusion that lies behind us.

Whether we are dealing with architecture or with music, with sculpture or painting, there is one thing that one should fundamentally never ignore: all true art must leave the mark of beauty on all its works, because the ideal for all of us must consist in the cultivation of the healthy. All that is healthy, however, is right and natural, and all that is right and natural is beautiful.

Source: Michael Walter, *Hitler in der Oper: Deutsches Musikleben, 1919-1945* (Stuttgart: J.B. Metzler, 1995), 195–197. Translated by David Scrase, University of Vermont.

WHAT ARE PEOPLE READING? A QUESTIONNAIRE IN BERLIN BOOK STORES

Christian Bock

The enquiry, the results of which are reproduced here, took place only in Greater Berlin. From the beginning the intention was not to produce complete figures; instead, a sample survey was carried out. The result is accordingly typical in individual cases, but not totally valid in general terms. (The survey could not otherwise have been limited to Greater Berlin.)

What are the best sellers?

In a bookstore adjacent to the Zoo railroad station, where two-thirds of the customers are those who simply drop in while regular customers comprise one-third, the following books were the ones most sold recently:

Céspedes: *Das andere Ufer*

Simpson: *Die Barrings*

Simpson: *Der Enkel*

Harsanji: *Ungarische Rhapsodie*

Harsanji: *Mit den Augen einer Frau*

Wiechert: *Das einfache Leben*

Gullvaag: *Es begann in einer Mittsommernacht*

Mungenast: *Der Zauberer Muzot*

Knittel: *Via Mala, Therese Etienne, Amadeus*

Philipp: *Scotland Yard*

Kluge: *Der Herr Kortüm*

Seidel: *Lennacker*

Caldwell: *Einst wird kommen der Tag*

Sales in this bookstore have increased by about 50 percent since the beginning of the war.

The increase in turnover in the book trade is clearly not to be attributed to regular buyers now buying more books; it is, rather, that new buyers (people, in other words, whose literature consumption in times of peace was so low that they could not be included in the statistics of regular book buyers) are now being added to the regulars. One might be forgiven for assuming that this would lead to a certain lowering in the quality of books in demand. It is quite astonishing that this is not the case. The demand is in every respect for good literature, and this is confirmed in all regions. Moreover the buyers are not stingy and pay a good price for their books. Expensive books are selling better than ever.

In a bookstore in Friedrichstrasse the following books were listed as most in demand (as in the above list, they are not in rank order):

Gritzbach: *Hermann Göring, Mensch und Werk* [sic]

Kuni Tremel-Eggert: *Bard* (novel)

Philipp: *Scotland Yard*

The Reich Press Chief Dietrich: *Auf den Strassen des Sieges*

Céspedes: *Das andere Ufer* (novel translated from the Italian)

Simpson: *Der Enkel*

Eugen Roth: *Ein Mensch*

Deutscher Geist (an anthology of literature from two centuries)

Emil Strauß: *Lebenstanz*

Günter Prien: *Mein Weg nach Scapa Flow*

Dr. Johanna Haarer: *Die deutsche Mutter und ihr erstes Kind*

Dibelius: *England*

Trevelyan: *Geschichte Englands*

Colonial literature

Books from series such as the Insel Library, Kröner Paperbacks, Dietrich Collection

The drop-ins of buyers at this bookstore comprise only about 40 percent. From a conversation with the owner, a number of remarkable facts emerged. War books about the last war are hardly ever in demand. But, yes, the interest in the present war is such a current and strongly political interest that, at this stage, people are asking almost exclusively for literature about England. Books about the war in France (and, of course, the campaign in Poland) are no longer selling at this point. To be sure, this interest will reappear, but as long as the battle against England continues, the interest in military and political events that have ended will remain weak.

Literature on England, on the other hand, from the standard works to the brochures, is still being bought. The bookstore in question is selling three times the number of books monthly it sold in peacetime. The increase varies in other bookstores from 50 percent to 300 percent.

In a Lending Library

Since a portion of the trade will involve books bought as gifts, it seemed appropriate to examine the same questions in a lending library, where those who are buying books intended for gifts or to be sent to servicemen at the front would be absent.

This lending library acquires all new publications immediately so there are no limiting factors that need to be taken into account. The most frequently borrowed books in the recent past are the following:

Simpson, *Die Barrings, Der Enkel*

Mungenast, *Der Zauberer Muzot*

Caldwell, *Einst wird kommen der Tag*

Boerner, *Das unwandelbare Herz*

Holzach, *Der goldene Rahmen*

Langenscheidt, *Königin der Meere*

Varé, *Der lachende Diplomat*

Prien, *Mein Weg nach Scapa Flow*

Here, too, more books are sought out and borrowed than earlier, and here, too, it has become obvious during the war that light reading is no longer in such demand. Overnight, the good book has been discovered.

Questionnaire

In a bookstore on Friedrichstrasse a questionnaire was displayed for several hours; the answers provided much that is of interest. Questions included whether the buyer was a man or a woman, and whether the book was purchased for the buyer as a gift for someone else or for someone in the military. A further question asked what led the buyer to choose that particular book, whether the buyer had heard or read about the book and come to the store to buy this specific work, or whether the decision had been made only after the buyer entered the store. Then there was the question as to whether the limited availability of other items because of the war had led to the decision to buy a book instead, or whether one would have bought the book no matter what.

Now, a questionnaire like this is somewhat rudimentary. Some buyers who bought Goethe's "Iphigenie," for example, did answer the question whether they had previously heard of this book with a "yes" and responded to the other question, whether they had made their decision while in the store, with a "no."

Sometimes a questionnaire had to be discarded for the purpose of our investigation: if it was a student buying Schiller's play *The Robbers*, or a dictionary, or if it was an office worker buying a "Duden" or some such reference work. A number of questionnaires that were inadequately filled out were also discarded. We ended up with 53 questionnaires.

Of the 53 book-buyers, 36 were men, and 17 were women. Twenty-seven books were bought as gifts (of these seven were to be sent to the battlefield); 26 of the purchasers bought the books for themselves.

Of the 53 buyers, 43 came in order to buy a specific title. A mere 10 made their decision only after entering the store. Only 6 answered the last question by saying they would not have bought a book but something else, had this possibility not been limited because of the war. In these cases the purchase was intended as a gift.

The books purchased were all of literary value.

Of course, this, too, was only a random survey, and the result has no general validity. The questionnaire was conducted in mid-November.

Debit and Credit

This bookstore on Alexanderplatz looks so typical—a bookstore like any other—but everything changes as soon as one is on the second floor and, flanked by the floor-to-ceiling shelves filled with books, enters the office of the owner as if through a portal. Suddenly you are standing in a tiny room totally lacking in all modern office splendor. Desk, bookcase, chairs—they are, to be sure, all there, but just as they stood there 20 years ago, when the bookstore was founded—a wonderful, homely permanence, as if taken out of [Gustav] Freytag's novel "Debit and Credit." Even the telephone seems to cower in deference.

The owner talks about how they decided 20 years ago, after reading Hamsun, to order 2,000 copies—at a time when Hamsun was still relatively unknown. It was a huge risk. Of course, a bookseller is not obliged to undergo such risks. He can let the opportunity slip, or he can wait to see whether Mr. Hamsun achieves success and then place an order. But if he wants more than assured business success he will risk all his cash for a book that impresses him, with the same idealism as the publisher.

Of the businesses that risk the greatest losses the book trade is in second place. (There are good and convincing reasons why glass and porcelain are in first place.)

Up here in this tiny room proofs of many a book have been read, and the three people who pronounce their verdicts—the owner, his son, and the business manager—have, with more idealism than realism, run many a risk. The owner speaks highly of the business manager, who is today on the battlefield, as it was he who stood up for Hamsun back then, and he was right: Hamsun sold.

One might have expected that here on Alexanderplatz the best sellers would be totally different, but they are more or less the same as those in the west of Berlin or on Friedrichstrasse:

Goebbels, *Kampf um Berlin*

Tremmel-Eggert, *Bard*

Gritzbach, Hermann *Göring, Mensch und Werk* [sic]

Céspedes, *Das andere Ufer*

Philipp, *Einst wie jetzt*

Harsanji, *Ungarische Rhapsodie, Deutscher Geist*

Fried, *Männer der Weltwirtschaft*

Schenzinger, *Metall*

Winschuh, *Manner, Traditionen, Signale*

Kluge, *Der Herr Kortüm*

Knittel, *Therese Etienne*

Varé, *Der lachende Diplomat*

Prien, *Mein Weg nach Scapa Flow*

Source: Das Reich, 15 December 1940. Translated by David Scrase, University of Vermont.

Contributors

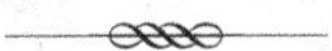

Jonathan Huener is Associate Professor of History at the University of Vermont. He is author of *Auschwitz, Poland, and the Politics of Commemoration, 1945-1979* (Ohio University Press, 2003), and coeditor with Francis R. Nicosia of *Medicine and Medical Ethics in Nazi Germany: Origins, Practices, Legacies* (Berghahn Books, 2002) and *Business and Industry in Nazi Germany* (Berghahn Books, 2004).

Michael H. Kater is Distinguished Research Professor Emeritus of History at York University, Toronto, and the author of numerous books on modern Germany. His latest is *Hitler Youth* (Harvard University Press, 2004; paper 2006). He is currently writing a biography of singer Lotte Lehmann (1888–1976).

Francis R. Nicosia is Professor of History at Saint Michael's College in Vermont. He is author of *The Third Reich and the Palestine Question* (University of Texas Press, 1985, Transaction Publishers, 2000) and coauthor with Donald Niewyk of *The Columbia Guide to the Holocaust* (Columbia University Press, 2000). He is also coeditor with Jonathan Huener of *Medicine and Medical Ethics in Nazi Germany: Origins, Practices, Legacies* (Berghahn Books, 2002) and *Business and Industry in Nazi Germany* (Berghahn Books, 2004).

Jonathan Petropoulos is the John V. Croul Professor of European History at Claremont McKenna College in Southern California, where he also serves as director of the Gould Center for Humanistic Studies and the Associate Director of the Center for the Study of the Holocaust, Genocide, and Human Rights. He is the author of *Art as Politics in the Third Reich* (University of North Carolina Press, 1996), and *The Faustian Bargain: The Art World in Nazi Germany* (Oxford University Press,

2000). Most recently, he published *Royals and the Reich: The Princes von Hessen in Nazi Germany* (Oxford University Press, 2006).

Pamela M. Potter is Professor of Music and German at the University of Wisconsin-Madison. She has written extensively on music and politics in twentieth-century Germany and is best known for her book *Most German of the Arts: Musicology and Society from the Weimar Republic to the End of Hitler's Reich* (Yale University Press, 1998, German ed.: Klett-Cotta, 2000). With Celia Applegate she is coeditor of *Music and German National Identity* (University of Chicago Press, 2002). She was the 1997 recipient of the Alfred Einstein Award of the American Musicological Society.

Eric Rentschler is the Arthur Kingsley Porter Professor and Chair of Germanic Languages and Literatures at Harvard University. He is the author of, among other books and articles, *The Ministry of Illusion: Nazi Cinema and Its Afterlife* (Harvard University Press, 1996). He is currently completing a book entitled *The Enduring Allure of Nazi Attractions* (to be published by Harvard University Press).

Alan E. Steinweis is the Hyman Rosenberg Professor of Modern European History and Judaic Studies at the University of Nebraska-Lincoln. He is the author of *Art, Ideology, and Economics in Nazi Germany: The Reich Chambers of Music, Theater, and the Visual Arts* (University of North Carolina Press, 1993) and *Studying the Jew: Scholarly Antisemitism in Nazi Germany* (Harvard University Press, 2006). He has also coedited *The Impact of Nazism: New Perspectives on the Third Reich and its Legacy* (University of Nebraska Press, 2003) and *Coping with the Nazi Past: West German Debates over Nazism and Generational Conflict, 1955-1975* (Berghahn Books, 2006).

Frank Trommler is Professor of German and Comparative Literature at the University of Pennsylvania. He has published widely in the fields of modern German literature, theater, and applied arts. He has dealt with National Socialism in his essays "Between Normality and Resistance: Catastrophic Gradualism in Nazi Germany" (*Journal of Modern History* 64, 1992) and "A New Epigraph for the Inner Emigration," in *Flight of Fantasy*, ed. Neil H. Donahue and Doris Kirchner (Berghahn Books, 2003).

SELECTED BIBLIOGRAPHY

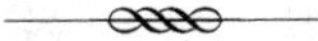

Culture, Ideology, and Propaganda

Baird, J. W. *The Mythical World of Nazi War Propaganda.* Minneapolis: University of Minnesota Press, 1974.

Balfour, Michael. *Propaganda in War, 1939-1945: Organisations, Policies, and Publics in Britain and Germany.* London: Routledge and Kegan Paul, 1979.

Bramsted, E. K. *Goebbels and National Socialist Propaganda, 1925-1945.* Lansing: Michigan State University Press, 1965.

Cuomo, Glen R., ed. *National Socialist Cultural Policy.* New York: St. Martin's Press, 1995.

Führer, Karl Christian. "A Medium of Modernity? Broadcasting in Weimar Germany, 1923–1943." *Journal of Modern History* 69, no. 4 (1997), 722–753.

Gassert, Philipp. *Amerika im Dritten Reich: Ideologie, Propaganda und Volksmeinung, 1933-1945.* Stuttgart: Steiner Verlag, 1997.

Gay, Peter. *Weimar Culture: The Outsider as Insider.* New York: Harper and Row, 1968.

Junker, Detlef. "The Continuity of Ambivalence: German Views of America, 1933–1945." In *Transatlantic Images and Perceptions: Germany and America since 1776,* edited by David E. Barclay and Elisabeth Glaser-Schmidt. Cambridge: Cambridge University Press, 1997.

Mosse, George. *The Crisis of German Ideology: Intellectual Origins of the Third Reich.* New York: Grosset and Dunlap, 1964.

———. *Nazi Culture: Intellectual, Cultural, and Social Life in the Third Reich.* New York: Grosset and Dunlap, 1966.

Nolan, Mary. *Visions of Modernity: American Business and the Modernization of Germany.* New York: Oxford University Press, 1994.

Schäfer, Hans Dieter. *Das gespaltene Bewusstsein: Über deutsche Kultur und Lebenswirklichkeit 1933-1945,* 2nd ed. Munich: Hanser, 1982.

Steinweis, Alan E. *Art, Ideology, and Economics in Nazi Germany: The Reich Chambers of Music, Theater, and the Visual Arts, 1933-1945.* Chapel Hill: University of North Carolina Press, 1993.

Stern, Fritz. *The Politics of Cultural Despair: A Study in the Rise of Germanic Ideology.* Berkeley: University of California Press, 1974.

Taylor, Brandon, and Wilfried van der Will, eds. *The Nazification of Art: Art, Design, Music, Architecture and Film in the Third Reich.* Winchester, UK: Winchester Press, 1990.

Welch, David, ed. *Nazi Propaganda: The Power and the Limitations.* Totowa, NJ: Barnes and Noble, 1983.

Zeman, Z. A. B. *Nazi Propaganda.* New York: Oxford University Press, 1973.

Culture and the Arts

Art

Aalders, Gerard. *Nazi Looting: The Plunder of Dutch Jewry during the Second World War.* Oxford and New York: Berg, 2004.

Barron, Stephanie, ed. *"Degenerate Art": The Fate of the Avant-Garde in Nazi Germany.* New York: Los Angeles County Museum of Art/Harry Abrams, 1991.

Barron, Stephanie, and Sabine Eckmann, eds. *Exiles and Emigrés: The Flight of European Artists from Hitler.* New York: Los Angeles County Museum of Art/Harry Abrams, 1997.

Blume, Eugen, and Dieter Scholz, eds. *Überbrückt: Ästhetische Moderne und Nationalsozialismus.* Cologne: Walther König, 1998.

Breker, Arno. *Paris, Hitler et Moi.* Paris: Plon, 1970.

———. *Im Strahlungsfeld der Ereignisse: Leben und Wirken eines Künstlers.* Preussisch Oldendorf: K. W. Schütz, 1972.

———. *Schriften,* edited by Volker Probst. Bonn: Marco, 1983.

Bushart, Magdalena, ed. *Skulptur und Macht.* Berlin: Fröhlich und Kaufmann, 1983.

Cassou, Jean, ed. *Le Pillage par les allemands des oeuvres d'art des bibliothèques appartenant á des juifs en France.* Paris: Centre Documentation Juive Contemporaine, 1947.

Francini, Esther Tisa, Anja Heuss, and Georg Kreis. *Fluchtgut—Raubgut: Der Transfer von Kulturgütern in und über die Schweiz 1933-1945 und die Frage der Restitution.* Zurich: Chronos, 2001.

Goldstein, Malcolm. *Landscape with Figures: A History of Art Dealing in the United States.* Oxford: Oxford University Press, 2000.

Haase, Günther. *Kunstraub und Kunstschutz: eine Dokumentation.* Hildesheim: Georg Olms Verlag, 1991.

Heilbut, Anthony. *Exiled in Paradise: German Refugee Artists and Intellectuals in America from the 1930s to the Present.* Boston: Beacon Press, 1983.

Heuss, Anja. "Die Reichskulturkammer und die Steuerung des Kunsthandels im Dritten Reich." In *Sediment: Mitteilung zur Geschichte des Kunsthandels 3*, edited by Zentralarchiv des Deutschen Internationalen Kunsthandels. Bonn: Zentralarchiv des Deutschen und Internationalen Kunsthandels, 1998, 49–61.

———. *Kunst- und Kulturgutraub: Eine vergleichende Studie zur Besatzungspolitik der Nationalsozialisten in Frankreich und der Sowjetunion.* Heidelberg: Universitäts-Verlag C. Winter, 2000.

Holz, Keith. *Modern German Art for Thirties Paris, Prague, and London: Resistance and Acquiescence in a Democratic Public Sphere.* Ann Arbor: University of Michigan Press, 2005.

Holz, Keith, and Wolfgang Schopf. *Im Auge des Exils: Josef Breitenbach und die Freie Deutsche Kultur in Paris 1933-1941.* Berlin: Aufbau Verlag, 2001.

Howe, Thomas Carr. *Salt Mines and Castles: The Discovery and Restitution of Looted European Art.* Indianapolis and New York: Bobbs-Merrill, 1946.

MacQueen, Michael. "The Conversion of Looted Jewish Assets to Run the German War Machine." *Holocaust and Genocide Studies* 18, no. 1 (2004): 27–45.

Michaud, Eric. *The Cult of Art in Nazi Germany.* Stanford, CA: Stanford University Press, 2004.

Peters, Hans Albert, and Stephan von Wiese, eds. *Alfred Flechtheim: Sammler, Kunsthändler, Verleger.* Düsseldorf: Westfälisches Landesmuseum, 1987.

Petropoulos, Jonathan. *Art as Politics in the Third Reich.* Chapel Hill: University of North Carolina Press, 1996.

———. *The Faustian Bargain: The Art World of Nazi Germany.* New York: Oxford University Press, 2000.

———. "The Nazi Kleptocracy: Reflections on Avarice and the Holocaust." In *Lessons and Legacies VII*, edited by Dagmar Herzog. Evanston, IL: Northwestern University Press, 2005.

Probst, Volker. *Der Bildhauer Arno Breker.* Bonn: Marco, 1978.

Schwarz, Birgit. *Hitlers Museum: Die Fotoalben Gemäldegalerie Linz.* Vienna: Böhlau, 2004.

———. "Hitler's Sonderbeauftragter Hans Posse." *Dresdner Hefte* 77, no.1 (2004): 77–85.

Städtische Kunstsammlung Augsburg, ed. *Gemälde der Stiftung Karl und Magdalene Haberstock.* Augsburg: Städtische Kunstsammlung, 1960.

———, ed. *Mythos und Bürgerliche Welt: Gemälde und Zeichnungen der Haberstock-Stiftung.* Augsburg: Städtische Kunstsammlung, 1991.

Weissler, Sabine. *Design in Deutschland: 1933-1945.* Giessen: Anabas-Verlag, 1990.

Wulf, Joseph. *Die bildenden Künste im Dritten Reich: eine Dokumentation.* Frankfurt am Main: Ullstein, 1963.

Film

Ahren, Yizhak, Stig Hornshøj-Møller, and Christoph B. Melchers. *"Der ewige Jude":
Wie Goebbels hetzte.* Aachen: Alano, 1990.

Albrecht, Gerd. *Nationalsozialistische Filmpolitik.* Stuttgart: Enke, 1969.

Belach, Helga, ed. *Wir tanzen um die Welt: Deutsche Revuefilme 1933-1945.* Munich:
Hanser, 1979.

Bock, Hans-Michael. *The Concise Cinegraph: An Encyclopedia of German Cinema.* New
York and Oxford: Berghahn Books, 2005.

Bock, Hans-Michael, and Michael Töteberg, eds. *Das Ufa Buch: Kunst und Kriesen,
Stars und Regisseure, Wirtschaft und Politik. Die Geschichte von Deutschlands grössten
Film-Konzern.* Frankfurt am Main: Zweitausendeins, 1992.

Bredow, Wilfried von, and Rolf Zurek, eds. *Film und Gesellschaft in Deutschland:
Dokumente und Materialen.* Hamburg: Hoffmann und Campe, 1975.

Cadars, Pierre, and Francis Courtade. *Geschichte des Films im Dritten Reich.* Munich:
Carl Hanser, 1975.

Drewniak, Boguslaw. *Der deutsche Film, 1938-1945: Eine Gesamtüberblick.* Düsseldorf: Droste, 1987.

Elsaesser, Thomas. *New German Cinema: A History.* New Brunswick, NJ: Rutgers
University Press, 1989.

Hake, Sabine. *The Cinema's Third Machine: Writing on Film in Germany, 1907-1933.*
Lincoln: University of Nebraska Press, 1993.

Hippler, Fritz. *Betrachtungen zum Filmschaffen.* Berlin: M. Hesse, 1942.

Hoffmann, Hilmar. *The Triumph of Propaganda: Film and National Socialism.* Trans.
John Broadwin and V. R. Berghahn. Providence and London: Berghahn Books,
1996.

Hull, David. *Film in the Third Reich.* Berkeley: University of California Press, 1969.

Kaes, Anton. "Mass Culture and Modernity: Notes Toward a Social History of Early
American and German Cinema." In *America and the Germans: An Assessment of a
Three-Hundred-Year History,* edited by Frank Trommler and Joseph McVeigh. 2
vols. Philadelphia: University of Pennsylvania Press, 1985.

Kanzog, Klaus. *"Staatspolitisch besonders wertvoll": Ein Handbuch zu 30 deutschen
Spielfilme der Jahre 1934 bis 1945.* Munich: Schaudig und Ledig, 1994.

Kater, Michael. "Film as an Object of Reflection in the Goebbels Diaries: Series II."
Central European History 33, no. 3 (2000): 391–414.

Kracauer, Siegfried. *From Caligari to Hitler: A Psychological History of the German Film.*
Princeton, NJ: Princeton University Press, 2004.

Kreimeier, Klaus. *The Ufa Story: A History of Germany's Greatest Film Company, 1918-
1945.* New York: Hill and Wang, 1996.

Loiperdinger, Martin. *Rituale der Mobilmachung: Der Parteitagsfilm "Triumph des Willens" von Leni Riefenstahl.* Opladen: Leske und Budrich, 1987.

Lowry, Stephen. *Pathos und Politik: Ideologie in Spielfilmen des Nationalsozialismus.* Tübingen: Niemeyer, 1991.

O'Brien, Mary-Elizabeth. *Nazi Cinema as Enchantment: The Politics of Entertainment in the Third Reich.* Rochester, NY: Camden House, 2004.

Petley, Julian. *Capital and Culture: German Cinema, 1933-1945.* London: British Film Institute, 1979.

Plummer, Thomas G. et al., eds. *Film and Politics in the Weimar Republic.* New York: Holmes and Meier, 1982.

Prawer, S. S. *Jewish Presences in German and Austrian Film, 1910-1933.* New York and Oxford: Berghahn Books, 2005.

Rentschler, Eric. "Mountains and Modernity: Relocating the *Bergfilm.*" *New German Critique* 51 (fall 1990): 137–161.

———. *The Ministry of Illusion: Nazi Cinema and its Afterlife.* Cambridge, MA: Harvard University Press, 1996.

Romani, Cinzia. *Tainted Goddesses: Female Film Stars of the Third Reich.* New York: Sarpedon, 1992.

Saunders, Thomas. J. *Hollywood in Berlin: American Cinema and Weimar Germany.* Berkeley: University of California Press, 1994.

Spiker, Jürgen. *Film und Kapital: Der Weg der deutschen Filmwirtschaft zum nationalsozialistischen Einheitskonzern.* Berlin: V. Spiess, 1975.

Trimborn, Jürgen. *Riefenstahl: Eine deutsche Karriere. Biographie.* Berlin: Aufbau, 2002.

Welch, David. *Propaganda and the German Cinema, 1933-1945.* Oxford: Clarendon Press, 1983.

Witte, Karsten. "Visual Pleasure Inhibited: Aspects of the German Revue Film." Trans. J. D. Steakley and Gabriele Hoover. *New German Critique* 24–25 (fall-winter 1981–1982): 238–263.

Literature

Amann, Klaus, and Albert Berger, eds. *Österreichische Literatur der dreissiger Jahre: Ideologische Verhältnisse, Institutionelle Voraussetzungen, Fallstudien.* Vienna: Böhlau, 1985.

Barbian, Jan-Pieter. *Literaturpolitik im "Dritten Reich": Institutionen, Kompetenzen, Betätigungsfelder.* Frankfurt am Main: Buchhändler-Vereinigung, 1993.

Bühler, Hans-Eugen. *Der Front Buchhandel 1939-1945: Organisationen, Kompetenzen, Verlage, Bücher. Eine Dokumentation* Frankfurt am Main: Buchhändler Vereinigung, 2002.

Caemmerer, Christiane, and Walter Delabar, eds. *Dichtung im Dritten Reich? Zur Literatur in Deutschland 1933-1945.* Opladen: Westdeutscher Verlag, 1996.

Dahm, Volker. *Das jüdische Buch im Dritten Reich.* Munich: Beck, 1993.

———. "Nationale Einheit und partikulare Vielfalt: Zur Frage der kulturpolitischen Gleichschaltung im Dritten Reich. *Vierteljahrshefte für Zeitgeschichte* 43, no. 2 (1995): 221–265.

Delabar, Walter, and Horst Denkler, eds. *Banalität mit Stil: Zur Widersprüchlichkeit der Literaturproduktion im Nationalsozialisums.* Bern: Lang, 1999.

Denkler, Horst, and Karl Prümm, eds. *Die deutsche Literatur im Dritten Reich: Themen – Traditionen – Wirkungen.* Stuttgart: Reclam, 1976.

Donahue, Neil H., and Doris Kirchner, eds. *Flight of Fantasy: New Perspectives on Inner Emigration in German Literature, 1933-1945.* New York: Berghahn Books, 2003.

Ehrke-Rotermund, Heidrun, and Erwin Rotermund. *Zwischenreiche und Gegenwelten: Texte und Vorstudien zur "Verdeckten Schreibweise" im "Dritten Reich."* Munich: Fink, 1999.

Fischer, William. *The Empire Strikes Out: Kurd Lasswitz, Hans Dominik, and the Development of German Science Fiction.* Bowling Green, OH: Bowling Green State University Press, 1984.

Hopster, Norbert, and Ulrich Nassen. *Literatur und Erziehung im Nationalsozialismus.* Paderborn: Schöningh, 1983.

Ketelsen, Uwe-Karsten. *Völkisch-nationale und nationalsozialistische Literatur in Deutschland 1890-1945.* Stuttgart: Metzler, 1976.

———. *Literatur und Drittes Reich.* Schernfeld: SH-Verlag, 1992.

Loewy, Ernst. *Literatur unterm Hakenkreuz: Das Dritte Reich und seine Dichtung. Eine Dokumentation.* Frankfurt am Main: Europäische Verlagsanstalt, 1966.

Reuveni, Gideon. *Reading Germany: Literature and Consumer Culture during the Weimar Republic.* New York and Oxford: Berghahn Books, 2005.

Rothe, Wolfgang, ed. *Die deutsche Literatur in der Weimarer Republik.* Stuttgart: Reclam, 1974.

Rüther, Günther, ed. *Literatur in der Diktatur: Schreiben im Nationalsozialismus und DDR-Sozialismus.* Paderborn: Schöningh, 1997.

Sauder, Gerhard, ed. *Die Bücherverbrennung. Zum 10. Mai 1933.* Munich and Vienna: Hanser, 1983.

Schneider, Tobias. "Bestseller im Dritten Reich: Ermittlung und Analyse der meistverkauften Romane in Deutschland 1933–1944." *Vierteljahrshefte für Zeitgeschichte* 52, no. 1 (2004): 77–97.

Schnell, Ralf. *Dichtung in finsteren Zeiten: Deutsche Literatur und Faschismus.* Reinbek: Rowohlt, 1998.

Schoeps, Karl-Heinz. *Literature and Film in the Third Reich.* Trans. Kathleen M. Dell'Orto. Rochester, NY: Camden, 2004.

Schweizer, Gerhard. *Bauernroman und Faschismus: Zur Ideologiekritik einer literarischen Gattung.* Tübingen: Tübinger Vereinigung für Volkskunde, 1976.

Strothmann, Dietrich. *Nationalsozialistische Literaturpolitik: Ein Beitrag zur Publizistik im Dritten Reich.* Bonn: Bouvier, 1960.

Thunecke, Jörg, ed. *Leid der Worte: Panorama des literarischen Nationalsozialismus.* Bonn: Bouvier, 1987.

Trommler, Frank. "Targeting the Reader, Entering History: A New Epitaph for the Inner Emigration." In *Flight of Fantasy: New Perspectives on Inner Emigration in German Literature, 1933-1945*, edited by Neil H. Donahue and Doris Kirchner. New York: Berghahn Books, 2003, 113–130.

Wulf, Joseph, ed. *Literatur und Dichtung im Dritten Reich: Eine Dokumentation.* Gütersloh: Sigbert Mohn, 1963.

Zimmermann, Peter. *Der Bauernroman: Antifeudalismus – Konservatismus – Faschismus.* Stuttgart: Metzler, 1975.

Music

Adorno, Theodor. *In Search of Wagner.* Trans. Rodney Livingstone. New York: Verso, 1981.

Brinkmann, Reinhold, and Christoph Wolff, eds. *Driven into Paradise: The Musical Migration from Nazi Germany to the United States.* Berkeley: University of California Press, 1999.

Bunge, Fritz. *Musik in der Waffen-SS.* Osnabrück: Munin, 1975.

Eichenauer, Richard. *Musik und Rasse.* Munich: Lehmanns, 1932.

Heister, Hanns-Werner, Claudia Maurer Zenck, and Peter Petersen, eds. *Musik im Exil: Folgen des Nazismus für die internationale Musikkultur.* Frankfurt am Main: Fischer Verlag, 1993.

Kater, Michael. *Composers of the Nazi Era: Eight Portraits.* New York: Oxford University Press, 2000.

———. "The Jazz Experience in Weimar Germany." *German History* 6, no. 2 (1988):145–158.

———. *Different Drummers: Jazz in the Culture of Nazi Germany.* New York: Oxford University Press, 1992.

———. *The Twisted Muse: Musicians and their Music in the Third Reich.* New York: Oxford University Press, 1997.

Kater, Michael, and Albrecht Riethmüller, eds. *Music and Nazism: Art under Tyranny, 1933-1945.* Laaber: Laaber Verlag, 2003.

Karbaum, Michael. *Studien zur Geschichte der Bayreuther Festspiele (1876-1976).* Regensburg: Bosse, 1976.

Karina, Lilian, and Marion Kant. *Hitler's Dancers: German Modern Dance and the Third Reich.* Trans. Jonathan Steinberg. New York and Oxford: Berghahn Books, 2004.

Katz, Jacob. *The Darker Side of Genius: Richard Wagner's Anti-Semitism.* Hanover, NH: University Press of New England, 1986.

Lühe, Barbara von der. *Die Emigration deutschsprachiger Musikschaffender in das britische Mandatsgebiet Palästina.* Frankfurt am Main: Peter Lang, 1999.

Ryding, Erik, and Rebecca Pechefsky. *Bruno Walter: A World Elsewhere*. New Haven: Yale University Press, 2001.

Osborne, Charles, ed. *Richard Wagner: Stories and Essays*. London: Owen, 1973.

Polster, Bernd, ed. *"Swing Heil": Jazz im Nationalsozialismus*. Berlin: Transit, 1989.

Potter, Pamela. "The Nazi 'Seizure' of the Berlin Philharmonic, or the Decline of a Bourgeois Musical Institution." In *National Socialist Cultural Policy*, edited by Glenn R. Cuomo. New York: St. Martin's Press, 1995, 39–66.

———. *Most German of the Arts: Musicology and Society from the Weimar Republic to the End of Hitler's Reich*. New Haven: Yale University Press, 1998.

Prieberg, Fred. *Musik im NS-Staat*. Frankfurt am Main: Fischer Verlag, 1982.

Sheffi, Na'ama. *The Ring of Myths: The Israelis, Wagner, and the Nazis*. Trans. Martha Grenzeback. Brighton: Sussex Academic Press, 2001.

Stock, Richard Wilhelm. *Richard Wagner und seine Meistersinger: Eine Erinnerungsgabe zu den Bayreuther Kriegsfestspielen 1943*. Nuremberg: Ulrich, 1938.

Traber, Habakuk, and Elmar Weingarten, eds. *Verdrängte Musik: Berliner Komponisten im Exil*. Berlin: Berliner Festspiele und Argon Verlag, 1987.

Walter, Michael. *Hitler in der Oper: deutsches Musikleben 1919-1945*. Stuttgart: J. B. Metzler, 1995.

Weber, Horst, ed. *Musik in der Emigration 1933-1945: Verfolgung, Vertreibung, Rückwirkung*. Stuttgart: J. B. Metzler, 1994.

Weiner, Mark A. *Wagner and the Anti-Semitic Imagination*. Lincoln: University of Nebraska Press, 1995.

Wulf, Joseph. *Musik im Dritten Reich: Eine Dokumentation*. Berlin: Ullstein, 1983.

Theater

Balfour, Michael, ed. *Theatre and War, 1933-1945*. New York and Oxford: Berghahn Books, 2001.

Berghaus, Günter. *Fascism and Theatre: Comparative Studies on the Aesthetics and Politics of Performance in Europe, 1925-1945*. Providence: Berghahn Books, 1996.

Gadberry, Glen, ed. *Theatre in the Third Reich, the Prewar Years: Essays on Theatre in Nazi Germany*. Westport, CT: Greenwood, 1995.

Hostetter, Elisabeth Schulz. *The Berlin State Theater under the Nazi Regime. A Study of the Administration, Key Productions, and Critical Responses from 1933-1944*. Lewiston, NY: Mellen Press, 2004.

London, John, ed. *Theatre under the Nazis*. Manchester and New York: Manchester University Press, 2000.

Mosse, George. *Masses and Man: Nationalist and Fascist Perception of Reality*. Detroit: Wayne State University Press, 1987.

Rennert, Hal, ed. *Essays on Twentieth Century German Drama and Theater: An American Reception, 1977-1999.* New York: Peter Lang, 2004.

Rischbieter, Henning, ed. *Theater im Dritten Reich: Theaterpolitik, Spielplanstruktur, NS-Dramatik* Seelze-Velber: Kallmeyer, 2000.

Schlösser, Rainer. *Das Volk und seine Bühne: Bemerkungen zum Aufbau des deutschen Theaters.* Berlin: Albert Langen, 1935.

Zortman, Bruce. *Theatre in Isolation: The Jüdischer Kulturbund of Nazi Germany.* Washington, D.C.: American Theater Association, 1972.

———. *Hitler's Theatre: Ideological Dramas in Nazi Germany.* El Paso, TX: Firestein Books, 1984.

Other Professions

Allen, Michael Thad. *The Business of Genocide: The SS, Slave Labor, and the Concentration Camps.* Chapel Hill: University of North Carolina Press, 2002.

Annas, George, and Michael Grodin. *The Nazi Doctors and the Nuremberg Code: Human Rights in Human Experimentation.* New York: Oxford University Press, 1992.

Bähr, Johannes. *Der Goldhandel der Dresdner Bank im Zweiten Weltkrieg. Ein Bericht des Hannah-Arendt-Instituts.* Leipzig: Kiepenheuer und Witsch, 1999.

Baldwin, Neil. *Henry Ford and the Jews: The Mass Production of Hate.* Boulder, CO: Westview Press, 2001.

Barkai, Avraham. *From Boycott to Annihilation: The Economic Struggle of German Jews, 1933-1943.* Hanover, NH: University Press of New England, 1989.

———. *Nazi Economics: Ideology, Theory, and Policy.* New Haven: Yale University Press, 1990.

———. "German Entrepreneurs and Jewish Policy in the Third Reich." *Yad Vashem Studies* 21 (1991): 122–155.

Barkan, Elazar. *The Guilt of Nations: Restitution and Negotiating Historical Injustices.* New York: Norton, 2000.

Benz, Wolfgang. *Sklavenarbeit im KZ.* Munich: Deutscher Taschenbuch Verlag, 1993.

Berghahn, Volker, ed. *Quest for Economic Empire: European Strategies of German Big Business in the Twentieth Century.* Oxford: Berghahn Books, 1996.

Beyerchen, Alan. *Scientists under Hitler: Politics and the Physics Community in the Third Reich.* New Haven: Yale University Press, 1977.

Billstein, Reinhold. *Working for the Enemy: Ford, General Motors, and Forced Labor in Germany during the Second World War.* New York: Berghahn Books, 2000.

Black, Edwin. *IBM and the Holocaust: The Strategic Alliance Between Nazi Germany and America's Most Powerful Corporation.* New York: Crown Publishers, 2001.

Boelcke, Willy. *Die Deutsche Wirtschaft 1930-1945: Interna des Reichswirtschaftsministeriums.* Düsseldorf: Droste, 1983.

Borkin, Joseph. *The Crime and Punishment of IG Farben: The Unholy Alliance of Adolf Hitler and Germany's Great Chemical Combine.* New York: Free Press, 1978.

Burleigh, Michael. *Death and Deliverance: "Euthanasia" in Germany, c. 1900-1945.* Cambridge: Cambridge University Press, 1994.

Caplan, Arthur L., ed. *When Medicine Went Mad: Bioethics and the Holocaust.* Totowa, NJ: Humana Press, 1992.

Deichmann, Uta. *Biologists Under Hitler.* Cambridge, MA: Harvard University Press, 1996.

Dobbs, Michael. "Ford and GM Scrutinized for Alleged Nazi Collaboration: Firms Deny Researchers' Claims on Aiding German War Effort." *Washington Post,* 30 November 1998, A1.

Eizenstat, Stuart. *Imperfect Justice: Looted Assets, Slave Labor, and the Unfinished Business of World War II.* New York: Public Affairs, 2003.

Feldenkirchen, Wilfried. *Siemens 1918-1945.* Columbus: Ohio State University Press, 1999.

Feldman, Gerald D. *Allianz and the German Insurance Business, 1933-1945.* New York: Cambridge University Press, 2001.

———. "The German Insurance Business in National Socialist Germany." *Bulletin of the German Historical Institute, Washington, D.C.* 31 (fall 2002): 19–33.

Friedlander, Henry, and Sybil Milton, eds. *The Holocaust: Ideology, Bureaucracy, and Genocide.* New York: Kraus International Publications, 1980.

Friedlander, Henry. "Step by Step: The Expansion of Murder, 1939–1941." *German Studies Review* 17, no. 3 (1994): 495–507.

———. *The Origins of Nazi Genocide: From Euthanasia to the Final Solution.* Chapel Hill: University of North Carolina Press, 1995.

———. "Die Entwicklung der Mordtechnik: Von der 'Euthanasie' zu den Vernichtungslagern der 'Endlösung'." In *Die nationalsozialistischen Konzentrationslager: Entwicklung und Struktur,* edited by Ulrich Herbert et al. 2 vols. Vol. 1, Göttingen: Wallstein Verlag, 1998, 493–507.

———. "Motive, Formen und Konsequenzen der NS-Euthanasie." In *NS- Euthanasie inWien,* edited by Eberhard Gabriel and Wolfgang Neugebauer. Vienna: Böhlau Verlag, 2000, 47–59.

Gabriel, Eberhard, and Wolfgang Neugebauer, eds. *NS-Euthanasie in Wien.* Vienna: Böhlau Verlag, 2000.

Gall, Lothar, Gerald D. Feldman, Harold James, Carl-Ludwig Holtfrerich, and Hans E. Büschgen, eds. *A History of the Deutsche Bank, 1870-1995.* London: Weidenfeld and Nicolson, 1995.

Gallagher, Hugh. *By Trust Betrayed: Patients, Physicians, and the License to Kill in the Third Reich.* New York: Henry Holt, 1990.

Geary, Dick. "The Industrial Elite and the Nazis in the Weimar Republic." In *The Nazi Machtergreifung*, edited by Peter D. Stachura. London: Allen and Unwin, 1983, 85–100.

Gregor, Neil. *Star and Swastika: Daimler Benz in the Third Reich*. New Haven: Yale University Press, 1998.

Gruner, Wolf. *Der geschlossene Arbeitseinsatz deutscher Juden. Zur Zwangsarbeit als Element der Verfolgung 1938-1943*. Berlin: Metropol, 1997.

———. *Zwangsarbeit und Verfolgung: Österreichische Juden im NS-Staat 1938-1945*. Innsbruck: Studienverlag, 2000.

Hayes, Peter. "Big Business and 'Aryanization' in Germany, 1933–1939." *Jahrbuch für Antisemitismusforschung* 3 (1994): 254–281.

———. "State Policy and Corporate Involvement in the Holocaust." In *The Holocaust and History: The Known, the Unknown, the Disputed, and the Reexamined*, edited by Michael Berenbaum and Abraham Peck. Bloomington, IN: Indiana University Press, 1998, 197–218.

———. "The Deutsche Bank and the Holocaust." In *Lessons and Legacies III: Memory, Memorialization and Denial*, edited by Peter Hayes. Evanston, IL: Northwestern University Press, 1999, 71–98.

———. *Industry and Ideology: IG Farben in the Nazi Era*. 2nd ed. New York: Cambridge University Press, 2001.

———. "The Degussa AG and the Holocaust." In *Lessons and Legacies V: The Holocaust and Justice*, edited by Ronald Smelser. Evanston, IL: Northwestern University Press, 2002, 140–177.

———. *From Cooperation to Complicity: Degussa in the Third Reich*. New York: Cambridge University Press, 2004.

Hayes, Peter, and Irmtrud Wojak, eds. *"Arisierung" im Nationalsozialismus: Volksgemeinschaft, Raub und Gedächtnis*. Frankfurt am Main: Campus, 2000.

Hentschel, Volker. "Daimler-Benz im Dritten Reich." *Vierteljahrsschrift für Sozial- und Wirtschaftsgeschichte* 75, no.1 (1988): 74–100.

Hepp, Michael. *Deutsche Bank und Dresdner Bank: Gewinne aus Raub, Enteignung und Zwangsarbeit 1933-1944*. Bremen: Stiftung für Sozialgeschichte des 20. Jahrhunderts, 1999.

Herbert, Ulrich. *Hitler's Foreign Workers: Enforced Labor in Germany under the Third Reich*. Cambridge: Cambridge University Press, 1997.

Hopmann, Barbara. *Zwangsarbeit bei Daimler-Benz*. Stuttgart: Franz Steiner Verlag, 1994.

Isabel, Vincent. *Hitler's Silent Partners: Swiss Banks, Nazi Gold, and the Pursuit of Justice*. New York: Morrow, 1997.

James, Harold. *The Deutsche Bank and the Nazi Economic War Against the Jews: The Expropriation of Jewish-Owned Property*. New York: Cambridge University Press, 2001.

———. *Verbandspolitik im Nationalsozialismus. Von der Interessenvertretung zur Wirtschaftsgruppe. Der Centralverband des Deutschen Bank- und Bankiergewerbes 1932-1945.* Munich and Zürich: Piper Verlag, 2001.

Jarausch, Konrad. *The Unfree Professions: German Lawyers, Teachers, and Engineers, 1900-1950.* New York: Oxford University Press, 1990.

———. "The Conundrum of Complicity: German Professionals and the Final Solution." Joseph and Rebecca Meyerhoff Annual Lecture. Washington, D.C.: United States Holocaust Memorial Museum, 2001.

Jaskot, Paul. *The Architecture of Oppression: The SS, Forced Labor and the Nazi Monumental Building Economy.* New York: Routledge, 2000.

Kalthoff, Jürgen, and Martin Werner. *Die Händler des Zyklon B. Tesch & Stabenow: Eine Firmengeschichte zwischen Hamburg und Auschwitz.* Hamburg: VSA, 1998.

Kater, Michael. "Dr. Leonardo Conti and His Nemesis: The Failure of Centralized Medicine in the Third Reich." *Central European History* 18, nos. 3–4 (1985): 299–325.

———. "Hitler's Early Doctors: Nazi Physicians in Pre-Depression Germany." *Journal of Modern History* 59, no. 1 (1987): 25–52.

———. "Medizin und Mediziner im Dritten Reich: Eine Bestandsaufnahme." *Historische Zeitschrift* 244, no. 2 (1987): 299–352.

———. *Doctors Under Hitler.* Chapel Hill: University of North Carolina Press, 1989.

Kobrak, Christopher. *National Cultures and International Competition: The Experience of Schering AG, 1851-1950.* New York: Cambridge University Press, 2002.

Kopper, Christopher. *Zwischen Marktwirtschaft und Dirigismus. Staat, Banken und Bankenpolitik im "Dritten Reich" von 1933 bis 1939.* Bonn: Bouvier, 1995.

Klee, Ernst. *"Euthanasie" im NS-Staat: Die "Vernichtung lebensunwerten Lebens."* Frankfurt am Main: S. Fischer Verlag, 1983.

———. *Auschwitz, die NS-Medizin und ihre Opfer.* Frankfurt am Main: S. Fischer Verlag, 1997.

LeBor, Adam. *Hitler's Secret Bankers: The Myth of Swiss Neutrality During the Holocaust.* Secaucus: Carol Publishing Group, 1997.

Lifton, Robert Jay. *The Nazi Doctors: Medical Killing and the Psychology of Genocide.* New York: Basic Books, 1986.

Lifton, Robert Jay, and Amy Hackett. "Nazi Doctors." In *Anatomy of the Auschwitz Death Camp*, edited by Yisrael Gutman and Michael Berenbaum. Bloomington, IN: Indiana University Press, 1998, 301–316.

Macrakis, Kristie. "The Rockefeller Foundation and German Physics under National Socialism." *Minerva* 27, no. 1 (1989): 33–57.

———. *Surviving the Swastika: Scientific Research in Nazi Germany.* New York: Oxford University Press, 1993.

McFarland-Icke, Bronwyn Rebekah. *Nurses in Nazi Germany: Moral Choice in History.* Princeton: Princeton University Press, 1999.

Mehl, Stefan. *Das Reichsfinanzministerium und die Verfolgung der Deutschen Juden 1933-1943*. Berlin: Zentralinstitut für Sozialwissenschaftliche Forschung, 1990.

Mollin, Gerhard. *Montankonzerne und "Drittes Reich": der Gegensatz zwischen Monopolindustrie und Befehlswirtschaft in der deutschen Rüstung und Expansion 1936-1944*. Göttingen: Vandenhoeck und Ruprecht, 1988.

Mommsen, Hans, and Manfred Grieger. *Das Volkswagenwerk und seine Arbeiter im Dritten Reich*. Düsseldorf: Econ, 1996.

Mönnich, Horst. *BMW: Eine Deutsche Geschichte*. Vienna and Darmstadt: Paul Zsolnay Verlag, 1989.

Müller-Hill, Benno. *Murderous Science: Elimination by Scientific Selection of Jews, Gypsies and Others, Germany 1933-1945*. New York: Oxford University Press, 1988.

Nicosia, Francis R., and Jonathan Huener, eds. *Medicine and Medical Ethics in Nazi Germany: Origins, Practices, Legacies*. New York: Berghahn Books, 2002.

————. *Business and Industry in Nazi Germany*. New York: Berghahn Books, 2004.

Perrenoud, Marc. *La place financière et les banques suisses à l'époque du nationalsocialisme*. Zurich: Chronos, 2002.

Platen-Hallermund, Alice. *Die Tötung Geisteskranker in Deutschland*. Bonn: Psychiatrie-Verlag, 1998.

Plumpe, Gottfried. *Die I.G. Farbenindustrie AG: Wirtschaft, Technik und Politik 1904-1945*. Berlin: Duncker & Humblot, 1990.

Pohl, Hans. *Die Daimler-Benz AG in den Jahren 1933-1945*. Wiesbaden: Steiner, 1986.

Proctor, Robert. *Racial Hygiene: Medicine Under the Nazis*. Cambridge, MA: Harvard University Press, 1988.

————. *The Nazi War on Cancer*. Princeton: Princeton University Press, 1999.

Roth, Karl Heinz. "Hehler des Holocaust: Degussa und Deutsche Bank." *Zeitschrift für Sozialgeschichte des 20. und 21. Jahrhunderts* 13, no. 4 (1998): 137–144.

Schmidt, Gerhard. *Selektion in der Heilanstalt, 1939-1945*. 2nd ed. Frankfurt am Main: Edition Suhrkamp, 1983.

Schulze, Winfried, and Otto Oexle, eds. *Deutsche Historiker im Nationalsozialismus*. Frankfurt am Main: Fischer Taschenbuch Verlag, 1999.

Schwarberg, Günther. *Der SS-Arzt und die Kinder: Bericht über den Mord vom Bullenhuser Damm*. Hamburg: Gruner und Jahr, 1979.

Seidelman, William. "Medical Selection: Auschwitz Antecedents and Effluent." *Holocaust and Genocide Studies* 4, no. 4 (1989), 435–448.

————. "Medicine and Murder in the Third Reich." *Dimensions: A Journal of Holocaust Studies* 13, no. 1 (1999): 9–13.

————. "Medicine and the Holocaust: Physician Involvement in Genocide." In *Encyclopedia of Genocide*, edited by Israel Charney. Santa Barbara, CA: ABC-CLIO, 2000, 412–415.

Siegfried, Klaus-Jörg. *Rüstungsproduktion und Zwangsarbeit im Volkswagenwerk 1939-1945.* Frankfurt am Main: Campus, 1999.

Sieman, Hans Ludwig. *Menschen blieben auf der Strecke…: Psychiatrie zwischen Reform und Nationalsozialismus.* Gütersloh: J. van Haddis, 1987.

Silverman, Dan. *Hitler's Economy: Nazi Work Creation Programs, 1933-1936.* Cambridge, MA: Harvard University Press, 1998.

Simpson, Christopher, ed. *War Crimes of the Deutsche Bank and the Dresdner Bank. Office of Military Government (U.S.) Reports.* New York: Holmes and Meier, 2001.

Steppe, Hildegard, ed. *Krankenpflege im Nationalsozialismus.* Frankfurt am Main: Mabuse-Verlag, 1989.

Thom, Achim, and Genadij Ivanovic Caregorodcev, eds. *Medizin unterm Hakenkreuz.* Berlin: Verlag Volk und Geschichte, 1989.

Turner, Henry A. *German Big Business and the Rise of Hitler.* New York: Oxford University Press, 1985.

Wagner, Bernd C. *IG Auschwitz: Zwangsarbeit und Vernichtung von Häftlingen des Lagers Monowitz 1941-1945.* Munich: K. G. Saur, 2000.

Weale, Adrian. *Science under the Swastika.* London: Channel 4 Books, 2001.

Weinreich, Max. *Hitler's Professors: The Part of Scholarship in Germany's Crimes against the Jewish People.* New Haven: Yale University Press, 1999.

Wiesen, Jonathan. *West German Industry and the Challenge of the Nazi Past, 1945-1955.* Chapel Hill: University of North Carolina Press, 2001.

Wilkins, Mira, and Frank Ernest Hill. *American Business Abroad: Ford on Six Continents.* Detroit: Wayne State University Press, 1964.

Wixforth, Harald. *Auftakt zur Ostexpansion. Die Dresdner Bank und die Umgestaltung des Bankwesens im Sudetenland 1938/39.* Dresden: Hannah-Arendt-Institut für Totalitarismusforschung, 2001.

Wolf, Mechthild. *Im Zeichen von Sonne und Mond: von der Frankfurter Münzscheiderei zum Weltunternehmen Degussa AG.* Frankfurt am Main: Degussa, 1993.

Ziegler, Dieter. "Die Verdrängung der Juden aus der Dresdner Bank 1933–1938." *Vierteljahrshefte für Zeitgeschichte* 47, no. 2 (1999): 187–216.

Racism and Anti-Semitism

Arendt, Hanna. *The Origins of Totalitarianism.* Part I: *Antisemitism.* New York: Harcourt Brace Jovanovich, 1973.

Bankier, David, ed. *Probing the Depths of German Antisemitism: German Society and the Persecution of the Jews, 1933-1941.* New York: Berghahn Books, 2000.

Barkan, Elazar. *The Retreat of Scientific Racism: Changing Concepts of Race in Britain and the United States between the World Wars.* Cambridge: Cambridge University Press, 1992.

Brustein, William. *Roots of Hate: Anti-Semitism in Europe before the Holocaust*. New York: Cambridge University Press, 2003.

Burrin, Philippe. *Nazi Anti-Semitism: From Prejudice to the Holocaust*. New York: New Press, 2005.

Efron, John. *Defenders of Race: Jewish Doctors and Race Science in Fin de Siècle Europe*. New Haven: Yale University Press, 1994.

Field, Geoffrey. *Evangelist of Race: The Germanic Vision of Houston Stewart Chamberlain*. New York: Columbia University Press, 1981.

Hertzberg, Arthur. *The French Enlightenment and the Jews: The Origins of Modern Antisemitism*. New York: Columbia University Press, 1990.

Massing, Paul. *Rehearsal for Destruction: A Study of Political Antisemitism in Imperial Germany*. New York: Harper, 1949.

Mosse, George. *Toward the Final Solution: A History of European Racism*. New York: Harper and Row, 1978.

Pauley, Bruce. *From Prejudice to Destruction: A History of Austrian Antisemitism*. Chapel Hill: University of North Carolina Press, 1992.

Poliakov, Leon. *The Aryan Myth: A History of Racist and Nationalist Ideas in Europe*. New York: Basic Books, 1971.

Pulzer, Peter. *The Rise of Political Antisemitism in Germany and Austria*. Cambridge, MA: Harvard University Press, 1988.

Rose, Paul Lawrence. *German Question – Jewish Question: Revolutionary Antisemitism from Kant to Wagner*. Princeton: Princeton University Press, 1992.

Zimmermann, Moshe. *Wilhelm Marr: The Patriarch of Antisemitism*. New York: Oxford University Press, 1986.

Holocaust, Final Solution, the German People

Adam, Uwe-Dietrich. *Judenpolitik im Dritten Reich*. Düsseldorf: Droste, 1972.

Aly, Götz. *"Final Solution": Nazi Population Policy and the Murder of the European Jews*. New York: Arnold, 1999.

Arendt, Hannah. *Eichmann in Jerusalem: A Report on the Banality of Evil*. New York: Penguin, 1994.

Bankier, David. *The Germans and the Final Solution: Public Opinion under Nazism*. Oxford: B. Blackwell, 1992.

Bartov, Omer. *Hitler's Army: Soldiers, Nazis and War in the Third Reich*. New York: Oxford University Press, 1991.

———. *Murder in Our Midst: The Holocaust, Industrial Killing, and Representation*. New York: Oxford University Press, 1996.

———, ed. *The Holocaust: Origins, Implementation, Aftermath*. New York: Routledge, 2000.

Browder, George. *Hitler's Enforcers: The Gestapo and the SS Security Service in the Nazi Revolution.* New York: Oxford University Press, 1996.

Browning, Christopher. *Fateful Months: Essays on the Emergence of the Final Solution.* New York: Holmes and Meier, 1985.

———. *Ordinary Men: Reserve Police Battalion 101 and the Final Solution in Poland.* New York: Harper Collins, 1992.

———. *The Path to Genocide: Essays on Launching the Final Solution.* New York: Cambridge University Press, 1992.

———. *Nazi Policy, Jewish Workers, German Killers.* New York: Cambridge University Press, 2000.

———. *The Origins of the Final Solution: The Evolution of Nazi Jewish Policy, September 1939-March 1942.* With contributions by Jürgen Matthäus. Lincoln: University of Nebraska Press, 2004.

Burleigh, Michael, and Wolfgang Wippermann. *The Racial State: Germany 1933-1945.* New York: Cambridge University Press, 1991.

Burleigh, Michael, ed. *Confronting the Nazi Past: New Debates on Modern German History.* New York: St. Martin's Press, 1996.

———. *Ethics and Extermination: Reflections on Nazi Genocide.* Cambridge: Cambridge University Press, 1997.

Cesarani, David, ed. *The Final Solution: Origins and Implementation.* London and New York: Routledge, 1994.

Dwork, Deborah, and Robert Jan van Pelt. *Holocaust: A History.* New York: W.W. Norton, 2002.

Friedländer, Saul. *Nazi Germany and the Jews: The Years of Persecution, 1933-1939.* New York: HarperCollins, 1997.

Gellately, Robert. *The Gestapo and German Society: Enforcing Racial Policy, 1933-1945.* New York: Oxford University Press, 1990.

———. *Backing Hitler: Consent and Coercion in Nazi Germany.* New York: Oxford University Press, 2001.

Goldhagen, Daniel. *Hitler's Willing Executioners: Ordinary Germans and the Holocaust.* New York: Alfred A. Knopf, 1996.

Gordon, Sarah. *Hitler, Germans, and the Jewish Question.* Princeton: Princeton University Press, 1984.

Hamburg Institute for Social Research, ed. *The German Army and Genocide: Crimes against War Prisoners, Jews, and Other Civilians in the East, 1939-1944.* New York: New Press, 1999.

Hilberg, Raul. *Perpetrators Victims Bystanders: The Jewish Catastrophe, 1933-1945.* New York: HarperCollins, 1992.

———. *The Destruction of the European Jews.* 3 vols. 3rd ed. New Haven: Yale University Press, 2003.

Höhne, Heinz. *The Order of the Death's Head: The Story of Hitler's SS.* London: Penguin, 1969.

Kershaw, Ian. *Popular Opinion and Political Dissent in the Third Reich: Bavaria, 1933-1945.* Oxford: Clarendon Press, 1983.

Langbein, Hermann. *People in Auschwitz.* Chapel Hill: University of North Carolina Press, 2004.

Lewy, Guenther. *The Nazi Persecution of the Gypsies.* New York: Oxford University Press, 2000.

Peukert, Detlev. *Inside Nazi Germany: Conformity, Opposition, and Racism in Everyday Life.* New Haven: Yale University Press, 1987.

Reitlinger, Gerald. *The Final Solution: The Attempt to Exterminate the Jews of Europe, 1939-1945.* New York: A.S. Barnes, 1961.

Rückerl, Adalbert. *Nationalsozialistische Vernichtungslager im Spiegel deutscher Strafprozesse: Belzec, Sobibor, Treblinka, Chelmno.* Munich: Deutscher Taschenbuch Verlag, 1977.

Steinert, Marlis. *Hitler's War and the Germans: Public Mood and Attitude during the Second World War.* Athens: Ohio University Press, 1977.

Yahil, Leni. *The Holocaust: The Fate of European Jewry.* New York: Oxford University Press, 1990.

INDEX

Index note: page references in *italics* indicate a figure or photograph.

CPSIA information can be obtained
at www.ICGtesting.com
Printed in the USA
JSHW062109200722
28320JS00005B/36